Tectonic Shift

TECTONIC SHIFT

THE GEOECONOMIC REALIGNMENT OF GLOBALIZING MARKETS

JAGDISH N. SHETH
Emory University

RAJENDRA S. SISODIA
Bentley College

Response Books
A division of Sage Publications
New Delhi/Thousand Oaks/London

Copyright © Jagdish N. Sheth and Rajendra S. Sisodia, 2006

All rights reserved. No part of this book may be reproduced or utilized in any form or by any means, electronic or mechanical, including photocopying, recording or by any information storage or retrieval system, without permission in writing from the publisher.

First published in 2006 by

Response Books
A division of Sage Publications India Pvt Ltd
B-42, Panchsheel Enclave
New Delhi 110 017

Sage Publications Inc
2455 Teller Road
Thousand Oaks
California 91320

Sage Publications Ltd
1 Oliver's Yard
55 City Road
London EC1Y 1SP

Published by Tejeshwar Singh for Response Books, typeset in 11/13 pts. Minion by Innovative Processors, New Delhi, and printed at Chaman Enterprises, New Delhi.

Library of Congress Cataloging-in-Publication Data

Sheth, Jagdish N.
The geoeconomic realignment of globalizing markets/Jagdish N. Sheth, Rajendra S. Sisodia.
p. cm.
1. International economic relations – Forecasting. 2. International trade – Forecasting. 3. Trade blocs – Forecasting. 4. International economic integration – Forecasting. 5. Economic forecasting. I. Sisodia, Rajendra. II. Title: Geoeconomic realignment of globalizing markets. III. Title.
HF1359.S5428 2005 382—dc22 2005037243

ISBN: 0–7619–3490–1 (US–Hb)

Production Team: Anupama Purohit, R.A.M. Brown, Jeevan Nair and Santosh Rawat

Dedication

Dedicated to the memory of my late brother-in-law, Mr. Sumatilal Mehta (founder of Safari Industries), who tirelessly served his community from Kutch, India.

Jagdish N. Sheth

Dedicated to the memory of my late father-in-law, Ram Chandra Malhotra, inspirational visionary and tireless humanitarian who devoted his life to reducing poverty around the world.

Rajendra S. Sisodia

Contents

Foreword

Why should you read this book? The answer is to gain a most insightful understanding of the forces and dynamics shaping today and tomorrow's world economy. Another reason is to be warned of the precarious future that the US and other Western economies face if they fail to make fundamental shifts in their global economic policies.

There have been many writings on geopolitical forces – how nations interact in the pursuit of power. Less has been written on geoeconomic forces – how national economies interact in the pursuit of economic gain. Yet it is the geoeconomic forces that shape and interact with the geopolitical forces. And it is to Sheth and Sisodia's credit that they offer a penetrating analysis on where the future of different countries is going under the pressure of geoeconomic forces.

Their argument is cogent. As long as developed nations mainly trade with each other, they won't be able to grow very fast. Developed nations are low on growth and high in prosperity. But the rapid decline in the West's fertility rate augurs aging societies and an inevitable decrease in prosperity. The health system, private pension plans, and the social security system in these developed nations are facing imminent decline.

Developed countries can avoid this fate if they start linking their economies with specific developing economies. Japan, a highly developed economy, is linking its future with China – a rapidly growing underdeveloped economy. The US is similarly linking its economy with Mexico, just as Western Europe is turning to Eastern Europe for growth.

Market forces are also propelling the growth of regional blocs. The members of a regional bloc – such as the ASEAN bloc – are reaching out to serve each other's interests. As more regional blocs form, they will deliver competitive advantages to their members that are not available to non-members.

Ultimately there will be three major regional blocs: a US/ North American bloc, a European/African bloc, and an Asian bloc. The emergence of a tripolar system promises a more stable world economy than one where there is only one superpower, or two superpowers in irreconcilable conflict with each other. There will be some loss of global free trade but better trade within blocs and between blocs will offset this.

The main hope is that the developed and developing worlds embrace each other. Otherwise no or slow growth in the developing world will increase poverty and the number of unemployed and disaffected youth and this is a huge destabilizing force that impacts on crime and terrorism and that will ultimately affect the West.

I am indebted to Sheth and Sisodia for their penetrating analysis of the global problem and the potential solutions.

Philip Kotler
S. C. Johnson Distinguished Professor
of International Marketing
Kellogg School of Management
Northwestern University

Preface

We are living in an era of unprecedented change and huge risks as well as opportunities. The world stands poised at a critical bifurcation. On the one hand, numerous forces have aligned in recent years with the potential to splinter the world along racial, ethnic, religious and economic fault lines. The recent riots in France, continued conflicts in the Middle East, sharp divisions between the Shia and Sunni sects within Islam, the retreat from free market principles in some Latin American countries, misplaced hysteria over outsourcing, escalating concern about the future of energy resources and concerns about the devastating impacts of climate change – all these factors could cause the developed and developing sections of the world to withdraw from active engagement with one another, and retreat into familiar but fruitless patterns of isolation, suspicion and neglect.

On the other hand, we could harness the positive forces that have been gaining momentum in recent years to craft a future in which partnering between developed and developing nations becomes the dominant paradigm. The Internet has democratized information and knowledge to a startling degree, in an astonishingly short amount of time. The telecommunications revolution, particularly wireless telephony, has brought the liberating and labour-saving fruits of technology to vast multitudes. The interconnectedness of the world has never been as evident as it is today. All the nations of the world exist in a symbiotic ecosystem, in which the health and well-being of one directly impacts and is impacted by the health and well-being of the others. Every country thus bears a responsibility to its own citizens as well as to the citizens of the world at large.

This book presents an optimistic and practical view of the future that is predicated on strengthened relationships between developed and developing countries that are based not on charity but on enlightened self-interest. We propose that the best way forward (i.e. the one that will generate the most prosperity for the largest number of people) lies in such 'North-South' integration. Moreover, this is most likely to be successful in the context of *regional* integration (though in some cases, countries that offer a strong strategic fit but are geographically distant will join a regional economic union), and will result in the formation of three huge regional economies bound together through the glue of free trade, a common currency, shared values, and shared developmental priorities and institutions.

The imperative on both sides is clear. For prosperous developed countries, the biggest need is for fresh economic growth. Most such countries have aging and shrinking populations. On the other hand, large emerging nations need investment and technology to raise their living standards and deliver the prosperity that their restive populations demand. Most such countries have young and still growing populations. The synergy between these two groups of countries is self-evident and widely recognized. For example, Goldman Sachs put out a very influential report in 2003 titled *Dreaming With BRICs: The Path to 2050*, which suggested that Brazil, Russia, India and China will account for a high proportion of economic growth over the next several decades, and their economies will rival and even overshadow the major industrialized economies of today.[1] But this optimistic prediction will not come to pass without the active involvement of developed countries.

[1] Dominic Wilson and Roopa Purushothaman, *Dreaming With BRICs: The Path to 2050*, October 1, 2003, Goldman Sachs Global Economics Paper No. 99.

Tectonic Shift represents a continuation of the journey started by *Commanding Heights*, Daniel Yergin and Joseph Stanislaw's masterful recounting of the economic history of the 20th century.[2] We offer a plausible scenario for how the global economy is likely to evolve in the first few decades of the 21st century. In many ways, the 20th century was hijacked by ideology: communism, Nazism, World War II, the Vietnam and Korean wars, the Cold War. The 20th century was an historical aberration in that it witnessed, first, a US domination of the world and, second, a bifurcation of the world into two opposing camps. The 21st century, we believe, will be characterized by a much higher degree of pragmatism and more uniform distribution of power. As the world population matures and stabilizes in the 21st century, the gross domestic product (GDP) of countries will grow only slowly. Economic growth and vitality will depend more than ever on renewed growth in trade. In some ways, the 21st century will be reminiscent of the 19th century, during which David Ricardo's theory of comparative advantage gave new impetus to trade as an extraordinarily powerful economic engine.

We show how several non-intuitive developments are likely to take place as what we call the 'regionalization with a twist' occurs. For example, the European Union will become fully integrated with Eastern Europe, including Russia. India will become a close strategic ally of the United States and a key member of the Free Trade Area of the Americas (FTAA). We discuss how this journey will not happen unless advanced countries are able to take a long-term view and muster the political courage to willingly vacate markets for developing countries to occupy. The worldview of powerful countries such as the US must shift from one of dominance to one that recognizes mutual interdependence. Rather than viewing everything through the lens of their own narrowly defined self-interest, they must adopt a win-win partnering mindset that is focused on expanding the overall pool

[2] Daniel Yergin and Joseph Stanislaw, *The Commanding Heights: The Battle for the World Economy*, New York: Simon & Schuster, 1998.

of prosperity. Finally, we will show that this evolution will depend heavily on a close and trusting relationship between one large developed and developing country in each of the three regional economies i.e. between Germany and Russia, between the US and India and between Japan and China.

The restructuring of the world into three huge regional economies of roughly equal size and power should not be viewed as a dangerous or ominous development, an Orwellian harbinger of an unimaginable future 'War of the Worlds.' If the transition is managed properly, it should result in fewer conflicts and rising prosperity. Each region will work collectively to remove sources of internal conflict, and will provide infrastructure investments and other forms of economic support to elevate the living standards in its weaker sections. The regions will continue to trade with one another, as well as engage in other forms of exchange.

Acknowledgements

We would like to acknowledge the highly valuable contribution of John Yow to this book. John assisted with the writing of portions of the book based on our ideas. We would also like to acknowledge the editorial and research assistance of Mark Hutcheson, Administrative Manager of the India, China and America Institute in Atlanta, USA. Finally, we would like to thank Chapal Mehra, the Managing Editor of Response Books, who worked diligently with us to get this book published in an expedited fashion.

CHAPTER 1

THE GEOECONOMIC REALITY OF GLOBALIZATION

'It's the Economy, Stupid'

In their landmark study, *The Commanding Heights: The Battle for the World Economy*, Daniel Yergin and Joseph Stanislaw convincingly demonstrated that, while state control of the world's economies advanced during the decades of rebuilding after World War II (WWII), the final decades of the 20th century saw a reversal of that trend: across the globe, governments were retreating from 'the commanding heights' and giving way to market forces. Why? Because government-controlled economies were failing to deliver growth and prosperity and those governments were being voted out of office, in Western democracies in particular.

This study will look beyond Yergin and Stanislaw's book, into the first decades of the 21st century, an era that brings new challenges. We believe that market forces will be increasingly ascendant and, as the world continues to flatten, in Thomas Friedman's phrase, progress toward globalization will likewise continue. But the new problem, which will vex the mature, advanced economies of the US, Western Europe and Japan, will be sustaining the growth that brought them to the pinnacle of the world's economy. More dramatically, how will developed nations continue to thrive in the era of globalization? Solving this problem will force interesting new alliances – strange bedfellows – as mature nations seek vibrant trading partners with young populations, unmet needs and still untapped resources. Of course, the two new giants – China and India – are already being courted, and we will predict to whom they will be wed. Yet our chief concern will be the newly evolving 'north-south' alignment of nations, via trade blocs, which we see as the regional path toward globalization.

To get started, let's look again at the upheaval of the 1990s, when incumbent political leaders and previously dominant political parties suddenly felt the ground give way under their feet. Consider the following:

- In 1991, in the wake of the first Gulf War, US President George H.W. Bush enjoyed a degree of popularity almost unheard of in modern times: well over 90 percent of the American public approved of his job performance, a level never even approached by his highly popular predecessor Ronald Reagan. But just over a year later, in the election year of 1992, Bush was rudely thrown from office, defeated by the virtually unknown governor of a small southern state, Bill Clinton, ending twelve years of Republican Party rule.
- With his approval rating dropping to an abysmal 11 percent, Canadian Prime Minister Brian Mulroney stepped down in the summer of 1993 after nine years in office. Kim Campbell, his finance minister who led the Progressive Conservative Party in the general election held that fall, replaced him. Neither she nor anyone else could have predicted the disaster that awaited. It wasn't simply that the Liberal Party, led by Jean Chretien, won a decisive majority of seats in Parliament. What was absolutely unprecedented was the scale of the Tories' defeat. Of 295 seats, Campbell's party retained two – not even enough to qualify for official party status in the House of Commons.
- In 1990, John Major succeeded Margaret Thatcher as Prime Minister of Great Britain after Thatcher had transformed

British society and served an unprecedented three consecutive terms. Major won reelection in 1992, the fourth victory in a row for the Conservatives. By the next election in 1996, the Conservative Party had ruled consecutively for 18 years. However, that election proved to be a veritable bloodbath for the Conservatives, as Tony Blair and the Labor Party swept into office with 418 seats in Parliament (a gain of 147), while the Conservatives lost 181 seats to stand at 165. Most recently, and despite his unpopular support of the US in the Iraq war, Blair was re-elected for the third time, mainly because the UK economy continues to do well.

- By 1998, Helmut Kohl had been Chancellor of Germany for 16 years, a post-war record. Had he been reelected, he would have surpassed Otto von Bismarck as Germany's longest-serving chancellor ever. Kohl had presided over the historic reunification of Germany in 1990. Defying his own economic advisors, Kohn made the controversial decision to allow an immediate 1-to-1 conversion of the East German Ostmark currency into Deutsche Marks, even though the prevailing black market rate ranged from five to ten Ostmarks per Deutsche Mark. The impact of this on the East German economy was disastrous; despite their much lower level of productivity, firms there had to operate with same cost structure as Western firms. This led to a precipitous drop in output, soaring unemployment and record budget deficits. Kohl's Christian Democratic Union party was soundly defeated in the 1998 election by the Social Democrat Party's Gerhard Schröder, who pledged to fight mass unemployment. Unfortunately, Schröder could not deliver economic growth and lost the election to Angela Merkel. After nearly two months of political gridlock, in late 2005, Merkel was poised to lead a coalition government as the first female chancellor of the German Republic.
- The Socialist Party's Francois Mitterand was elected President of France in 1981. In 1992, Francois Mitterrand's Socialist Party was soundly defeated. From their Parliamen-

tary majority established in the previous election, the Socialists plummeted to 70 seats against the 484 won by the combined forces of the right. Mitterrand remained in office until 1995, when Jacques Chirac was elected President. Again, with an anemic economy and rising ethnic discord, it is unlikely that Chirac's party will be re-elected in the next election.

- Japan's post-war leadership was dominated by the Liberal Democratic party, which held power from its formation in 1955. Japan's long economic miracle finally ran out of steam in 1991, when the economy began a lengthy and deep downturn. In 1993, the LDP's 38-year monopoly on power suddenly ended, ushering in a period of coalition governments and political instability; as many as 18 new political parties were formed and disbanded between 1993 and 1999, when the LDP returned to power. In April 2001, the youthful and reform-minded Junichiro Koizumi was elected Prime Minister, signaling a generational change in Japanese politics. Again, in the most recent elections, Koizumi won a landslide victory mostly because Japan's economy is breathing again and the Tokyo stock exchange is filling the wallets of the nation.

To put together an explanation of such political upheaval across the industrialized world, let's recall a few facts. In Canada, voters were suffering from a lingering recession that was made more painful by Tories' imposition of the Goods and Services Tax, a national sales tax. In France, although Mitterrand had long since abandoned Socialist economic principles, unemployment still hovered at 10 percent, and the national budget was strained to pay jobless benefits. In Germany, Kohl's popularity crested with reunification, but when he allowed the mark in East Germany to be of equal value to that in the West, he invited economic disaster – and spiraling unemployment. He injured himself further when he broke his promise and raised taxes to help defray the costs of reunification. In the US, as the first President Bush geared up for re-election, unemployment was close to 8 percent, and the economy was still mired in a two-year-old recession. Of course, like Chancellor Kohl, Bush was undone when he broke the infamous pledge, 'Read my lips. No new taxes.'

Clearly, when voters in Western democracies go to the polls, they are influenced not so much by ideology as by their stomachs and their wallets; and the political turmoil that roiled the industrialized world in the early 1990s was certainly an economic revolt against the stagnation and unemployment that seemed to have become endemic. But the problem was – and continues to be – larger than a temporary economic downturn, and it will not be solved by quick-fixes like tampering with the money supply or the exchange rates. In surveying the global landscape prior to the G-7 meeting in Munich in 1992, *Wall Street Journal* columnist Gerald Seib pointed in the direction of the real problem: 'There is a widespread sense that Western economies are moving into a post-industrial phase in which many lost jobs aren't coming back – and that current political leaders, geared to a Cold War military-industrial complex, don't know how to generate new ones.'[1]

Simply put, among the major industrialized countries – the 'triad' consisting of North America, Japan, and the European Union – there is little room left for growth. As Kenichi Ohmae analyzed the problem in his book, *Triad Power*, 'These countries have very similar problems: a mature and stagnant economy, escalating social costs, an aging population, lack of jobs for skilled workers, and at the same time, dynamic technological developments coupled with the ever-escalating costs of research and development (R&D) and modern production facilities.'[2]

Meanwhile, dramatic changes were taking place in developing countries as well:

- Since 1929, the Institutional Revolutionary Party (known by its Spanish initials, PRI) ruled Mexico. The party became so deeply rooted in the country's institutions that it became synonymous with the State. Institutions that were aligned with the party represented all government employees, peasants and workers. By 1997, the PRI was the world's longest-ruling party, but in elections that year, it lost power in the lower house of Congress. Then, in the 2000 election, the party was forced out of power completely, losing the election to the conservative National Action Party (PAN). Vicente Fox, a rancher and former Coca-Cola executive, was elected President. Unfortunately, despite the positive impact of the North American Free Trade Agreement (NAFTA) on the Mexican economy (it is now the second largest trading partner of the US, behind Canada, and neck and neck with China), the Fox government has been unable to deliver an economic miracle in Mexico. It is, therefore, less likely that his party will be re-elected.

- The socialist-minded Congress party had ruled India since independence from England in 1947 until 1996, except for three years in the late 1970s. What's more, the Prime Ministership was held, except for a brief time in the 1960s, by the Nehru family: Jawaharlal Nehru from 1947 to 1964, his daughter Indira Gandhi from 1966–77 and again from 1980–84, and her son Rajiv Gandhi from 1984–89. In 1991, following Rajiv Gandhi's assassination during the election campaign, the Congress' P. V. Narasimha Rao became Prime Minister. With the help of the IMF, Rao and Finance Minister Manmohan Singh initiated wide-ranging economic reforms. But economic growth was not rapid enough, and the Congress party was defeated in the 1996 elections. After that, a coalition led by the nationalist Bharatiya Janta Party (BJP) and its charismatic leader, Prime Minister Atal Behari Vajpayee, ruled India. The BJP accelerated the pace of economic reform, and was seemingly poised to win a large majority in Parliament in the 2004 elections – but instead lost by a wide margin in one of the biggest electoral shocks of recent times. In retrospect, the BJP failed to deliver economic benefits to rural India, and the Congress party is back in power as the leader of a coalition that will attempt to do just that. If the current government, despite its coalition with the Communists, continues to deliver growth through employment and wealth creation that is especially beneficial to the rural population, it is likely to survive and may even weather any scandals or external events.

- The great economic miracle that is China today was mired in insularity and stagnation as recently as 1978. That was when Deng Xiaoping and other pragmatists within the Communist Party of China (CPC) initiated major economic changes that continue to this day. Their vision was clear: China needed to generate surplus value in its economy to invest in modernization. Deng's approach was simple: motivate factory workers and farmers to produce more. Farmers were given incentives to become more productive by allowing them to retain a good portion of the fruits of that improved productivity. In industry, managers were given more autonomy and were allowed to reduce their work force if needed and give bonuses to more productive workers. Gradually, China also started to adopt more of an open door policy to allow direct investment by foreign companies and encourage international trade. In the 1980s, China created more market institutions and gradually moved from an administratively driven command economy to a price-driven market economy. In the 1990s, China focused on building a viable banking system driven by profit and loss rather than by political mandates. In the late 1990s and early 2000s, China focused on industrial reform, including shutting down non-viable state-owned factories. The liberalization of the economy and the injection of market forces have thus progressed in a steady and gradual way, greatly raising national output and living standards. This reflects Deng's original tenets of reform: pragmatism and incrementalism. Today, China is investing heavily to upgrade its infrastructure, with new superhighways, airports and telecommunications facilities. China's enormous ambitions for the future are dramatically symbolized by its deployment of the world's first commercial magnetic levitation train service. The train, capable of traveling at 300 miles per hour in virtual silence, zips people from Shanghai's airport to the city center in less than 10 minutes.[3] Among all the emerging economies, it seems that China is the most likely to continue to deliver economic growth with more jobs and wealth creation, especially among the interior Chinese population.

- When Dr. Mahathir Mohamad became Prime Minister of Malaysia in 1981, the country was just recovering from race riots and fighting a Communist insurgency. Mahathir gradually transformed the country into an oasis of peace, prosperity and economic growth. He moved Malaysia away from its dependence on commodities such as crude oil, rubber and palm oil, encouraging export-oriented manufacturing instead. His government kept inflation low and avoided balance-of-payments problems. He invested heavily in infrastructure, building high quality roads, an excellent railroad system and a world-class phone system. The results were outstanding: GDP rose from $12 billion in 1980 to $210 billion in 2002, with a per capita income of $3,540, the third highest in South Asia.[4] Today, Malaysia has one of the world's most open economies. As it finds itself squeezed by lower-cost manufacturing destinations such as China, Malaysia is trying to emulate Singapore, South Korea and Taiwan by moving up to more sophisticated, higher value activities. The government is increasing its spending on R&D, now 0.5 percent of GDP, compared to 0.1 percent in Indonesia.[5] Also, unlike many other Islamic countries, Malaysia's economic policies are secular in nature and seem to benefit significantly as a gateway between ASEAN and China for the moderate Middle East trading countries.

The common denominator in all these examples is that the only way for politicians to get in office and stay there is to deliver jobs and economic growth. Bill Clinton rode into the White House in 1992 by focusing relentlessly on a single message, summed up by his campaign manager James Carville in the now-immortal phrase, 'It's the economy, stupid.' Not only that, Clinton was comfortably re-elected in 1996 despite his personal problems, because the economy was doing well.

Carville was on to something big in pressing that theme. As democracy takes root in more and more parts of the world, politicians who cannot deliver economic growth quickly lose their jobs. Ideological considerations have gradually lost out to economic ones, and as a result, economic and political dogmatism is giving way to pragmatism, especially after the collapse of the Communist bloc. For example, India shed its socialist, protectionist and isolationist stance, while China gave up on collectivism (while continuing to pay lip-service to communism and maintain strict limits on political expression).

Why have economic forces become such a dominant factor in determining the outcomes of elections and the fates of politicians? Economics drives politics, and economic malaise inexorably leads to political instability. When democratic governments fail to deliver economic growth – when people lose jobs – those governments are turned out of office. Political instability, in turn, adds the additional economic stress of capital flight. Money goes underground, out of the country, under the mattress, rather than being invested in productive work, and growth is therefore further stymied.

While the changes were brewing before, we trace the turning point back to the energy crisis of the early 1970s. This, coupled with currency deflation after President Nixon took the US dollar off the gold standard, led to stagflation (slow economic growth and high inflation) in the mid and late 1970s. Though stagflation originated in Nixon's policies and the twin energy shocks of the 1970s, Jimmy Carter ultimately paid the price for it, and lost the 1980 election (he calls this being 'involuntarily retired by the public') amidst record levels of inflation and unemployment.

In this light, when he leaves office in 2008, George W. Bush will leave his party an interesting legacy. To this point his administration has skirted economic disaster, but massive deficits and a huge trade imbalance will be a drag on economic recovery, depress wages, and slow job creation. Such conditions on the micro level will compound the macroeconomic problem we addressed at the outset: How will the US and other advanced nations continue to grow their economies in the 21st century? To find the answer, let's look back, then forward.

Economic Growth Engines – Past, Present and Future

Prior to the industrial revolution in the late 18th century, there was little economic growth in the world. For thousands of years, the average standard of living rose very little, and the vast majority of people lived a subsistence-level existence, with few luxuries if any. Then, after the industrial revolution, per capita income and consumption increased dramatically over the succeeding two centuries.[6] Gradually, ordinary citizens in industrialized countries could aspire to levels of comfort and prosperity that only a few rich people experienced earlier.

Before the industrial revolution, there was very little democracy; political rights and the ownership of land and property were all with the monarchy by birthright. The democratization of wealth gradually allowed the private sector to enter infrastructure businesses such as shipping and railroads.

After the industrial revolution, the first big economic growth engine for the world was Western Europe (Figure 1.1). The Europeans began to gradually outsource manufacturing; rather than get raw materials from the 'new world,' they began to set up factories there. The British in particular invested heavily in the US, in railroads, mines, cattle ranches, mineral processing, packing meat, and flour making. The US was able to grow as an export-oriented economy. Likewise, many colonies of European countries around the world experienced economic growth by exporting first raw materials and later some finished goods to Europe.

In the 1900s, the growth engine was North America, primarily the US. Especially in the second half of the century, the US began to open up its market to imports. In industries where it was no longer competitive, it began to outsource, and countries such as South Korea, Singapore, Taiwan, Japan and Hong Kong

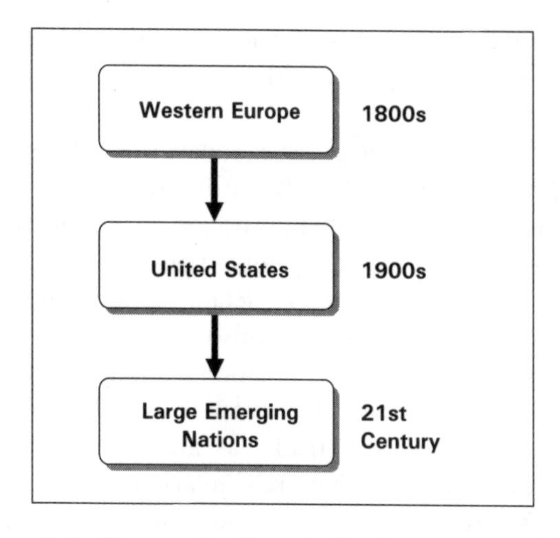

Figure 1.1: Economic Growth Engines for the World

all grew into major economies by exporting to the US market. At that time, trade policy was clearly linked with the Cold War; if a country was a political or military ally, the US market was opened up to it; otherwise, it was closed. Thus, the US had very little trade with the USSR, enormous trade with South Korea and none with North Korea.

The 21st century will bring a radical change: for the first time in history, economic growth will be driven by large emerging nations rather than by advanced countries (Figure 1.1). How revolutionary is this change? If you were to draw a map of the post-colonial, post-industrial-revolution world based on economic strength and world trade instead of on physical size or population, it would consist largely of Western Europe, the US and Canada and Japan. These fifteen countries utterly controlled the world economy. As of 1987, they represented 75 percent of world trade and 70 percent of world GDP.[7] In economic terms, the rest of the world almost didn't matter; on such a map China and India would look puny, while Mexico would be virtually invisible.

Indeed the fruits of the industrial revolution were concentrated in these advanced countries, whose GDPs grew enormously, while the rest of the world lagged far behind. These countries primarily traded with one another, and largely ignored the 80 percent or so of the world's population that lived outside their borders.

To reiterate the central issue: today, these fifteen countries have little inherent growth left within their own economies. Without economic growth, there is no job or wealth creation, and without employment or wealth, politicians are soon out of a job.

As we shall explain in more detail, economic growth in the world's advanced countries is seriously hampered by their aging and, in many cases, declining populations. But the problem is more complicated than that. Even if population is still rising (as it is in the US via immigration), trade, as an engine of growth, is ineffective among nations that are similarly mature and similarly advanced. As economists Baumol and Gomory have shown, the net gains from trade are far greater when it occurs between a developed and a less developed economy, rather than between two comparably developed economies.[8]

Thus, if trading among themselves is no longer the solution because they all have similar strengths and weaknesses, the world's advanced economies will have to search elsewhere for continued economic health. To put it point-blank, the world's leading powers will be able to sustain economic growth only through trading partnerships with large developing nations. This fact will drive the realignment of nations as the world 'goes global.'

Until recently, the economic output and potential of these large developing nations were severely underestimated, based on comparing their economic output in terms of their nominal GDP. Then the World Bank, IMF, WHO, and UNDP started using a different index with which to measure the new world economic order. This new index is called Purchasing Power Parity (PPP). Traditional assessments of the size of an economy and therefore its attractiveness as a market were based on how much people earn per capita; on that score, many developing countries were sliding back further and further, and the gap between rich and poor nations was rising. Countries such as China, India, Brazil, Indonesia and Mexico were measuring poorly in terms of per capita income because the denominator (population) was rising nearly as fast as the numerator (GDP denominated in US dollars). Instead of measuring how much people earn, the PPP index measures what they can buy with what they earn. For example, Coca Cola promotes the idea that it takes four minutes of work for a worker in China to buy a bottle of Coke, compared with three minutes in the US. The forecast is that in the next ten years, it will be cheaper for the Chinese worker to buy Coke than for the American worker.

Rank	*Country*	*Economic Output (PPP) (In millions of US dollars)*
1	US	11,628,083
2	China	7,123,172
3	Japan	3,774,086
4	India	3,363,960
5	Germany	2,325,828
6	United Kingdom	1,832,252
7	France	1,744,352
8	Italy	1,621,372
9	Brazil	1,483,859
10	Russia	1,408,603
11	Spain	1,046,249
12	Mexico	1,014,514
13	Canada	993,079
14	South Korea	980,694
15	Indonesia	779,719
16	Australia	605,942
17	Turkey	552,990
18	Netherlands	520,918
19	Thailand	510,268
20	South Africa	510,102

Source: The World Bank

Figure 1.2: Size of Economies based on PPP (2004)

Using this index, China emerged in 2002 as the second-largest economy (after the US), up from 4th in 1994. It has now surpassed Germany and Japan, and the forecast is that by 2040 (maybe sooner), it will be the single largest economy, surpassing the US. India is now the fourth-largest economy (larger than Germany, the UK and France), and it too has huge potential to grow in the future. India will certainly overtake Japan and become the third-largest economy during the present decade. The PPP index indicates that even other developing nations – like Mexico, Indonesia and Brazil – are becoming much more significant players on the world economic stage than acknowledged ever before (Figure 1.2).

The Population Paradox

For decades now, we have become accustomed to hearing about the world's population crisis. For most, this means one thing and one thing only: the world's population has been exploding at an unprecedented and unsustainable rate.

Indeed, if we look at the statistics from the century just concluded, we can certainly find cause for alarm. The world added by far more human beings to its population in the century than ever before; the global population rose from 1.6 billion in 1900 to over six billion in 2000 (the population would have been even greater in 2000 were it not for the more than 200 million people killed in wars and by governments in the 20th century). Improved medical care contributed greatly to this growth, as life expectancy at birth rose from 30 years to 65 years during the century.

However, there was a big change around the middle of the century. The average fertility level dropped by about 40 percent in the second half of the century i.e. each woman gave birth to two fewer children – on an average – than in the first-half of the century. This fertility decline occurred earliest and was most pronounced in the industrialized and prosperous countries of the West and in Japan. By the 1970s, the birth rate in many countries had dipped below the replacement rate of 2.1 live births per woman. Today, about half the world lives in nations with sub-replacement fertility. The stark reality is that citizens in virtually every developed nation have ceased replacing themselves.

While life expectancy has been going up steadily for 300 years, the decline in the number of young people is a new and completely unprecedented phenomenon. Developed nations are in an economy-depressing process of 'deyouthing,' and many countries face the prospect of acute population shrinkage. For example, by 2050, Japan's population will shrink by 30 million from its present 125 million population, and Russia's will decline by 42 million from its present 146 million. Europe's elderly (those over 65) will increase from 20 percent of total population in 1998, to 25 percent by 2020. By 2030, people over 65 in Germany will account for almost half the adult population, compared with one-fifth now. Fertility rates all across Europe are shockingly low: just 1.15 in Spain, 1.2 in Italy, 1.3 in Germany, 1.35 in Russia, 1.37 in Portugal and 1.41 in Austria (Figure 1.3).

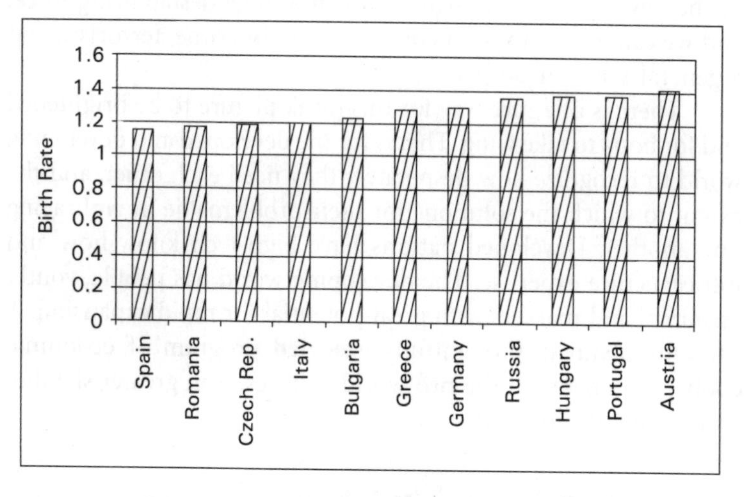

Figure 1.3: The 'Deyouthing' of Europe

While the rate of growth of the population has slowed even in developing countries, their populations do continue to grow. Overall, the world's population is expected to climb to 7.8 billion in 2025. At the same time, the absolute number of people in 'more developed countries' (as the UN calls them) will start to decline in 2017, and the median age in these countries will continue to rise rapidly. Only about 15 percent of the world's population will be in these more developed countries, down from over 18 percent today. The world population is likely to peak at 9 billion around 2050 and then start to decline.

So the reality that the world faces is that there will be, in effect, a 'population implosion' in developed countries, while overpopulation will continue to be the norm in most developing countries. Developed countries will have very high median ages, enormous health care burdens and an unsustainably high ratio of retirees to workers. Developing countries will have large young populations with insufficient economic opportunities and high levels of environmental degradation. This widening of the economic divide could give rise to a host of social and political problems. The unemployed, under-employed and disaffected youth of the developing world will represent a huge destabilizing force, and we can expect to see a continued rise in crime, terrorism and a general sense of despair.

There is one sure way for this bleak picture to be brightened and for hope to take wing. That is for the developed and developing world to recognize how desperately they need each other, and the extent to which the solutions for their problems lie in embracing one another. Developed nations have high-tech know-how and infrastructure expertise. The developing world has people, youth, resources and markets with great potential for rapid expansion. A carefully planned, thoughtfully executed program of economic cooperation between the two worlds can result in greater stability and prosperity for both.

A Great Opportunity

Such stability and prosperity constitute the ultimate rationale for globalization, of course, but now let's look more closely at the evolving 'north-south' economic integration that will temporarily interrupt but ultimately pave the way for global cooperation. Over the past 200 years, the world has been organized along what may be termed an 'east-west' axis, trade and investment flows largely stayed either above the equator or below the equator, with very little crossover. This is shorthand to suggest that countries tended to be in close trading relationships only with other countries in similar economic conditions. Thus, developed countries traded mostly with other developed countries; they certainly never attempted any degree of economic integration with countries that were not comparably developed. This mindset was expressed in 1992 by US presidential candidate Ross Perot, who harshly criticized the then proposed North American Free Trade Agreement (which would bring Mexico in the trade pact already established between the US and Canada). Perot warned voters that there would be a 'giant sucking sound' as US jobs flowed to Mexico. He argued that the US should never economically integrate with another country unless that country's standard of living was comparable to its own.

Such thinking is fundamentally flawed, because it ignores the huge potential for synergy that exists when economies with truly complementary strengths and weaknesses get together. Indeed, the world is now becoming fundamentally realigned along a 'north-south' axis, and it is in this realignment that we see the beginnings of a propitious marriage between the developed and the developing worlds. Young countries are seeking out older ones. Countries with low or declining birth rates are aligning with countries with high birth rates. Overcrowded countries are seeing the attractions of those with sparse populations.

There are two axes along which to think about this: growth and prosperity. For continued economic progress (and in order to lift people out of abject poverty), the world needs both growth and prosperity. Most developed countries have high prosperity but low growth, while many developing countries have high growth but low prosperity (Figure 1.4). The surest and fastest way to benefit the largest number of people is to create true synergy by speeding integration between countries from both categories.

A Win-Win Approach

The notion of a win-win approach is finally coming to be accepted by countries where internal growth has almost stopped. Countries that now must seek opportunities elsewhere, in high-growth

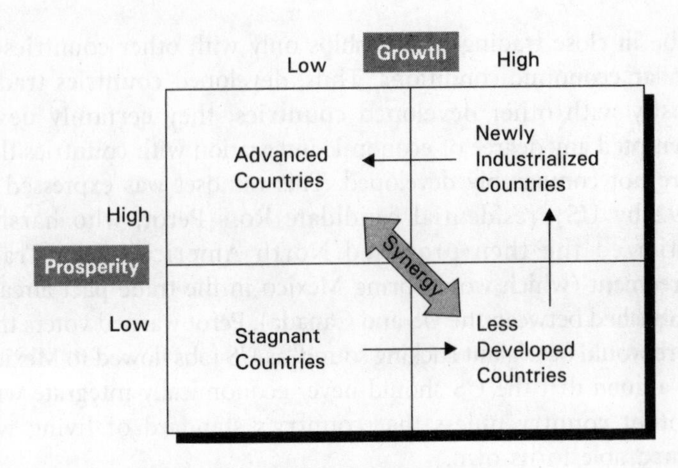

Figure 1.4: Classifying Nations

economies, are beginning to realize the shortsightedness of the old colonial mindset i.e. a win for them but a long-term loss for the other country. The only viable option today is mutually beneficial arrangements. Developing countries need ways to rapidly increase their prosperity. Advanced countries need growth. In the win-win situation, the advanced country gets its growth by participating in a developing country's domestic market. The developing country gets technology, know-how, and capital which are key to its prosperity and economic development. Soon it begins to improve its prosperity, primarily through the transfer of product and process technologies.

Indeed, it has to happen. Otherwise, slowing growth in the advanced economies will have dire consequences – the sorts of things we are already seeing with under-funded pension plans and a social security system in critical health. Increasingly, new wealth creation and job creation will come from emerging economies, and unless two-way partnerships are formed, both brains and capital will be drained from the old world to the new. The high-tech highway leads to developing nations, and developed nations must make sure that traffic continues to flow in both directions. That kind of full integration constitutes a win-win situation.

Not that it will be easy. The win-win scenario demands a convergence of values, goals, and ideas that has not historically characterized relationships between developed and developing nations. There is lingering mistrust in the post-colonial world; deep-seated suspicions that developed nations want only to take advantage of the markets and resources that the developing world has to offer. There are political differences – specifically, the Communism that still prevails in China and to some extent lingers in India. In the Middle East and other parts of the world, there is open hostility to the West, to Western values, and to Western-style consumption.

In essence, both sides must understand that they can be winners. The developing world, in particular, must see that it will not be exploited. Perhaps the clearest demonstration of the new paradigm can be found in Japan's rewriting of Ricardo – the theory of vacating markets. Here, outsourcing means not cheap labor and resource extraction, but the transfer of entire industries to the developing world. As developed nations 'vacate' traditional manufacturing and move up toward 'knowledge' industries, the developing world follows, progressing from agriculture to industry, from industry to service, as India already illustrates so dramatically.

The road to world prosperity is likely to be long, but also fascinating. One of its most interesting features is taking shape right now, in the geoeconomic realignment of nations that we describe as a 'tectonic shift.'

Alternatives to American Dominance

On major strategic and international questions today, Americans are from Mars and Europeans are from Venus: They agree on little, and understand one another less and less.

Robert Kagan[9]

At the outset, let us admit that competition – even armed aggression – between nations is not suddenly going to disappear as the WTO waves the magic wand of globalization. Indeed, the tri-polar North-South alignment that is our subject here is not simply a matter of enlightened economic cooperation. We hope that its evolution will continue in that direction, but, frankly, its origins lie in the economic and political rivalry between the US and Europe.

The US was the dominant economic player on the world stage for much of the 20th century, especially after World War II (WWII). It had many unique advantages: a huge and prosperous domestic market, abundant natural resources, a common language and currency, well-developed infrastructures for the transportation of people, goods and information, an outstanding educational system, strong financial markets and so on. No country in the world even came close to matching these advantages.

While the US emerged from World War II at the zenith of its power and influence, Europe and Japan were down and nearly out. The US created the Marshall Plan to help rebuild Europe and, at the same time, occupied Japan till 1952 and oversaw the rebuilding of that economy into the formidable competitor that it soon became.

The Europeans, while grateful to the US for helping them get back on their feet, started to assert themselves soon after the end of the war. To counter US dominance in the world economy, they created the Common Market, built on a vision first articulated by Winston Churchill in 1946 in a famous speech in Zurich:

> I wish to speak to you today about the tragedy of Europe... Yet all the while there is a remedy which, if it were generally and spontaneously adopted by the great majority of people in many lands, would as if by a miracle transform the whole scene, and would in a few years make all Europe, or the greater part of it, as free and as happy as Switzerland is today. What is this sovereign remedy? It is to recreate the European Family, or as much of it as we can, and to provide it with a structure under which it can dwell in peace, in safety and in freedom. We must build a kind of US of Europe… The first step in the recreation of the European Family must be a partnership between France and Germany.[10]

As European nationalism became more pronounced after World War II, the US began to look eastward more and more. It began to outsource basic manufacturing to Asia, initially to Japan, followed by Taiwan and then South Korea after the Korean War. Economic policy was heavily dictated by strategic military considerations, which were mostly driven by the Cold War between the West and the Union of Soviet Socialist Republics (USSR)-led Communist bloc. (Indeed, the Cold War itself was an engine of growth for the US, since it required huge spending on defense and therefore the robust health of defense-related industries.)

With the US looking to the Far East and with the Marshall Plan coming to an end, it seemed that Europe could no longer depend on America. They were also worried about the potential threat from Japan, which had surpassed Germany, France and the UK to become the world's second largest economy. It was time for European nations to take charge of their own destiny.

As a decisive first step, Europe sought to match the US advantage by 're-launching' itself with the Treaty of Rome and the creation of the Common Market, or European Economic Community. Seeing that the game was afoot, the US moved to expand its 'home' market by integrating Canada. This cooperative agreement began in the auto industry in 1965, followed by the signing of the comprehensive CUFTA (Canada-US Free Trade Agreement) in 1989. The US then raised the stakes by bringing Mexico into NAFTA in December 1992. Seeking to trump these moves, Europe created a common currency and made plans to expand east and south. In response, the US has renewed its efforts to create the Free Trade Area of the Americas (FTAA), spanning the northern tip of Alaska to the southern tip of South America. So this has become an iterative process with elements of one-upmanship.

Let's pause to note, though, that the integration of Mexico into the existing free trade agreement between the US and Canada was a watershed event; it marked the first time that developed countries had welcomed a developing country into such an agreement. While some countries within the European rubric (e.g. Portugal) are less developed than others, the differences are not nearly as stark as those that existed between the US and Mexico. Significantly, here is where the benefits of economic cooperation between developed and developing nations elbow aside the competitive posturing of the superpowers. The European Union has now embraced this 'North-South' thinking with its push to include less developed Eastern European countries to the East and Turkey to the South.

Meanwhile, Japan's economic explosion in the last quarter of the 20th century set it at the center of the Asian axis – an axis that extends north-to-south from China all the way to Australia. Moreover, what emerging China offers to already-developed Japan is analogous to what Mexico offers the US. As we are already seeing, however, the huge economic potential of China (and India, too, to a lesser extent) will have the effect of breaking down alignments based on regional trade blocs and of pushing toward real globalization. But we're getting ahead of the story.

Why Regional Trade Blocs Will Prevail in the Meantime

It makes sense to crawl before we walk. It makes sense to first have the Canada-US Free Trade Agreement (CUFTA), then NAFTA, and then FTAA. It makes sense to learn how free trade works on a regional level before mandating it globally. We know that trade is good. It will be better if we work out the kinks. That's why over the past few decades, we've seen the creation of a plethora of regional trade pacts, including The Southern Common Market (MERCOSUR), the Andean Pact, the Caribbean Community and Common Market (CARICOM), NAFTA, the Baltic Free Trade Area (BFTA), the Central European Free Trade Area (CEFTA), the Economic Community of West African States (ECOWAS), the South African Development Community (SADC), Asia Pacific Economic Cooperation (APEC), the Closer Economic Relations Agreement (CER) between Australia and New Zealand, the South Asian Association for Regional Cooperation (SAARC) and many others.

Following the same logic, we can expect to see many of these regional trade pacts merge into three major regional economies: the FTAA, AFTA (Asian Free Trade Area) and the as-yet unnamed Europe-centered trade region. To reiterate, each will be organized geographically on a (roughly) north-south axis, and each will demonstrate the dynamic benefits that accrue when developed nations partner with developing nations.

It is also quite likely that these three regional trade economies will become strong economic rivals; we already see some evidence of economic battles among them. But note: in the past, economic wars have often led to military wars. But in this case military wars are highly unlikely because of the very fact that *three* groups are emerging. If it were just Europeans versus Americans, it might be like Russia and the US all over again. But fortunately, a counter-balancing third force is emerging in Asia.

In fact, the world today is in a precariously unipolar state, with one superpower – the US. The rise of anti-American sentiment globally is inevitable in such a world. With rising European assertiveness and the undeniable power of what is happening in China, two rival centers of power are rapidly rising. The combined force (economic and military) of Europe and Asia will not have to be subservient to the US, and the unipolar world will be replaced by a safer tripolar one.

So what about the much discussed World Trade Organization (WTO)? Ultimately, as it mediates trade disputes among disparate nations, the WTO will serve as the great arbiter of globalization. In the meantime, it is in fact *not* a hindrance to regional free trade agreements (FTAs), since it incorporates two key provisions: developed countries can give tariff preferences to developing countries, and countries entering into regional FTAs do not need to extend the preferences negotiated in this context to all other WTO member states.[11]

How Regional Integration Will Play Out

As the rivalry among the three major trade economies increases, each will want to generate a significant domestic base of its own from which to export. For advanced countries, the domestic base has to be a lot larger than the export base. As an advanced country, the only way to create domestic growth is to de-emphasize national boundaries through free trade agreements. Europe was the first to move in this direction, because growth there plateaued sooner than in the US or in Japan, 25 to 30 years ago. Europe saw that the way for it to grow was to remove the economic barriers between nations and give companies the freedom to invest across national boundaries. As a consequence, there have been numerous mergers and acquisitions in industry after industry all across Europe – deals not only sanctioned by governments but, in some cases, financed (at least in part) by them. This effective erasure of national boundaries has successfully created a more efficient, larger domestic market for companies in all of Europe's member states. Ultimately, this process leads to the kind of full economic integration now underway in Europe, with *de facto* free movement of money, people, products, resources and information. It creates domestic growth as well as improved products for the world market. At the same time, there is a protective tendency to create a 'fortress' around the trade bloc, which means only intra-bloc companies can participate in the market.

In fact, competition will encourage each of the three trade blocs to create its own fortress. The size and scope of the enlarged regional market will foster the notion that trade outside the region is unnecessary: a notion that eventually will prove illusory. An unwillingness or inability to export outside the region will make companies within the trade bloc fatally vulnerable to competitors that become truly global.

For now, however, the division of the world economy into three trade blocs seems a certainty. Given how far we have already come, and the dynamic that is already in motion, where is this transition headed? The broad outlines are already quite clear:

- NAFTA will expand to include all of the Americas – North, Central and South, as well as the Caribbean nations and even Cuba (post Castro) – in the FTAA, which will be led by the US, Canada and Brazil or India (in that order).
- The European Union will expand to include Eastern Europe and Russia, in a free trade zone led by Germany, France and Russia (in that order).

- Almost all Asian countries will come together (with the exception of countries in South Asia), including Australia and New Zealand, in a free trade zone that will be led by China, Japan and South Korea (in that order).

Note that it is the economic coalition and integration of one advanced and one large emerging economy that is likely to create growth in each bloc. Also, while the developed economies of the US and Germany will lead their coalitions, our forecast is that it will be China that will lead Japan and South Korea.

Who is Left Out?

Two categories of countries are in danger of being ignored or even shunned from entry into one of the three major economic alliances: ideology-driven nations and 'Fourth World' countries.

As for the first group, any country that is ideology-driven today is likely to be a pariah. Today, ideology just does not sell well. After World War II and all through the Cold War, ideology was a great 'sales mechanism' that countries could use to align themselves with one group or another. The ideology might have been political (for example, Communism), religious (Christianity or Islam), isolationist (North Korea or Burma, now Myanmar) or even social or cultural (Latin America). Today, ideology has been replaced in much of the world by *economic pragmatism*. Still, however, in countries like Israel, the Arab states, and many Central African nations, ideologies remain obstacles in the path of economic growth.

Formerly Communist countries have rapidly shed their ideological baggage. Russia is moving toward a market economy, followed by the other Eastern European countries. China is undergoing the same metamorphosis silently; while it does still have single-party rule, the Chinese government is fervently pursuing market-based economic reform. A similar ideological change has taken place in India, which has moved away from Fabian socialism to embrace a free-market vision. Change is coming even to the Middle East. The Gulf States, such as UAE, are booming, and Turkey is at the cusp of major economic transformation. Cuba is likely to be integrated with the North American economy. The most dramatic example of this is Communist-ruled and formerly isolationist Vietnam, which we believe will be totally integrated into the Asian-Pacific economy.

A second category of countries that have little to offer by way of either import or export potential are what we call 'Fourth World' countries. These countries – typified by Nepal, Sudan, Rwanda and Malawi – have the misfortune of being so poor that they represent an economic burden rather than an opportunity. Their populations are too small to be attractive as potential markets. They are unlikely to be integrated for quite some time, unless a wealth of natural resources tempts investment by advanced countries.

Who Joins Whom?

The north-south realignment we foresee will, by definition be influenced by geography. In fact, the pressure of proximity will create some strange and perhaps wonderful alliances. For example, Australia and New Zealand are discovering that despite their overwhelmingly Caucasian populations and Western value systems, their destiny lies in fostering ever-closer linkages with their Asian brethren. Similarly, a hoped-for trade pact between India and Pakistan has the potential to ease the bitter tensions between these sometimes-hostile neighbors, and lead to amicable relations and mutual economic development. The same holds for North and South Korea, and for Ireland and the UK.

Yet let us consider a few interesting examples where the rules of strict geography might be violated.

The UK

In a fascinating development, the UK has basically been relegated to the sidelines in the EU theater. The European Union (EU) – as a bloc – is primarily driven by Germany, in close partnership with France. Talk about strange bedfellows; when the Germans and the French can get together in this manner, anything is possible!

Neither of them is willing to cede much political power to Europe's third major economic entity, the UK. The UK thus has a tough time crossing the English Channel, even though it is formally part of the Union. Reflecting its own ambivalence towards Europe, the UK has so far refused to join the European monetary union, continuing to use its own currency.

In fact, this has been a major source of contention between the UK and Europe. Each trade bloc needs to have its own common currency so that members do not have to deal with currency fluctuations. Margaret Thatcher, a true 'Euro-skeptic,' resented the unwillingness of the EU to embrace the pound as the natural *de facto* common currency. The Germans didn't want it, and they toppled the pound in February 1993. The British saw that as a sign to that their future lay less with Europe and more with the Americans.

In terms of both investment and trade, the UK economy is becoming tightly integrated with the US. The amount of US FDI (foreign direct investment) assets in the UK alone is larger than US overseas assets in Asia, Africa and the Middle East combined. International mergers and acquisitions are commonplace. British Petroleum bought out Amoco and, more recently, ARCO. Vodafone and Virgin Atlantic are likely to make significant investments in the US.

Politically, it is already evident that the US and the UK walk together (just like the Germans and the French), regardless of which political parties are in power on either side of the Atlantic. Margaret Thatcher and Ronald Reagan were ideological allies who greatly influenced one another. The close relationship continued under John Major and Bill Clinton, then under Tony Blair and Clinton, and now under Blair and George Bush.

Spain and Portugal

Since Germans are driving the evolution of the EU, the power base is moving more towards northern Europe, which is why the Spanish and Portuguese are becoming somewhat nervous about their future. As a result, those countries are forging closer ties with Latin America. Going forward, in fact, we are likely to find that Spain and Portugal will align themselves more closely with the UK and the emerging FTAA than with the EU. Their colonial ties with the region, and resulting cultural and language similarities, make this a very likely outcome. At the same time, these countries will remain in the EU fold.

The Middle East

If and when the Middle East is able to move beyond its ideological battles and embrace economic pragmatism, it will find a natural home in the European (including Russia) trade bloc. We include even Israel in this prediction. While some might expect that Israel to be more likely to ally with the US, in fact the historical linkages of Israel's immigrant population are much stronger with Europe and Russia.

Africa

The future of Africa is uncertain. Northern Africa (above the Sahara) is similar to the Middle East; this includes Morocco, Algeria, even Libya. On the other hand, South Africa has a more advanced, liberalized economy and has given signals that it would like to align with one of the trade blocs. We believe that it is more likely to align with the Europeans than with the Americas. The same is true of Zimbabwe and other Southern African countries, many of which are already in trading relationships together (similar to MERCOSUR in South America). The value systems, cultures, regulatory processes, etc. are very compatible with Europe's.

Chaotic Middle Africa will continue to be 'no man's land.' However, any country there that announces that it wants to liberalize and become a free-market economy will see quick interest from the Europeans, especially if it is resource-rich – a situation developing right now in Nigeria.

India

'India and the US – nations that barely interacted 15 years ago – could turn out to be the ideal economic partners for the new century.'

'The Rise of India,' *Business Week* (2003)

As recently as ten years ago, India was in the uncomfortable position of not being needed or wanted by its Asian neighbors. The border of the Association of South East Asian Nations (ASEAN) bloc grew to include Laos, Cambodia, Vietnam and Burma (Myanmar), but stopped there. India is not wanted or needed there, because Asia already has the huge China market. Ethnically and culturally, South Asia is very distinct from East and Southwest Asia. India is a poor fit in the European trade bloc as well, because Europe is now absorbing many East European economies that can offer many of the same advantages that India has – like low wages and an educated workforce – and they are neighbors with similar cultures, religions, and so on.

So rather than remain isolated, India is moving into a strategic partnership with the US that includes both military and economic interdependence. US companies are already heavily outsourcing their call centers and business process outsourcing (BPO) to India. Indians in the US as well as companies in India are developing software; India currently exports more than $15 billion of software a year, mostly to the US – a number that is expected to grow to $50 billion a year in less than five years. If that sounds unrealistic, think about how little trade the US used to have with China, and how much it trades now.

We believe that India will supplant China as a major economic partner of the US; it will likely invest in the US in mature industries such as textiles, gems and jewelry, leather goods, and granite and marble. Rather than shipping out raw material, India will export finished products. India is the largest diamond cutter in the world; 90 percent of the world's diamonds are cut and polished there. It is one of the largest leather goods exporters and ranks number two in exports of granite and marble. Since many of these have already been outsourced from the US, there will be no significant negative political impact.

India is also a huge agriculture producer. The largest bakery in the world is India's Modern Bakery, now owned by Unilever. India is the largest producer and consumer of milk and dairy products, and is now creating a large dairy industry through cooperatives and companies such as Amul. Brands such as

Marlboro are likely to be 'Made in India' or 'Made in Brazil' – not just raw tobacco, but the entire product.

Human capital is one of India's major resources. The Indian government has primarily targeted three areas of relevance here: software and information technology, R&D and management talent. For example, Cisco is investing in India to create tens of thousands of Cisco-certified IT professionals; IBM, Oracle and Microsoft have made similar commitments. As a result of its long-standing emphasis on higher technological and scientific education, India is becoming recognized as a great place to do R&D, and many major laboratories are moving into the country. In pharmaceuticals, India is already enjoying a reverse flow: patents generated by Indian scientists are being licensed to the world.

Russia

The alignment of Russia does not violate geography, but Russia's journey toward a market economy is so interesting that we can't resist mentioning it.

Communism was on its way out long before Gorbachev. Leonid Brezhnev's successor, Yuri Andropov, had already decided to liberalize the economy while sustaining the one-party Communist system (which is exactly what Deng in China did subsequently). However, Andropov suddenly died after just one year on the job, and Mikhail Gorbachev came in and essentially reversed the sequence: he ushered in an era of *glasnost* or political openness, while doing little on the economic front, other than giving signals that he wanted to align more with the Americans and British. Ultimately, the more economically pragmatic Boris Yeltsin and then Vladimir Putin, who had clearly indicated that Russia's future lies with Europe, replaced him. This was starkly illustrated when he joined France and Germany in presenting a united front opposing US action in Iraq.

We believe that Russia will definitely align with the Europeans. With the Putin government now, the deal seems pretty much done. The early indication of economic alignment is always trade; the US only accounts for about 8 percent of Russia's imports and exports, while Germany alone accounts for 9 percent of exports and 14 percent of imports.[12]

The End Game

We believe that by 2025, most countries of the world will be loosely or tightly aligned with one of the three trade blocs. The table below provides details of each trade bloc in terms of its constituents. The population trends (Table 1.1) clearly indicate that the American bloc will have an advantage going forward.

Is the New Alignment a Good Thing?

The transformation of the world into three mega economic blocs is certainly not without controversy. Many are concerned that this move towards self-contained economic blocs comes at the expense of 'true' globalization. But as we have argued, regional trade paves the way for global trade.

In any case, the reality right now is that the forces propelling economic blocs based (shared geographies, common heritage, complementary economic characteristics, and rivalry with other regions) are more potent than those propelling globalization. While we expect that the WTO will be successful in gradually lowering barriers around the world, its impact for the immediate future will continue to be overshadowed by the rise of economic blocs.

The ultimate yardstick by which this development needs to be assessed is a simple one: will it lead to a more rapid and broader uplift of the economic fortunes of a larger number of people? On this score, the answer is likely to be a resounding 'yes.' Why? Because it will help solve the problem we put forward at the beginning of this chapter. It will create, promote, and sustain economic growth.

One key to this affirmative vision is, as we have noted, the north-south integration that will characterize the evolution of the three economic blocs. Until recently, trade blocs were, in effect, clubs for wealthy nations. Members jealously guarded their

Table 1.1: Population Trends

	Trade Bloc	*Population in Mid-2003*	*Population in 2025 (projected)*	*Population in 2050 (projected)*
Americas	North America	323,000,000	387,000,000	459,000,000
	Central America	144,000,000	192,000,000	230,000,000
	South America	358,000,000	452,000,000	507,000,000
	Bangladesh	146,700,000	208,300,000	254,600,000
	India	1,068,600,000	1,363,000,000	1,628,000,000
	Pakistan	149,100,000	249,700,000	348,600,000
	Sri Lanka	19,300,000	21,700,000	21,400,000
	UK	59,200,000	62,900,000	63,700,000
	Total	**2,267,900,000**	**2,936,600,000**	**3,512,300,000**
Europe	Africa	861,000,000	1,289,000,000	1,883,000,000
	Western Asia	204,000,000	308,000,000	418,000,000
	Europe	727,000,000	722,000,000	664,000,000
	Total	**1,792,000,000**	**2,319,000,000**	**2,965,000,000**
Asia	Southeast Asia	544,000,000	697,000,000	792,000,000
	East Asia	1,519,000,000	1,688,000,000	1,597,000,000
	Oceania	32,000,000	42,000,000	50,000,000
	Total	**2,095,000,000**	**2,427,000,000**	**2,439,000,00**

Source: PRB 2003 World Population Data Sheet (http://www.prb.org/)

exclusivity and subjected aspiring nations to stringent tests that essentially measured how similar new members would be to old ones. That insular mindset, fortunately, has been broken, most dramatically when the US and Canada took the bold step of integrating with Mexico under NAFTA. In the process, a new paradigm was established: partnerships between developed and developing nations. And the seemingly intractable problem – where mature economies would find future growth opportunities – was simultaneously solved. Going forward, we shall see increasingly rapid integration of a new and diverse set of members. This will pay rich dividends on all sides, since north-south integration, by reaching out to developing nations, offers far more potential to lift living standards than east-west integration, which simply raises economic efficiency for companies and lower prices for consumers.

(It bears repeating that although we call them trade blocs with a north-south delineation, the three areas are not *strictly* geographical entities. And when geography is violated – as in an alliance between the US and India, or between Europe and Africa – the same overarching purpose is served: the mature and fully developed economies of the West are finding new growth in developing nations, and those emerging nations are, in turn, being given the opportunity to develop and prosper.)

A second and equally important consequence of the creation of these three mega powers is that the world has the potential to be a much more stable and peaceful place than it has been at any time in the past. In a unipolar world (such as exists currently), the tendency towards unilateral action – however well-intentioned – invariably breeds resentment and foments rebellion and even terrorism. In a bipolar world, with two evenly matched rivals, there is real potential for destructive competition – economic or military. In a tripolar world, however, a high degree of stability is built in. If any one of the three powers becomes overly belligerent, it will likely be countered by a united front of the other two. A tripolar world thus offers an inherent deterrence against military or economic adventurism.

Given that the trilateral powers will have little to gain and much to lose from aggression, it follows that resources will in all probability be diverted away from military spending and towards economic development. In a world that succeeds in filling stomachs and wallets, minds are less likely to be filled with fundamentalist ideology or the politics of jihad. Illiteracy will be reduced. Poverty will be reduced, not through aid but through job and wealth creation.

In his landmark book *1984*, George Orwell envisioned a world divided into three super-states, each a totalitarian regime ('Big Brother') and all perpetually at war with each other:

- Oceania: The Americas and England
- Eurasia: Russia and Europe
- Eastasia: The Far East

On the other hand, Bjorn Hettne and his co-authors have argued that 'new regionalism' (defined as a multidimensional form of integration that includes the economic, political, social and cultural levels) will contribute to peace, development and ecological sustainability.[13] Our view is much more closely aligned with this perspective than that of Orwell. The fact is that past approaches based on shunning trade, trading only with similarly developed trade partners, or relying purely on multilateral trade agreements to open markets have simply not succeeded in lifting enough people out of poverty; for the most part, they have been ineffectual or simply made the rich richer and the poor poorer.

Structure of the Book

The first half of the book – chapter two to chapter six – is historical in nature. Chapter two revisits the 'magic of Ricardo' showing how free trade between countries results in mutually beneficial outcomes. The succeeding three chapters trace how each of the three trade blocs has evolved to the point where they are at now. Chapter six looks at some of the countries that are not yet part of the design of the trade blocs.

The second half of the book focuses on what each trade bloc must do to make itself globally competitive. Chapter seven provides an overview of the needed changes, and chapters eight through eleven deal, in turn, with each of the four key aspects of strong bloc integration. The book concludes with chapter twelve, which addresses the obstacles to this emerging realignment, and how they can be overcome.

Chapter 2

Trade as the Engine of Economic Growth

The Magic of Ricardo

Britain had been a trading nation since the establishment of its first colonies – but a decidedly protectionist one. Import duties were levied against nearly a thousand articles and commodities, and at the same time the long-standing Navigation Laws mandated that British trade be undertaken in British ships. At the pre-dawn of the Industrial Age, pressures began to wear against such barriers, and Adam Smith's *The Wealth of Nations* (1776), with its soothing concept of the 'invisible hand' and its reasoned advocacy of *laissez-faire* was the first clarion call for a free-market economy.

The long Napoleonic Wars, ending with Napoleon's defeat at Waterloo in 1815, added their own unique strains to Britain's trading economy. In the first place, by creating demand for virtually every kind of manufacture, they gave a tremendous boost to Britain's burgeoning industrial economy. And second, meeting these industrial needs added vastly to Britain's store of investment capital. Both of these trends added to the growing power of the business class.

At the same time, the long war disrupted the flow of goods – particularly agricultural products – coming in to Britain, and food prices began to rise. The one segment not hurt by this curtailment of imports was the aristocratic landowners, who profited from the higher prices of their domestic produce. When the war finally ended, the landowners were reluctant to see their profits decline, so they appealed for the passage of the so-called Corn Laws – duties imposed on imported grain and controls on exports which gave the landowners a virtual monopoly over the domestic market. But the balance of power was shifting; the engines of industrialization – machines, manufacturers, merchants, traders – came to be aligned against the exclusive interests of the landlords. Into this fray stepped David Ricardo, who, having made a fortune on the London Exchange by the age of 26, retired to a country estate, bought himself a seat in Parliament in 1819, and spent his remaining few years (he died in 1823 at age 51) contemplating the larger issues of economics.

A closer look at the problem that absorbed him not only helps explain Ricardo's formulation of his famous 'theory of comparative advantage' but also helps show the timeliness of his work today. What he found in the Corn Laws – and in the larger problem of the 'rents' paid to landlords for the grain produced on their property – was an economic system that inevitably brought about its own stagnation. In the absence of competitively priced imported grain, the monopolistic landlords would meet rising demand by putting more and more acreage into cultivation. The grain raised on this poorer land would be more expensive to bring to market and would effect a general rise in prices. Consequently, the subsistence wages of workers in the urban shops and factories would have to rise, and that rise in wages would come directly out of the profits of their employers – the capitalist class. Since these very profits represented the money the capitalist would have poured back into the business – creating more jobs, more output, more growth – the eradication of these profits resulted in the end of expansion.

So the fundamental problem Ricardo was addressing was one of economic growth, and he saw the sort of protectionist policy exemplified by the Corn Laws as ultimately damaging to Britain's own economy. It is not surprising then, that he advocated open trade policies. But his theory of comparative advantage went even further – to suggest the benefits of specialization and resource allocation. Ricardo not only demonstrated that a country should export what it has in abundance and import what it has in scarcity, but also showed that it should concentrate its resources on what it does efficiently and trade its surplus for what its neighbor does efficiently. To use a modern example, if the neighbor makes a cheaper car, a country's response should not be to impose tariffs on it to protect its own inefficient car industry. Its response should be to buy cars from the neighbor, get out of the car business, and put its own resources to better use.

This, of course, is perfectly analogous to today's widely accepted practice of outsourcing, and it has great implications for the car example. Let's assume that your real genius lies in service, or in customer relations, and that you would be better off in the car rental business than in the car manufacturing business. You still need cars, but you see now that you need to buy them, not make them, and that you can buy them from your neighbor who was already making them more cheaply and efficiently than you were. True, the people you had hired to build your cars are going to be out of work, but unlike your uncompetitive car manufacturing business, your new car rental business is going to expand and produce more jobs – and higher-value ones at that.

Ricardo saw clearly the limits of the 'closed economy,' wherein a country produces its own raw materials, shapes them into finished goods, and sells them in its own market. He saw, too, that in the sort of open system he favored, capital would flow from mature economies to developing nations, which in turn would be brought to higher levels of production. Ricardo's theory, like outsourcing today, creates a 'win-win' scenario.'[14]

As a historical footnote, because of the entrenched power of Britain's landed aristocracy, the Corn Laws weren't repealed until 1846. But long before then the free-market policies advocated by Adam Smith and systematized by Ricardo were propelling the remarkable expansion of the British Empire.

The British – Enlightened Colonialists

The key point here – and one often overlooked in the vision of Britain as a 'colonial' power – is that Britain's hegemony in the nineteenth-century global economy was not built merely on the 'colonial' model of trade. That is, Britain was not content to import raw materials from its colonies, turn them into finished products, and then consume or export the manufactures. Britain's financiers and industrialists, following the Ricardian model of outsourcing, saw that they could export technology – *and capital* – to their trading partners, especially resource-and-labor-rich nations like the US. In effect, Britain exported the Industrial Revolution, and thereby blew open the world economy.

So, while it's true that in the half-century after Waterloo Britain's own manufacturing output rose spectacularly, more important were the advances in transportation and communications, especially the rapid transfer of industrial technology, which allowed its growth to be seeded around the globe. The huge increase in productivity that resulted from the invention of the steam engine stimulated a worldwide demand for more machines, more raw materials, more iron, more shipping, more everything. By mid-century, when the Corn Laws and Navigation Acts were repealed, restrictions on the export of advanced technology (textile machinery, for example) had also been lifted, and the furnace of the world economy was stoked anew.

Equally significant is the growth in Britain's foreign investment during these decades. The 6 million pounds annually invested abroad in the decade after Waterloo rose to 30 million by mid-century, and to 75 million a year by 1870. Moreover, the income from this investment – 50 million pounds a year by the 1870s – was promptly reinvested overseas, providing even greater stimulus to global trade. It goes without saying that this massive export of technology and capital was driving the economic expansion of other nations, and no doubt some Tory hard-liners looked askance at what was happening in the US. In the earlier part of the century, US exports had consisted mostly of raw materials (especially cotton), and the nation was still an importer of finished manufactures. But after the Civil War – thanks to Britain's infusion of capital and technology – this pattern changed astonishingly, and in a few short decades the US became the world's largest producer of manufactures – including farm machinery, iron and steel goods, machine tools, and more.

Did Britain ultimately damage its own position as a world power by 'outsourcing' the Industrial Revolution? No. Britain grew the world economy throughout the nineteenth century, and it prospered mightily at the same time. In 1900 Britain's empire was the largest the world had ever seen, and with some twelve million square miles of land and close to a quarter of the world's population, the Union Jack flew literally around the globe. Britain's merchant marine, far larger than any other, still assured its place as the world's greatest trading nation, and London's financial houses established Britain as the biggest investor, banker, insurer, and commodity dealer in the global economy. It was indeed the empire on which the sun never set.[15]

And indeed, up until the outbreak of World War I (WWI), Britain's global trading empire continued to grow – and to bring the world economy along with it. In the first years of the new century, some 4 billion pounds of British capital were invested overseas, and in the twenty years leading up to the war British exports had expanded by 120 percent. It cannot be overemphasized that this remarkable economic achievement was carried out in a spirit 'cosmopolitan rather than national... willingly admitting others to its enterprises, if only to share the risk.' And whatever criticisms and revilements the Empire might suffer a century later, historian Stuart Legg seems right that the British economic system, 'with its passionate belief in *laissez faire*, free trade, open competition – laid the economic foundations and raised the physical infrastructure of the free world of today.'[16]

Hijacking History

What, exactly shook those foundations? The obvious answer is, of course, the cataclysm of World War I and – following closely behind – the devastating dislocations of the Great Depression. Yet this is not a satisfactory answer. After all, the world had always known war. The horrendous and never-ending Napoleonic Wars failed to rattle the philosophic underpinnings of Britain's economic liberalism; in fact, that long conflict seemed only to strengthen them and to add fuel to Britain's economic engine. When we glance across the world's stage during and immediately after World War I, looking for the new player in the politico-economic drama, we see the bearded, dark-complexioned face of Karl Marx.

Of course we see his ghost, which suddenly commanded a much greater share of the world's attention than the man ever did in his lifetime. Marx died in 1883, having managed to publish only the first volume (of four) of his masterpiece *Das Kapital.* Thirty-five years earlier, Marx and Friedrich Engels had published *The Communist Manifesto* with its ominous warning: 'Let the ruling classes tremble at a Communist revolution. The proletarians have nothing to lose but their chains.' And for a while it seemed that the ruling classes did tremble, but then the uprisings of 1848 subsided, the old order was largely restored, and the workers of the world went back to work.

However, as world pressures began to coalesce at the turn of the century, political and economic thinkers were ready to consider what Marx had to say. One of these was Lenin, who began studying Marx in the 1890s and found a penetrating critique of the capitalist system itself.

It is important to understand that *Das Kapital* is not an exercise in histrionics. The living conditions of the working poor in England and across Europe would certainly have justified a furious polemic – which, in fact, had already been supplied by Engels in his *The Condition of the Working Class in England in 1844*. But Marx's work has staying power because it is a careful analysis, an intricately detailed argument pointing to the inevitable collapse of the capitalist system. In its barest outline – that capitalists, locked in competition, must eat or be eaten, inevitably reducing their own numbers; that the working class, swelled by workers from businesses forced under, continues to grow; that eventually a crisis point is reached at which the system collapses in on itself – the argument has great force. Moreover, one of Marx's supporting arguments – that an inherent weakness of capitalism is that it is 'unplanned' – must have been of particular interest to Lenin and later to Stalin, whose 'five-year plans' epitomized state control of the economy.[17]

In the aftermath of World War I, then, we appear to have a reversion to protectionism as war-torn nations turned inward to set about rebuilding themselves. Our evidence for this view is the erection of trade barriers and a plunge in the volume of world trade. In fact, however, we have a much more striking phenomenon, one whose effects will be felt for most of the remainder of the twentieth century. It is the appearance of a new economic *Weltanschauung* – the idea that free-market capitalism, unrestrained, leads to excess and imbalance, and therefore needs guidance by the reins of government. In this view, the 'roaring twenties' in the US can be understood as a sort of tarantella – a last, feverish fling – and the crash in 1929 as the death knell of the free market. If it needed a grave marker, the Smoot-Hawley Act of 1930, a US tariff measure that raised the average duty on imported goods from 39 percent to 59 percent, might have served.

The power of Marx's ideas – especially state control of the means of production – is not only illustrated by the success of the 1917 revolution in Russia. As we know, the revolution was worldwide, achieving another great victory with the establishment of the People's Republic of China in 1949. In Europe, that same year saw the establishment of COMECON (Council for Mutual Economic Assistance), an economically based organization of the continent's Communist states, not only including Russia but also Bulgaria, Czechoslovakia, Hungary, Poland, and Romania. (Interestingly, Cuba became the last nation to join, in 1972). This bloc, willfully shutting itself off from the rest of the world, evolved into the world's largest-ever closed economy.

Even more pertinent to this discussion, however, is the fact that under the influence of the Marxist critique, even the 'open' economies of the Western democracies ceased to be quite so open as they had been in the nineteenth century. Surely the jaundiced view of capitalism that spread outward from Marx's attack lay somewhere in the thinking of John Maynard Keynes and other mid-century advocates of the 'mixed' economy. This more general thesis – that after the disruptions early in the century, the question of economic control has dominated policy-making in western governments – is fully developed in Daniel Yergin and Joseph Stanislaw's *The Commanding Heights: The Battle for the World Economy.* As the authors explain, the title phrase comes from Lenin, who reassured his comrades (after his New Economic Policy granted some modicum of freedom to small tradesmen and farmers) that the state would continue to control the 'commanding heights' of the economy.[18]

Mixed-Up Economies

To haul the world economy out of the Great Depression and then to rebuild the European infrastructure after World War II, the mixed economy seems to have been the right medicine. Nationalization of key industries in Europe, the ascension of the welfare state in Britain, Roosevelt's programs in the US – all these helped solve the world's No. 1 problem: unemployment, and brought about general recovery. The General Agreement on Tariffs and Trade (GATT), instituted in 1948, helped immeasurably in this recovery by offering a framework through which barriers to international trade could gradually be brought down. 'By 1955,' write Yergin and Stanislaw, 'all the Western European countries had exceeded their prewar levels of production.... This record of success... vindicated the idea that government must take an active role in overseeing or directing the economy – and in many cases own part of it – in order to provide prosperity for all. On the strength of this unprecedented economic expansion, the mixed economy established itself as the new incumbent system and one whose reach would grow in the ensuing years. The state was either in control of the commanding heights or managing the levers of fiscal policy. Government had created and assumed the responsibilities of the welfare state, and it was dedicated to correcting the 'failures' of the market. All this added up to a formula for economic success that consigned the deplorable interwar years and the destruction of World War II to the past.'[19]

Yet trouble began to brew for the mixed economy in the early 1970s. In August 1971, President Richard Nixon ended a speculative run on US gold by halting the practice of selling it to foreign central banks for dollars, and at the same time the dollar was devalued against foreign currencies by about 8 percent. Within two more years, the dollar was 'floating' against foreign currencies, which meant that the gold standard – and with it the agreement hammered out at Bretton Woods 30 years earlier – had been abandoned.

A much greater blow to the world economy occurred in October 1973, when war broke out between Israel and the Arab countries. As a result of the oil embargo levied against the US and the Netherlands (which supported Israel), buyers began to bid up oil prices in an attempt to build up their reserves, and the Organization of Petroleum Exporting Countries (OPEC) began raising the price. By March 1974, the price of oil had quadrupled from $3 to $12 per barrel. This first 'oil shock' toppled the world economy into recession and created a new economic phenomenon, which pundits were quick to find a name for. Normally, inflation would fall during a recession, but this time prices continued to rise, along with unemployment. The resulting 'stagflation' – stagnating output and high inflation – brought renewed focus on the problem of economic growth.

Since the primary problem was seen to be inflation, the solution was to restrict the money supply. Tight money does curb inflation; but, of course, it also slows growth. Conversely, a loosened money supply promotes economic activity but spurs inflation. The US was expanding its way out of the worldwide slump in late 1970s – and again incurring high inflation – when the Shah of Iran was overthrown in 1979. With the disruption of oil flows from that country came the second oil shock: a rise in prices from $13 per barrel in 1978 to $32 in 1980. The shock precipitated another round of stagflation. Unemployment soared, along with prices. Restrictive monetary policies curbed inflation, but plunged the world economy into a deep and prolonged slump. It goes without saying that President Jimmy Carter, who oversaw this economic turmoil, was decisively turned out of office.

And so it goes. President Reagan kept his promise to cut taxes, but he also accelerated defense spending – hoping, in Keynesian fashion, to spend the economy back to health. The result was a ballooning deficit. By 1987, the US had become a net debtor to foreign countries. Moreover, the infusion of money in 1985 and 1986 pushed inflation up by 1987 and 1988. When the Federal Reserve Board responded by tightening down on the supply, the economy sank into a prolonged downturn by the summer of 1990. As mentioned earlier, the political power of the pocket book was once again in evidence in the presidential election of 1992, when incumbent former Arkansas governor Bill Clinton defeated George Bush.

As the steady economic growth of the post-World War II years has given way to the fits of turmoil and stagnation that marked the 1970s, 1980s, and 1990s, one ray of global prosperity has shone steadily: world trade. This contention is borne out by figures from the World Trade Organization, the ten-year-old child of GATT. In the fifty years since GATT's inception, despite the array of barriers that have risen and fallen, merchandise exports have grown at an annual average of 6 percent, and total world trade in the year 2000 was 22 times greater than the level in 1950. Moreover, since the creation of the WTO in 1994, forty nations have successfully concluded negotiations for tariff-free trade in information technology products, and seventy member nations have signed an agreement to liberalize trade in banking and financial services information.

Furthermore, world trade provides the only answer to the overriding problem articulated at the beginning of this chapter. The mature industrial economies of the world can – and must – create growth by means of trade with emerging nations. This return to Ricardian outsourcing will again prove to be a 'win-win' situation. In fact, it is already proving to be so, as we see in the following case histories of China and Mexico.

China

No wonder US shoe retailers were besieging the Commerce Department in September and October of 2002. The shoes they hoped to sell for Christmas were sitting in the tankers that couldn't unload during the West Coast shutdown that closed 29 ports from San Diego to Seattle. But if US importers and retailers were upset, consider the feelings of the Asian exporters. The surprising fact is that two-thirds of all of the shoes worn in the US today are made in China.

In fact, while the rest of the world was falling into economic doldrums, China's economy expanded by a robust 8 percent during 2002, and has now elbowed out Japan to become Asia's biggest exporter to the US. But it didn't happen overnight.

Deng Xiaoping was a senior party leader and a devoted follower of Chairman Mao, when the Communists defeated the Nationalists and established the People's Republic in 1949. But Deng stood on the sidelines and kept his thoughts to himself when Mao launched the Great Leap Forward. He saw little sense in herding farmers into communes and depriving them of the last vestiges of autonomy and self-empowerment, and was not surprised when the Great Leap went backward, when agricultural and industrial production plummeted and tens of millions of people died of starvation. The question of moving China's economy forward was in his mind when he uttered his famous aphorism: 'It doesn't matter whether a cat is black or white so long as it catches mice.'

Deng would get his chance to find the right cat two years after Mao's death when he became China's paramount leader in 1978. He began his reforms in the agricultural sector, with the re-establishment of the kind of incentive that had not been seen since before the Great Leap Forward. This was the so-called 'household responsibility system,' which allowed a family to hold on to some of the fruits of its labor. After delivering to the state the required amount of their production, farmers could keep the rest – or sell it. The next step, and a more important one, was Deng's creation of Special Economic Zones. Located in coastal areas – one across from Hong Kong, another across from Taiwan – these SEZs, by promoting trade, would engage China in the world economy.

The results have been stunning. Between 1978 – Deng's first year as paramount leader – and 2000 – three years after his death – China's foreign trade increased from $36 billion to $474 billion. Perhaps even more remarkable, per capita income doubled between 1978 and 1987, then doubled again over the next ten years. As Yergin and Stanislaw put it, 'Deng did something no one else in history has ever accomplished – he lifted more than 300 million people out of poverty in just two decades.[20]

To be sure, the restructuring was not universal. The state-owned industrial sector remained virtually untouched by reform. That would be left to Deng's successors, President Jiang Zemin and Premier Zhu Rongji, who still must face many a hurdle before China is fully integrated into the world economy. Yet *New York Times'* columnist Thomas Friedman also tells a story that illustrates the inevitability of change in China – fundamental grassroots change. In 1998, he traveled with a team of international monitors to observe local elections in northeastern China. The incumbent chief in one village called for 'fiber-optic cable so everyone can have a telephone.' The challenger went further: he promised to bring technology, to be 'very non-ideological,' to improve the schools because 'knowledge is important.' Even more remarkable, in another village, the incumbent all but hailed the emergence of free-market capitalism: 'If elected, we need to introduce more science and technology into agriculture, get more enterprises here and speed up procedures for generating wealth...(because) the whole world is turning into one big market for merchandise.'[21]

Reform at the grassroots and government levels became all the more imperative – and inevitable – with China's official entry into the World Trade Organization in November 2001. In pushing for membership, China's leaders indicated their ultimate desire for full participation in the global economy – a far cry from the 'household responsibility system' of just twenty years earlier.

Of course, China is already a huge player in the world economy. Its international trade has quadrupled in ten years and its 1.3 billion population constitutes the world's largest consumer market, one whose purchasing power is steadily increasing. It has now become a world leader in virtually every category of manufactured goods – including shoes.

China's stream of imports is also widening rapidly. Thanks to its membership in the WTO, tariffs have dropped to an average of about 15 percent, one fourth of their peak level in the 1980s. China is now the chief market for exports from South Korea and Taiwan, and, more remarkably, it passed the US in 2002 as the world's largest importer of steel.[22]

Most impressive of all, China attracted a record $53 billion in foreign investment in 2004. A recent *Wall Street Journal* article tells the story of Nebraska-based Behlen Manufacturing Co., just one of the many midsize manufacturing companies rushing to open operations in China. The company's CEO explained that orders from China, for his prefabricated metal buildings dropped when one of his US-based competitors opened a factory there. So now he has also opened a factory there. Note that this is a joint venture with several Chinese companies in Beijing, which will eventually employ 200 people. Orders, says the CEO, are streaming in.

At the other end of the scale, General Motors doesn't disclose the exact amount of its annual investment in China but a company spokesman acknowledged that it was in the hundreds of millions. He also noted that while GM has been reducing car-building operations in Europe, in China the company is investing in new plants as well as in companies that already have plants.[23]

As we see, then, China's market reforms over the past 25 years have produced stunning results. The nation's role as the mighty dragon of the Asian economic bloc will be discussed in chapter five.

Mexico

Mexico's story is a familiar one: A one-party political system (the Institutional Revolutionary Party, or PRI), government ownership of industry, a protective policy of import substitution (i.e. 'building our own and protecting our own' rather than paying for imports), and, in 1982, a debt crisis that crippled the reform efforts of forward-looking finance minister Jesus Silva Herzog for most of the rest of the decade.

But Herzog's reform policies were continued, and intensified, under his successor, Carlos Salinas, who had worked alongside Herzog as budget minister. Salinas sold off the national holdings in industries like telecommunications and banking, and with the proceeds he paid off the country's debt, balanced the budget, and reined in inflation. Even more important, in 1993 he negotiated the North American Free Trade Agreement with the US.

Salinas's successor, Ernesto Zedillo Ponce de Leon, came to power in 1994 only to confront the sudden and unexpected plunge of the peso. In an analysis for *Business Economics*, Jonathan Heath writes that Mexico suffered an increase in inflation from 7 percent in 1994 to 52 percent in 1995. The value of the peso dropped from 3.45 pesos to the dollar in November 1994 to 7.65 pesos a year later, and suddenly Mexico was floundering in its deepest recession since the 1930s. But unlike the debt crisis of 1982, which mired Mexico's economy during most of the decade, Mexico pulled out of the 1995 slump in only a year.

Why the difference? The government's response in 1982 was to implement exchange controls, clamp down on imports, and nationalize the banking system, all of which flew in the face of market-oriented policy. In 1995, by contrast, the government introduced no exchange controls and no import controls. The free-trade agreements were upheld, and no barriers were erected. This market-oriented policy response, including the continuation of privatization and other on-going reforms, had Mexico's economy back on track in short order.[24]

As a sign of the times, Thomas Friedman, who had visited Mexico at the depth of the crisis in 1995, returned in May of 1996, when the struggle to rebound was at its fiercest. There were demonstrations in the streets and placards that read 'death to Ortiz' (Mexico's finance minister). But Ortiz was far from disquieted by disturbances in the street. Mexico had just placed its first 30-year bond on Wall Street since the collapse of the peso a year earlier.[25]

Mexico's story is also typical in that it offers another instance of economic turmoil bringing about political change. Zedillo would prove to be the last in the long line of PRI-designated presidents. During his term, elections were placed under the authority of an independent commission, the political field was opened up, and, consequently, the Partido Accion Nacional (PAN) was in a position to challenge the PRI in the 2000 presidential election. As it happened, PAN's candidate, Vicente Fox, was freely and democratically elected, effectively bringing to an end Mexico's one-party system.

PAN's market-oriented philosophy is complemented by Fox's business background. The former president of Coca-Cola Mexico and champion of deregulation came into office in time to cheer the tremendous jolt that NAFTA had already given to the country's economy: the tripling of Mexico's exports over six years, led not by petroleum but by manufactures; the huge surge in exports to the US; and billions of new dollars of foreign investment in Mexico. In fact, as of today Mexico has emerged as the US' second-largest trading partner after Canada.

Not surprisingly, there is no bigger proponent of global trade than Vicente Fox, who notes that his country is the only one in the world to have trade agreements with both North America and with Europe. 'Now we want to go further,' says Fox of NAFTA's success. 'In the long term, what we are looking for is convergence of our two economies.... Of course, this is a ten-, twenty-year program. But when we reach that level, then we can just erase the border, open up that border for free flow of products, merchandise, capital, as well as people.'[26]

If we see the stock market crash of 1929 as the death knell of *laissez faire* capitalism, we may also see the fall of the Berlin wall in 1989, the subsequent collapse of the Soviet Union as the beginning of the end of the Keynesian mixed economy and, yes, the resurrection of David Ricardo.

The world economy is shaping a new geopolitical order based on international trade, and leaders who fail to grasp this are being pushed out of office. Consider Japan: For four decades, the Ministry of International Trade and Industry (MITI) oversaw its rebuilding from the destruction of World War II. It worked well. Japan's economy grew dramatically, and the nation resumed its place as an industrial power. But in the 1990s – as elsewhere in the world – Japan's growth slowed, and the weaknesses of MITI's centralized, protectionist system began to show. From 1992 to 1999, Japan averaged a 1 percent growth rate. Prime Minister Hashimoto, elected in 1996, struggled for reform but couldn't overcome the legacy of unsound business practices, especially in the banking sector with its huge portfolios of bad loans. Hashimoto resigned in 1998 and, in quick succession, two prime ministers failed to stem the tide and were similarly voted out of office.

Perhaps the current Prime Minister, Junichiro Koizumi, has got the message. He promises to open up the rest of Japan's economy to competition and to privatize Japan's postal savings system – which, with more than $3 trillion in deposits, is the world's largest financial institution. Most important, Koizumi appears to have grasped the concept of outsourcing to the developing world. The *Wall Street Journal* reports that exports to Japan's Asian neighbors rose 14 percent in 2002, including a 32 percent jump (to $41.3 billion) in exports to China. Honda Motor Company's auto production facility in Guangzhou doubled its production in 2003 – up to 112,000 vehicles. Here Japan is growing its own economy, and it is growing China.[27]

A Future Shaped by Geoeconomics

On a global scale, here is what we see happening. The industrialized world is reshaping itself into three large zones or blocs. They are the European Union, expanded to include East European countries and Russia; North America (including the US, Canada, and Mexico); and Asia. The urgent necessity for economic growth will force each member of the Triad to seek out trading partners in the developing world. Europe will leverage its traditional ties to Africa and the Middle East and integrate them into its fold. For

North America, of course, we can predict that the Free Trade Agreement of the Americas will bring Central and South America into alignment with North America. In Asia, Japan is already linking its economy with China, South Korea and the ten nations in the ASEAN bloc.

This new alignment constitutes a radical geoeconomic restructuring. Historically, trade between nations has flowed on East-West lines (Europe-North America-Japan). Now, as each Triad power seeks its developing-world partners, the flow will be predominantly North-South.

As this new pattern of trade takes shape, it should be emphasized that the colonial model is dead and the point is not to overrun the developing world and extract its resources. The Cold War model of offering assistance to developing nations in order to gain military and ideological advantage is also dead. In fact, we must understand that an even more recent paradigm – the search for, and exploitation of, cheap labor – is also out of date. Kenichi Ohmae points out that a company that migrates in search of low-cost labor typically has a competitive half-life of only five years. Therefore, simply treating developing nations as low-wage production centers will not enhance a corporation's global competitive power.

The new paradigm is true economic integration, or what Ohmae calls being a 'true insider.' In other words, the new paradigm is the old paradigm of Ricardian outsourcing, with a geoeconomic twist. As Ohmae suggests, 'Why not choose a few developing nations and get to know them very well? Once you do so, then you think about building a global-scale operation taking advantage of your in-depth knowledge of one or several select countries, your relationships with its people and the relative cost advantage of the chosen host countries. Be prepared to contribute to the attainment of the nation's goals, as you would undoubtedly do for your own home country.'[28]

Paul Krugman and Maurice Obstfeld, in their useful survey *International Economics*, ask whether the coming realignment is a good thing. 'Most analysts believe the direct effects of NAFTA and '1992' (i.e. the European Union) will be clearly positive. That is, the gains from trade creation will outweigh any losses from trade diversion. The concern is instead that the large economic blocs being formed may turn protectionist against the outside world – for example, that 1992 will pave the way for 'Fortress Europe.' All of the policymakers involved deny that this will happen; it remains to be seen if they are right.'[29]

Yes, we will certainly see instances of protectionism as this new alignment comes into balance. We will have trade skirmishes that will threaten to push the world economy backward instead of forward. But more important, in the notion of each member of the Triad seeking its partners in the developing world, we see the solution to the fundamental problem of economic growth. And in the long run, 'the power of three' is likely to be a source of global economic stability.

In any case, a return to the free market principles of Smith and Ricardo seems inevitable. Protectionism, Keynesianism, 'closed' and 'mixed' economies have served their purpose and their time has passed. As Yergin and Stanislaw point out, since the 1990s government has been retreating from the 'commanding heights' of the economy, and market forces have been flexing their muscle. We see this in the fall of the Soviet Union, in the freeing of the Chinese economy, and in worldwide privatization – 'the greatest fire sale in the history of the world.' The decamping of the state from the commanding heights, write Yergin and Stanislaw, 'marks a great divide between the twentieth and twenty-first centuries. It is opening the doors of many formerly closed countries to trade and investment, vastly increasing, in the process, the size of the global market.'[30] Liberalized trade is the future. Economic integration is the future.

The three chapters that follow will be devoted to the evolution of the three major trade blocs – Europe, the Americas, and the Pacific realm. We will then take a closer look at the remaining pieces, the nations (or continents) that remain geographically or politically isolated. Who will partner with India, for example? Or Africa? How will the bridge between Europe and the Middle East be reconstructed?

The journey will be turbulent, but the outlook is ultimately positive. The prognosis is for the stability and equilibrium inherent in the triangle. More important, the prognosis is for the resumption of vigorous economic growth.

CHAPTER 3

FLEXING ITS MUSCLE: THE EUROPEAN UNION

From hormone-laced beef to biotech corn to electric power, Europe is pulling up the drawbridge in the face of US-made products. Fortress Europe? Why not? With the agreements ratified at 'EC '92,' the European Union suddenly became the world's largest single market. Not surprising that it would exercise its newfound power in the world economy.

In this chapter, we will trace the three-stage process by which Europe, since World War II, has evolved from a collection of inward-looking nation-states to an outward-looking confederation expanding its sphere of economic influence far beyond its continental borders.

Rebuilding at the Local Level

With the Communist bloc consolidating its power throughout Eastern Europe after World War II, rebuilding – quickly – the democratic states of Western Europe was of utmost importance. Of course, the job fell to the US, which, under the auspices of the Marshall Plan, distributed some $13 billion in aid to repair the economies of its European allies – including West Germany –

between 1948 and 1951. During that four-year period, the beneficiary nations experienced a rise in their gross national products of 15 to 25 percent. West Germany's recovery was particularly spectacular. Even by 1950 industrial production had rebounded from 45 percent to 75 percent of the 1936 level. However, despite this strong start, European economic growth after World War II had faltered by the end of the 1960s. Let us consider why.

One obvious reason is, of course, that the devastation suffered by Europe's economic infrastructure was severe and the rebuilding job was simply bigger and more time-consuming than anyone could have predicted. But there were other reasons, too.

Perhaps inevitably after the long war, there was – across Europe – a return to the 'nation of origin' concept. In the effort to rebuild, individual nations were more worried about taking care of themselves, rather than about Europe as a whole. Each country had domestic issues to resolve, and a renewed nationalism emerged.

This nationalism was abetted by the prevailing micro-economic structure. In many European countries, a large concentration of economic activity lay in the hands of a small number of family-owned corporations. The widespread policy throughout Western Europe was to rebuild the domestic economy by encouraging these companies to diversify into a range of businesses. (We still see this in Korea today, where 60 percent of business activity is generated by four companies, as well as in Japan. Western European governments promoted this model, and the designated 'national champion' corporations benefited tremendously from government support. Many of these same firms would eventually go international, but the model was first domestic.

In Italy after World War II, for example, Adriano Olivetti, son of the company founder, expanded the typewriter manufacturer into calculators, computers, and, ultimately, electronics. By 1958, Olivetti employed 24,000 workers and was one of the engines of Italy's rebirth. Similarly, Fiat, which was in the hands of the Agnelli family since its inception in 1899, diversified into jets, railway cars, and newspapers. Today, the $50 billion conglomerate remains Italy's largest private employer. In Germany, steel makers Krupp and Thyssen (now merged into the ThyssenKrupp Group), both of which were founded in the nineteenth century, were key players in the revitalization of the industrial heartland. By the mid-1960s, Thyssen was the largest steel producer in Germany and the fifth-largest in the world. In the Netherlands, Royal Dutch/Shell, which had merged in 1907, enjoyed huge growth in the 1950s and 1960s as it expanded into natural gas, coal, and metals. The point to be emphasized is that throughout these post-war economies, a few key industrial conglomerates, family owned and interlocked with the government, dominated each country.

In some cases, government support took the form of actual ownership – at least in part – of its national champions. In Britain, Clement Atlee's Labour Party nationalized the coal industry, as well as iron and steel, railroads, and utilities. In France, where some of the old family firms were regarded as rigid and self-protective, Charles de Gaulle's nationalization acts of 1945 and 1946 took control of banking, electricity, gas, and coal. In Italy, under the direction of Enrico Mattei, the state-owned oil company ENI (Ente Nazionale Idrocarburi) grew into a huge conglomerate of 36 companies in businesses ranging from oil and gas to hotels and highways.[31]

Industries that were not nationalized were protected, and this paradigm generally succeeded in rebuilding the European economy on a country-by-country basis. But its limits were obvious. Whether because government control was too restrictive or because the large, diversified conglomerates saturated their local domestic economies, growth had slowed dramatically by the end of the 1960s. The smaller the country, the more quickly this phenomenon occurred, and the sooner the corporation in question was pushed to go international. For example, Philips, in the Netherlands, had already acquired Magnavox by 1974. In the larger countries like Germany, domestic growth was still possible through diversification. (Interestingly, the push for diversification hit the wall internationally some years ago, as is reflected in the US stock market. This has become known as the 'conglomerate discount.' Highly diversified companies are now in bad odor among investors, who are pressuring boards of directors to return to their core business.)

Moreover, when we see interlocking connections between the governments and a few key industries in each country, we see the influence of Keynesianism, with its guiding principle that government can, and should, play a role in the direction and growth of the economy. In a time of crippled industry and little private capital for investment, Keynes advocated that governments borrow the necessary capital to get businesses going again. This deficit spending would create the jobs that would, among other things, create the tax base from which the government debt would be repaid. This was not the time for governments to be worrying about balancing their budgets. It was a good idea for the mid-century, but Keynesianism, like the mixed economy it supported, ultimately ran into the problem of finite domestic growth.

Tiny Belgium, incidentally, carved out its own path to post-war economic stability. To all of the US companies rushing in to claim a share of European markets, it offered itself as a business hub and port of entry into Europe. Belgium's offer became all the more convenient once NATO relocated to Brussels from Paris in 1967, and many US companies established their headquarters there. But notice how times have changed. Under the influence of continental unification, Belgium retreated into the bosom of Europe and subsequently became the capital of the European Union. A far different climate prevails there now, and US businesses have hurried to relocate their international headquarters in London – a much more US-friendly environment.

To reiterate, the prevailing program throughout post-war Europe was to encourage the large, existing, family-owned corporations to expand and diversify and – with government support in the form of low-interest loans and other subsidies, if not outright ownership – to take care of the critical business of reconstruction. By the 1970s this program had finished its work. By the 1980s, there was no domestic growth left.

Yet another factor contributed to the initial success and ultimate stagnation of the post-war economic model. As we saw in Chapter Two, the communist thought propagated by Karl Marx was tremendously influential in mid-century Europe, and in many Western European countries – notably Italy, France, Spain, and Germany – Communist parties were established and respected components of coalition governments. The result, in broad terms, was the creation of the welfare state. Ideology became a force in the shaping of economic policy, and suddenly governments found themselves underwriting a wide range of worker benefits – minimum wages, guaranteed employment, pensions – as well as larger social programs like health care and education. At the same time, unions began to flex their muscle.

For the sake of comparison, we may observe that the US government did not go down this path. In America, employee benefits were left to the corporations, as we see in medical insurance and pension plans.

In Europe, as costs for social programs rose faster than income-tax-based revenues, we have seen the imposition of value-added taxes – taxes on consumption, in addition to income tax. Nations struggling with stagnating growth – facing not only the traditional military expenditures but also vast payouts to keep the welfare state alive – have no choice except to impose taxes. Government has become too expensive – a predicament exacerbated by an unanticipated feature of generous social programs: the influx of foreign labor.

In Germany, for example, when growth was steady and unemployment was low during the 1960s (also when the building of the Berlin Wall in 1961 had virtually eliminated migration from East Germany), the government began recruiting foreign labor – especially Turks – under the 'Gastarbeiter' program. The Turks were delighted to come – and to receive wages eight to ten times higher than at home, not to mention the additional worker benefits. By the time Germany curtailed the program in 1973, more than 800,000 Turks had 'officially' moved to Europe – not to mention the half-million more who had migrated without work permits but nevertheless found work and stayed on. The problems caused by such high number of foreign workers once growth had stagnated and unemployment began to rise – problems complicated by difficulties of assimilation – continue to perplex Germany today. In fact, the likelihood of another huge migration of Turks into Europe is one of the current arguments against the entry of Turkey into the European Union.[32]

These related phenomena – postwar nationalism, the dominance in each country of a few highly diversified corporations, Keynesian advocacy of government influence in the economy, the ascendance of the welfare state – help us understand the situation of Western Europe's economy in the decades after World War II, and they also show its fundamental weakness. To be sure, European leaders saw the need for longer-range vision early on – one that would unite rather than divide the individual countries and that would seek to consolidate the economic strength of the continent as a whole.

In fact, we can see the first step in the journey toward the European Union as early as 1957. In that same year, six nations – Germany, France, Italy, Belgium, the Netherlands and Luxembourg – signed the Treaty of Rome; creating the European Economic Community, or Common Market. However, though the treaty stipulated the removal of traditional customs duties among the signatory nations, for another two decades a European Common Market was an idea that existed mostly on paper. Until galvanized by the oil shocks of the 1970s, movement toward a federal Europe stalled, bogged down in squabbling over authority, budgets, and how much member governments should contribute. At one point, Margaret Thatcher, disgruntled over the huge amounts spent to subsidize uneconomic but politically critical farmers in Germany and France, declared, 'I want my money back.'[33] (We will return to Mrs. Thatcher's attitude toward European unification at the end of the chapter.)

Besides, until the 1970s, Keynesianism and the welfare state were entrenched and they were working. The three decades after the war became known in France as *Les Trente Glorieuses* – 'the thirty glorious years' – and Germany at the same time was experiencing the *Wirtschaftswunder,* or 'economic miracle.'

So while the vision may have looked toward union, economies remained local. As late as the early 1970s, when one of the authors was consulting for Shell in the Netherlands, the managers complained to him that they were forced to have separate subsidiaries for Norway, for Denmark, for Sweden – each with its own facilities, duplications, and enormous overhead costs. It was a case of old Europe's traditional localism – and one of the continent's ingrained economic weaknesses. In fact, when Europe's big corporations began to go international, rather than looking to European neighbors for healthy growth, they found it easier to expand into America and into Japan. Companies like Philips, ABB, and Siemens even moved into emerging nations.

Moving Toward Union

A solution to European localism – and a significant step toward European unity – emerged in 1978, when French president Valery Giscard d'Estaing and German chancellor Helmut Schmidt negotiated the European Monetary System (EMS), which tied the franc and other West European currencies to the Deutsche Mark. Now, symbolically as well as practically, Europe could be seen coming together economically. The inefficiency of isolated markets could be overcome. The limitations of GDP-orientation could be overcome. Problems of economies of scale could be overcome. And the growth engine of trade – among the nations of Europe – could at last be revved up. (In retrospect, it is fascinating to watch France ally so closely with Germany – not so long ago its bitterest foe. Since 1992, French-German trade has been growing at 15 percent a year. At the same time, France's trade with America has been declining; French exports to the US fell by 11 percent and US exports to France fell by 12 percent between 2001 and 2002.[34])

Crucial to stoking this engine was the realization (a reminder from David Ricardo) that individual nations would benefit from specializing in industries in which they already enjoyed an advantageous position and from embracing the entire European community as their market. (By this point, by the way, Britain, Denmark, and Ireland had joined the EEC, bringing the number of member nations to nine.)

Consider Finland-based Nokia, for example. Founded in 1865 when Fredrick Idestam opened a pulp mill, the company has since had a long and steady history of diversification. Idestam's son-in-law assumed control of the company in 1895 and expanded to power generation. By the time of the 1966 merger with Finnish Cable Works, the Nokia Group – as it then became known – had expanded from paper and power to rubber, cable, forestry, and electronics. It was CEO Simo Vuorilento who, in 1989, came to the realization that all this diversification was a dilution of resources. Since the company was established in electronics, why not concentrate on cell phones and become the dominant provider of this hot commodity for the huge European market? In fact, Nokia subsequently surpassed Motorola and is now the world's No. 1 cell phone manufacturer.

This is the core competency theory at work. Ironically, COMECON, the economic organization of the Communist bloc established in 1949, provided something of a model here. Like Europe would later, the bloc nations joined to form one market and sought to specialize rather than compete. This is what Lester Thurow calls 'niche competition,' which he describes as 'win-win. Everyone has a place where they can excel; no one is going to be driven out of business. Head-to-head competition is win-lose. Not everyone will get those seven key industries. Some will win; some will lose.'[35]

Germany and France provide an example of this kind of economic cooperation on a grand scale. Both nations had a large stake in both the aerospace and automobile industries. But it's our belief Germany would hold the dominant hand in automobiles, and France would take the lead in aerospace. Look what has happened. Daimler-Benz, already dominant, acquired Chrysler in 1998 and has become the world's second-largest auto company (after General Motors; though Toyota may soon ascend to the No. 1 position). Volkswagen, after its acquisition of Rolls Royce, is No. 5 in the world. At the same time, German manufacturers Bosch and Siemens are world leaders in automotive electronics. France, meanwhile, put together the European consortium behind Arianespace, the world's first commercial space transportation company. Founded in 1980, Arianespace now lifts more than half the world's satellites into orbit.

An initial consequence of this international cooperation, largely driven by labor considerations, was that heavy manufacturing industries were encouraged to concentrate below the Alps. Labor was cheaper in Spain, Southern France, and Italy, for example, and there was also an abundance of foreign labor – Algerians in Southern France, Yugoslavs in Italy. In northern Europe, by contrast, a smaller, more educated, higher-earning workforce helped stimulate the development of such non-labor-intensive industries as financial services, high technology, and higher education.

In fact, in 1986 three of these southerly nations – Spain, Portugal, and Greece – joined the European Economic Community (EEC), and the following year, in July 1987, all twelve member-nations signed the Single European Act. According to its provisions, all economic barriers between EEC nations were to be eliminated by the end of 1992. The march toward unity was continuing. The South was being brought into the economic mainstream. Northern Italy became a manufacturing and design hub. Spain was revitalized. Europe's pulse was beating.

But then something unforeseen took place, which radically shifted the shape and direction of Europe's economic growth. In 1989, the Berlin Wall fell, and West German chancellor Helmut Kohl seized the political opportunity of a lifetime – to unite East and West Germany and vastly increase the size and power of his nation. We might note in passing that to win the allegiance of East Germany's 16 million citizens, Kohl made one critical mistake: he gave the East German mark one-to-one parity with the currency of the West. The disaster that ensued – the utter collapse of the East German economy and an unemployment rate of over 10 percent – would sweep Kohl's party out of power in the 1991 elections.

Nevertheless, in the unification process, Kohl changed the whole strategy of Europe's economic thrust. He no longer wanted to shift manufacturing industries to the south. He sent them northeast instead, in order to rebuild the economy of his newly acquired territory. In fact, Kohl steered two major corporations – Daimler-Benz and Volkswagen – to eastern Germany, where they were victimized by rising wages and low productivity. This core problem – wage parity between East and West, combined with productivity *disparity* – is one that Gerhard Schroeder would still be dealing with, more than a decade later.

Still, the point to emphasize is that Kohl's determination caused a seismic shift. The German capital relocated to the north, to Berlin instead of Bonn, and the eyes of the European economy turned in the same direction. Consequently, when the Soviet Union collapsed two years later, Western Europe was already in position to expand its economy north and east, into the newly autonomous states of Central and Eastern Europe. This movement is in full flower today, as we see in the fact that ten nations (including former Soviet satellites Poland, Hungary, the Czech Republic, Slovakia, Slovenia, Lithuania, Latvia, and Estonia) entered the European Union in May 2004. Russia itself, of course, huge and rich in natural resources, will be the ultimate prize.

It is fascinating to see how this shift in Europe's economic structure is reflected in the conflict in Iraq in 2003. Which European powers were most outspoken in their criticism of George W. Bush's haste to invade Iraq? Germany, followed by its ever-closer ally France, and then Russia. Was this a simple matter of idealistic European leaders taking the moral high ground? Not likely. Their real motive will come under discussion later in this chapter. (Of course, Britain, followed by Spain, joined President Bush's coalition.)

Meanwhile, the provisions of 1987's Single European Act came to fruition with the signing of the Maastricht Treaty at the end of 1991. Not only was a firm plan – and schedule put in place to further consolidate Europe with a single currency, but suddenly, with the creation of 'EC '92,' Europe became by far the world's largest economic market.

The underlying idea of the ever-stronger European Community (EC) was to increase trade *within* the bloc, at the expense of trade between the bloc and the rest of the world. To further this aim, a number of interesting barriers have been put in place. For instance, there is ISO 9000, a quality certification process instituted by the European Union's International Organization for Standardization. The process involves a review by an outside auditor of the whole range of a company's procedures – contracting, management, inspection, customer service, and document control. With other types of barriers falling among the European Union nations, some sort of quality control would seem necessary. But, not surprisingly, EC products were given the tremendous advantage of being the first to be certified. For example, a spokesman for IBM's branch banking software unit told *American Banker* that it took a full year for his group to receive the certification.[36]

Another barrier was erected in the form of the EC 'Utilities Directive,' covering purchases by water, transport, energy, and telecommunications authorities. According to the directive, EC procuring utilities may simply ignore, for no further reason, bids that include less than 50 percent local (i.e. EC) content, and any bid with a majority of local content must receive a 3 percent price preference over non-EC bids. Continuing a long tradition of protection against US utilities firms, the directive keeps the EC effectively closed to US competition.[37]

That European markets would become harder to penetrate from outside is simply a statement of the obvious. 'An American firm and a German firm that were equally competitive in Italy before integration will find that in 1993 the German firm has an advantage. The barriers facing German products will have gone down, while the barriers facing American products will remain unchanged. Similarly, if an Italian and Japanese firm were equally competitive in Germany before integration, then the Italian firm will have an edge after 1992.' Umberto Agnelli, president of Fiat, Europe's largest industrial company, states the case point-blank: 'The single market must first offer an advantage to European companies. This is a message we must insist upon without hesitation.'[38]

If this sounds like blatant protectionism, that's exactly what it is. In the US, the accepted wisdom is that the Japanese wrote the book on protectionism, but in our opinion the Japanese learned everything they know from the French, who are the real masters. To illustrate, consider the story of the VCR.

France's Thomson CSF – which, along with Philips, was one of Europe's two major electronics firm – saw that its own opportunity in the VCR (video cassette recorder) race was vanishing as Japanese manufacturers were fast dominating the market. But the French had another idea. Their customs inspectors threw up a smoke screen in the form of a product safety issue. Japanese VCRs, they announced, were prone to create a fire hazard. They went on to add that, because of the unfamiliar Japanese technology, there was only one technician in all of France who could inspect these machines properly and that, unfortunately, he lived in a remote village and was not willing to relocate. As a result, all of the VCRs coming into Marseilles, France's major southeastern port, would have to be unloaded, shipped out to this small town, inspected, and shipped back again to the market. Not only were the added cost and the delay untenable, but an artificial quota was also created based on the number of VCRs – that could trickle through this complicated net. Without the net, Marseilles would be the gateway to the whole European Union.

It should be noted that all this maneuvering was widely publicized. There was nothing covert about it. Indeed, France was trying to send a very clear message to the Japanese: We in France are not as foolish as the people in the US – where the Japanese had completely taken over the consumer electronics industry. If Japan wanted to capture France's – and Europe's – VCR market, it would have to make a deal. It would have to license Thomson as its European licensee. The deal was struck, and Thomson got the license to make VCRs for the European market, paying royalties to Japan.

That's the protectionism game played by a master. But the French are not the only players, and the Japanese are not the only targets. When the Arabs threatened to buy a controlling interest in Mercedes-Benz, Deutsche Bank intervened on behalf of the German economy to buy up the shares that were for sale. Moreover, the size of the playing field – and the stakes – continues to increase.

Thurow reports that in 1990 two of the world's largest business groups (the Mitsubishi group from Japan and the Daimler Benz-Deutsche Bank group from Germany) held a secret meeting in Singapore to talk about a global alliance. Among other things, both were interested in expanding their market share in civilian aircraft production. 'From an American perspective,' writes Thurow, 'everything about that Singapore meeting was criminally illegal. It violated both antitrust and banking laws.... Yet in today's world Americans cannot force the rest of the world to play the economic game as Americans think it should be played.'[39]

(Interestingly, Daniel Burstein, writing in 1991, predicted that the Daimler-Benz/Mitsubishi alliance, by outflanking America and setting a precedent for joint Japanese-European exploitation of the Soviet market, would prove to be the 'deal of the decade.')[40]

As the European Union rises as a major economic bloc, the 'economic game' will become intensely competitive. The rules – as written by the WTO, for example – are likely to be subverted by any number of means, even psychological warfare. This is what we are witnessing in the on-going battle between US-based Boeing and Europe's Airbus, the two dominant players in aircraft manufacturing. It is a story worth looking at in detail.

First, a little background. Airbus Industrie, headquartered in Toulouse, France, is 80 percent owned by European Aeronautic Defense and Space Co. (EADS), a French-German-Spanish conglomerate, and 20 percent by BAE Systems PLC of Britain. Founded in 1970, it was conceived as a way to break the American monopoly and get Europe back into civilian aircraft manufacturing.

Whittling away at Boeing's dominant market share whenever and wherever it could, Airbus scored a coup in 1999 when it won the JetBlue contract – the company's first foothold in the fast-growing low-fare sector. The foothold became an imprint in 2002, when Britain's low-fare airliner easyJet struck a deal to buy 120 passenger jets from Airbus, with an option to buy 120 more for a fixed price over the next decade. This deal not only gave Airbus a strong presence in Europe's budget sector; easyJet was also the first low-fare carrier to switch from Boeing to Airbus.

But the story gets more interesting in July 2002, when *Wall Street Journal* reported that Taiwan-based China Airlines had announced it would buy 16 jetliners from Airbus. In response to Airbus's move into the potentially huge Asian market, sixteen US senators and at least four members of the House of Representatives sent letters to Taiwan President Chen Shui-bian pressing him to reverse the decision and give the business to Boeing. One of the letters read, in part, 'It is our hope that a decision in favor of Boeing will provide an additional demonstration of the important and beneficial implications of an enhanced US-Taiwan economic relationship.' The arm-twisting continued with the suggestion that buying from Boeing 'could increase momentum toward the successful negotiation of the US-Taiwan Free Trade Agreement.' It was signed by Senate Finance Committee Chairman Max Baucus (D., Mont.), as well as by senators from states like Washington and California in which Boeing is a major employer.

According to the story, China Airlines denied having finalized the deal, but meanwhile Airbus was vigorously protesting the lobbying on behalf of Boeing by the US government. Airbus claimed the US lawmakers were in violation of a 1992 international agreement that prohibits governments from using politics to influence what should be commercial purchasing decisions.

The reporter put the dispute in context by noting that it could well exacerbate tension between the US and Europe over other simmering trade issues, including US tariffs on steel and farm-product subsidies.[41]

At the beginning of 2003, Airbus turned up the heat. While Boeing announced it would scale back production for the year to 280 planes, Airbus held firm to its projection schedule of 300, giving it a legitimate claim to the title of 'world's biggest aircraft producer.' 'It's clearly a demonstration that Airbus is the leader in the commercial aircraft industry,' boasted Philippe Camus, co-chief executive of EADS. Of course, Boeing accused its rival of glutting the market at a time when, according to its spokesperson, airlines worldwide have parked more than 2,000 aircraft. Nevertheless, at the end of 2002, Airbus's order backlog stood at 1,468, while Boeing's was only 1,152.[42] More salt in Boeing's wounds came with the April 2003 announcement that Airbus had signed an agreement valued at $1.7 billion to sell 30 aircraft to four state-controlled airlines in China. For the first time, the Airbus A330 was joining the fleet of a Chinese carrier.

And here's a further installment: In a May 28, 2003, story, the *New York Times* reported that a day earlier seven European countries had agreed to purchase 180 military transport planes from Airbus in a colossal deal worth $24 billion. The new A400M would replace old military transport planes like the Hercules C-130, and its customers would be Belgium, Britain, France, Germany, Luxembourg, Spain and Turkey. Described as one of Europe's most ambitious military projects, the agreement would give Airbus and its parent, EADS, a huge lift at a time when its civilian business has been battered by a slump in air travel and by the sorry plight of airlines around the world.

Needless to say, Washington disapproved of the deal, suggesting that Europe's shrinking military spending should be channeled into more innovative technology. It's likely that Washington also disapproved of the fact that Airbus awarded a $3.6 billion contract to build the engines for the planes to a European consortium of manufacturers led by Snecma of France and Rolls Royce of Britain, even though a rival bid by US firm Pratt & Whitney came in at 20 percent lower.[43]

Perhaps not so coincidentally, the same day this deal was announced, May 27, *USA Today* ran a cover story that Airbus knew for almost five years, but did not disclose, that the tailfin on one of its jets had almost snapped off in flight.

According to the story, not until after American Airlines Flight 587 crashed in 2001 – a catastrophe investigators say was caused when the tailfin broke off the A300 jet – did Airbus reveal its findings from an incident in 1997, when pilots lost control of another A300, Eastern Airlines' Flight 903, in the skies over Miami before finally landing the aircraft safely.

The story alleges that while Airbus was sufficiently concerned about the 1997 incident to urge American Airlines to inspect the tail fin to make sure it had not been damaged, it did not disclose until the investigation into Flight 587 that the actions of the pilots in1997 – fully engaging the rudder, first one way then the other, to bring the plane back under control – had pushed the stress on the tail fin to the 'ultimate limit.'

The story also reports that though the inspection by Eastern found no damage to the tail fin, Airbus's own examination, conducted in March 2004 as part of the Flight 587 investigation, found two crescent-shaped cracks where the tail fin attaches to the fuselage. Thus, while most analysts agree that pilot error was the probable cause for both incidents, the *USA Today* story implies that, first, a fuller disclosure from Airbus in 1997 might somehow have prevented the 2001 catastrophe, and, second, that Airbus was flying a damaged plane for almost five years.[44]

Three days later, a letter to *USA Today* from Airbus vice president for Safety and Technical Affairs called the story 'hugely misleading.' But had the damage been done? Will air passengers now think twice before boarding Airbus-made aircraft? Will carriers think twice before ordering planes from Airbus?

More generally, as competition between Europe and America heats up, will the psychology of fear become one of the strategies in the trade wars?

In *The End of Globalization*, Alan Rugman puts the problem in perspective: 'One of the biggest problems in international business in the triad is the ability of domestic producers to lobby their home governments to erect barriers to trade. In the past, textile, apparel, and shoe industries were able to obtain protection from cheaper imports through tariffs, quotas, and special measures. Now multilateral trade agreements under the GATT and WTO... outlaw such blatant instruments of protection. They have been replaced by more subtle ones.'[45]

But let us return to the big picture. In its effort to rebuild after World War II, the first phase of Europe's growth was domestic. Each country's major corporations diversified – with the government's blessing – and dominated the local economy. This 'national champion' concept did its job well, but once the reconstruction work was done, Europe was ready to move from domestic to regional growth. This second stage was defined by an emphasis upon trade among the European nations, with each nation focusing on key industries and seeing its market as not confined to its own borders but expanding to the European Community as a whole.

The tearing down of barriers between EC member nations eliminated the inefficiencies of the closed domestic markets. Industries threw off the government paternalism that first helped, but then hindered, their growth. The grip of Keynesianism was weakening. Now, instead of investing in their favorite industries, governments were divesting, and their holdings were privatized. Impoverished by having to empty their treasuries to support the welfare state, governments were refilling their coffers by selling off the railroads, the postal service, and the communications industries. The all-powerful unions, which had become accustomed to dictating the fate of politicians, were weakening. Their intra-national organization was much less effective on the international playing field.

This model – based on revitalized trade among European nations – stimulated growth, but, predictably, that growth too has slowed. There are several reasons for the slowdown. One is that in its struggle to contain the damage from reunification, the Bundesbank, Europe's dominant bank, adopted a stringent monetary policy to curb inflation. The price of this policy was soaring unemployment and stalled growth rippling out across Western Europe. This leads directly to the larger problem that lies at the core of the present study. As we noted in chapter one, the political upheaval that roiled the western world in the early 1990s was a symptom of worldwide economic malaise: no more room for growth among the industrialized nations.

Moreover, a model based on trade *among* European nations is ultimately as limited as the previous model – domestic growth on a country-by-country basis. Trade statistics from the International Monetary Fund show that the European Union's trade is overwhelmingly intra-European. More than 60 percent of EU exports go to another country within the union, and another 13 percent go to other parts of Europe. Import statistics show the same picture.[46]

Finally, growth will have to come from trade *outside* the bloc. Which brings us to the third phase of Europe's post-war economic evolution.

Expanding Europe – and Beyond

What is happening in Europe, today, is so radical that it would have been hard to imagine just a few years ago.

In 1949, the European nations of Belgium, Denmark, France, Greece, Iceland, Italy, Luxembourg, The Netherlands, Norway, Portugal, Turkey, and Britain joined with the US and Canada to create the North Atlantic Treaty Organization (NATO). Its purpose was clear: to establish a counterweight against the Soviet military presence in Eastern Europe. When West Germany joined NATO in 1955, pressing against the border of the Communist bloc, the Soviets countered with the creation of the Warsaw Pact. Its purpose was equally transparent: to draw the Soviet Union and its satellites – Bulgaria, Czechoslovakia, East Germany, Hungary, Poland, and Romania – into a tight-knit defensive league against any encroachment from NATO powers. This ushered in the Cold War, which dominated global military and economic strategy for the second half of the twentieth century.

Now it all seems like an unpleasant dream from which the world has woken up. Arch enemies are acting like old friends. Warsaw Pact nations like Hungary, the Czech Republic, Slovakia, and Poland are being invited to become part of NATO. And while NATO is primarily a military/defense organization, the European Union – an economic organization – is also opening its doors to Central and Eastern Europe. The consequences for Europe – and the world – will be far-reaching.

In the European Union's thrust toward the northeast, of course, we see a perfect illustration of the tripolar organization that is coming to shape the globe. Not only will the expanding Europe become one of the three dominant blocs, but, as we predict, its economic flow within that bloc – its trade and industry – will move north-south rather than along the historic east-west corridors.

For Europe, the former Soviet states will provide the 'developing world' through which its stagnating economy will refuel itself – but with an important difference. Unlike the truly undeveloped nations of the world, these Central and Eastern European countries are already industrialized, with highly educated populations. The largest bus manufacturer in the world is in the Czech Republic, for example. Indeed, a major problem in these nations is the *post*-industrial issue of pollution and environmental degradation. Of course, what is undeveloped in these countries – from the EU's point of view – is their economies. But as these nations reform their economies in the direction of the free-market model, the EU will have huge new markets into which to expand, just as new EU members will have all of Europe as their new market. This is the recipe for growing the total pie.

West Europe's expansion began, of course, with East Germany. But consider Poland and Hungary, whose inclination westward could be seen as early as 1956, when uprisings in those countries incited a Soviet crackdown. In the 1980s, Poland's 'solidarity' movement under the leadership of Lech Walesa was another step to the west. Czechoslovakia's urge for free expression – and freer markets – brought Soviet tanks across the border in 1968. Since the nation split into the Czech Republic and Slovakia, market reforms have continued and both have begun to prosper. When Western Europeans look across the divide that was once the Iron Curtain, they see people like themselves – with good education, of similar ethnic descent, of similar religious background. Quite logically, European industrialists say to themselves, 'Let's move the factories there, just like the US is doing in Mexico. Let us put the jobs there.' Otherwise, of course, a flood of Eastern European immigrants would overwhelm the job market in the west.

Let's take a closer look at these three countries, all three of which have been extended membership in the EU, and all three of which sit right on western Europe's border.

Poland was the early frontrunner toward a market economy. *The Economist* reported in 1993 that it was 'leading Eastern Europe's transition,' with a growth rate in the first half of that year 4 percent higher than the same period a year earlier and industrial output 9.4 percent higher. Unemployment remained high (15 percent) and inflation even higher (35 percent), but with 1.7 million private firms in operation, accounting for 45 percent of GDP, the report concluded that 'the vitality of the private sector is a sure sign that the Polish economy has been structurally transformed.'[47] Unfortunately, by 2002 Poland's economic picture – like that across Europe – had dimmed. Unemployment stood at 17 percent, and companies were failing, including the important Szczecin shipyard in the northeast. Poland's export-driven economy was struggling as its trade deficit rose to $6 billion. The budget deficit was projected to rise to $10 billion, 5 percent of GDP. For 2002 growth was predicted at an unsatisfactory 1.5 percent, when 5 percent was needed to make headway against unemployment. This scenario would make Poland's 2004 accession into the European Union all the more critical.[48]

With EU membership looming, the picture in the Czech Republic was brighter. The economy was growing at approximately 4 percent in 2002, and state coffers continued to be replenished by privatization, including the government's 68 percent stake in the electricity company – valued at $5.5 billion. Exports were growing steadily and foreign investment, relative to population, was the highest in the region. Cementing more than 10 years of reforms, the Czech Republic's economy was firmly anchored in the West, and looking quite stable.[49]

The real tiger in the region, however, turns out to be Hungary. This nation, according to a 2002 report in *Global Finance*, has completed one of the most profound and orderly shifts to a market economy in Central and Eastern Europe. 'The most important thing,' explains Vilmos Skulteti, CEO of Hungary's Investment and Trade Development agency ITDH, 'is that the privatization process already has been completed here.' More than 85 percent of Hungary's GDP is in the hands of the private sector now, and as a result, GDP has been growing about 5 percent a year, twice as fast as the European Union average. All the figures are promising: unemployment down to 5.7 percent; wages up 6 percent over the previous year; inflation down to 6.8. Of course, all of this makes

Hungary very attractive to foreign capital, bringing in about $2 billion a year in foreign direct investment. Meanwhile, exports – mostly machinery and equipment – account for more than 60 percent of GDP, and more than 75 percent of exports go to the EU. Skulteti understands perfectly the significance of EU membership: 'There is a combined market of 600 million people within five or six hours' traveling time from Hungary.'[50]

None of these three countries are likely to vote against their accession. But EU expansion will not be simply a stroll in the park. Already other nations – notably Turkey, Bulgaria, and Romania – are banging on the door, and each new entry brings a unique set of problems. Europe finds itself in the position of being able to wring concessions from petitioning nations – in Turkey's case, a smaller role of the military in government and sustained economic growth – that can seem burdensome. At the December 2002 summit in Copenhagen, when told that his nation would have to wait until 2004 just to begin negotiations for membership, Turkey's prime minister, Abdullah Gul called the offer 'far from satisfactory.'[51]

Moreover, once the nations of Central and Eastern Europe are in fact offered membership, they face a host of gearing-up problems. One is the low production capacity that is a serious legacy of the Soviet era. How can you build an economy when you have too little output? Another is the very logical inclination of workers in the East to migrate to the better jobs and living conditions of the West. Yet another is the East's under-developed work ethic – as illustrated in the popular Soviet joke: 'We pretend to work. They pretend to pay us.' Perhaps most troubling will be the problem of instituting the fundamental right of private property. Without financial institutions, without credit histories, how does the huge transition from state to private ownership take place?

In the end, says Lester Thurow, Western Europe will have no choice but to help. 'Preventing westward migration, reducing border tensions, and lowering ethnic hatreds all demand economic success in Middle and Eastern Europe. A mixture of altruism and fear of the Russian military bear led to the original Marshall Plan.

A mixture of altruism and a fear of chaos on immediate borders will lead to a similar plan for Middle and Eastern Europe.'[52]

But it is our contention that the European sphere of influence will not end with Eastern Europe. Ultimately, Europe will be driven by three powers: Germany, France, and Russia. As mentioned earlier in the context of the war in Iraq, we already see this new alignment taking shape. Interestingly, Gorbochev sought an alliance with Britain and America, but Boris Yeltsin began the move back toward Europe. His appointed successor, Putin, is clearly carrying out that plan.

Differences – and areas of disagreement – remain between Russia and Europe, and these differences come into sharp focus as the European Union expands right up against Russia's borders. For example, Putin would like to ease travel restrictions between Russia and Europe, especially out of Kaliningrad, the small Russian enclave on the Baltic Sea that will soon be completely surrounded by the new EU member states. However, fears of crime and illegal migration make European Union leaders balk at the prospect of unlimited travel, and their offer – at the 2003 Russia-EU summit – of multiple-entry visas for Russians traveling in and out of Kaliningrad left Putin so miffed that he compared the visa requirement to a diplomatic version of the Berlin Wall.[53] Russia is also at odds – with both Europe and the US – over its proposed entry into the World Trade Organization. The western powers argue that Russia wants to retain too much protection for financial industries like banking and insurance, while Russia argues for limiting foreign participation on the grounds that its firms are not yet strong enough to compete with international rivals. Another bone of contention is Russia's low domestic energy prices – approximately one-sixth the average level in Europe. Europe calls this an unfair subsidy of a local industry; Russia calls it a competitive advantage.[54]

Larger forces, however, steadily push for the solution to such problems. We see these forces at the political level in Russia's accession to the G-8, and with the creation of the NATO-Russia Council, which gives Russia a seat and a voice – but no veto – at the 19-nation NATO table. More broadly, we see economic forces strengthening the bonds between Russia and the EU.

Vassily Likhachev, Russia's Permanent Representative provides an overview of these economic ties to the European Communities. Likhachev reports that, as of the end of 2002, the European Union accounted for 35 percent of Russian foreign trade and one-third of all foreign investment in Russia. In 2001, Russia's exports to Europe totaled 54 billion euros and imports from Europe totaled 28 billion. On the other side of the equation, 21 percent of Europe's oil and 41 percent of its natural gas come from Russia. Europe's keen interest in developing the relationship is reflected in its two-year, 88-million euro allotment to support Russia's administrative and legal reforms. Likhachev also hailed the commitment to Russia-EU cooperation that came out of the 2002 summit – most notably, their joint effort on a North European gas pipeline from the Leningrad Region to Germany to be laid on the bottom of the Baltic Sea.[55]

Europe's embrace of her northern neighbor has, of course, been stimulated by Russia's impressive economic rebound after the disastrous 1998 crash. The nation has enjoyed three straight years of robust growth and now has a budget surplus and all-time high foreign-exchange reserves. Putin's continued reforms – an income tax cut to 13 percent (Europe's lowest), approval of the sale of agricultural land, and an overhaul of the judicial system to better protect property rights – have the stated goal of keeping Russia's economy on its current course.[56]

On the other hand, Russia's over-heavy dependence on its gas and oil reserves – as well as the hangover effect from the 1998 collapse – leave one lingering weakness in its economic recovery: relatively little foreign direct investment. However, the recent mega-deal between Britain's BP PLC and Russia's Alfa Group and Access-Renova seems to indicate that reluctance to invest in Russia may at last be disappearing. For $6.75 billion, BP will get a 50 percent stake in a joint venture that will create Russia's third-largest oil producer. Of particular interest, the new Russian company, which owns a huge Siberian oil field near the Chinese border, will give the partners a platform from which to reach the energy-starved markets of the Far East. The deal – signaling global approval for doing business in Russia – was regarded as such a milestone that Putin and Britain's Tony Blair got on the phone to give it their blessing.[57]

The developing alliance between Europe and Russia has yet further significance. Why? Because it is Russia that is going to help cement Europe's ties to the Middle East, and, through its network in the Middle East, the European Union will cultivate its relationship to the rich developing markets in North Africa. The Russia connection is one of the keys to Europe's future in these regions.

How important is the Middle East to Russia? Consider that Russia is the world's largest provider of natural gas and that its crude oil reserves are also tremendous. An alliance with the Middle East would create tremendous leverage in terms of world energy. The US' alliance with Mexico and Venezuela – even with the Alaska pipeline thrown in – pales in comparison. The Bush administration sees this clearly, recently scrapping an eight-year, $1.5 billion project to develop high-mileage gas-powered cars in favor of a $1.7 billion, five-year federal subsidy for fuel-cell research and development.

In fact, Russia's historic ties to the Middle East are now being renewed and strengthened. Witness its help building a nuclear reactor in Iran, over the protests of the US. Witness Russian officials' presence in Saudi Arabia, where they met with OPEC ministers to agree on mutually profitable oil output levels. Witness the deals between Iraq – shortly before Washington decided to attack – and three different Russian oil companies. Perhaps now we begin to understand Putin's reluctance to support President Bush's invasion. Russia used to make arms deals with Middle Eastern countries; now it finds an advantage in making oil and gas deals. Perhaps the European Union, behind the Russian phalanx, hopes to drive a wedge between the Middle East and the US.

Moreover, it is our belief – though many people find it unbelievable – that thanks to Russia's influence, even Israel will pull away from its relationship with the US. But we are getting ahead of ourselves. In chapter six, we will take a more detailed look at the place of the Middle East – as well as of Africa, India, and other regions of the world – in the coming tri-polar economic alignment.

To reiterate, then, out of simple economic necessity Europe has evolved from a nation-state mentality into a single market – and a very powerful one. The younger generation – growing up with euros in their pockets – is thinking 'European' now, and schools and universities are encouraging this viewpoint. Moreover, all old obligations to the US – born of World War II – are fading away as the older generation fades away, and the attitude toward America among young Europeans seems a mixture of loathing and envy. Not to mention resentment that the US still struts like a puppet master on the world's stage.

Europe is flexing its muscle now, growing into its role as one of the world's three great geoeconomic powers. And just as the Soviet Union was America's military rival during the Cold War, Europe will emerge as an equally determined economic rival. Of course, in the long run, China and Japan will merge into a formidable foe on the opposite horizon, and how these three great economic powerhouses compete and collide over the coming years should provide a spectacular show.

Meanwhile... As for Britain

In October 1990, almost on her way out of office, British Prime Minister Margaret Thatcher agreed to have sterling enter into the European Exchange Rate Mechanism (ERM) a move she had resisted since her first election in 1979. In fact, under Thatcher, Britain had never been a completely happy member of the European Community, despite her enthusiasm for what she saw as the guiding spirit of the 1957 Treaty of Rome – i.e. free trade among European nations. The problem was, as Thatcher recalls in her memoir, *Downing Street Years,* 'Britain's unique trading pattern made her a very large net contributor to the EC budget – so large that the situation was indeed unacceptable.' There was also the thorny issue of the CAP (Common Agricultural Policy); a sizable portion of the EC's budget was being spent to subsidize, as Thatcher saw it, inefficient German and French farmers.

Having set her country on the road to a remarkable economic recovery during the 1980s, Thatcher resisted the loss of national power and autonomy, which, for her, joining the ERM would entail. 'Sterling's participation in the ERM,' she writes, 'was seen partly as proof that we were "good Europeans"... But it was also seen as a way of abdicating control over our own monetary policy, in order to have it determined by the German Bundesbank. This is what was meant when people said we would gain credibility for our policies if we were – to adopt another Euro-metaphor – 'anchored' to the Deutsche Mark.' In reality, Thatcher's chief misgiving was that entry into the ERM would lead Britain inexorably into the European Monetary Union. 'Eventually, I was to go along with what (Chancellor of the Exchequer) John (Major) wanted (and enter sterling into the ERM). On EMU, however, which for me went to the very heart not just of the debate about Europe's future but about Britain's future as a democratic, sovereign state, I was not prepared to compromise.'

A pan-Europe exchange rate was bad enough, in other words, but a single European currency went beyond the pale. For Thatcher, it was an absolutely fundamental issue. The EMU, as she saw it, 'which involves the loss of the power to issue your own currency and acceptance of one European currency, one central bank and one set of interest rates – means the end of a country's economic independence and thus the increasing irrelevance of its parliamentary democracy. Control of its economy is transferred from the elected government, answerable to Parliament and the electorate, to unaccountable supra-national institutions.'

Bucking what she perceived as the continental drift as early as 1983, Thatcher was reporting to Parliament that 'I do not in any way believe in a federated Europe.' Still, as a committed free-trader, she had signed the 1985 Single European Act, which she believed worked to keep Europe 'on course for the Single Market by 1992.' The Single Market – which Britain pioneered, according to Thatcher – harkened back to the Treaty of Rome and was meant to revive its liberal, free trade, deregulatory purpose. But even as she signed the document, she was increasingly disturbed by the federalizing tendencies of the European Commission and its leader Jacques Delors (formerly finance minister under Francois Mitterand), whom she saw as one of the 'new breed of unaccountable politicians.' Furthermore, writes Thatcher, 'In the two years of European politicking that led up to the Single European Act, I had witnessed a profound shift in how European policy was conducted – and therefore in the kind of Europe that was taking shape. A Franco-German bloc with its own agenda had re-emerged to set the direction of the Community. The European Commission, which had always had a yen for centralized power, was now led by a tough, talented European federalist (Delors), whose philosophy justified centralism.'

In her memoir, Thatcher looks back at her second term as Prime Minister (1983–87) as a time during which the European Community 'subtly but surely shifted its direction away from being a Community of open trade, light regulation and freely co-operating sovereign nation-states toward statism and centralism.' The forces of federalism and bureaucracy were gaining in strength, she says, as Socialist and Christian Democrat governments in France, Spain, Italy and Germany forced the pace of integration into a centralist mindset. In particular, Thatcher saw worrisome evidence of a 're-emergence of a Franco-German axis with its own covert federalist and protectionist agenda.'

The collapse of the Soviet Union at the end of the decade only served to strengthen Thatcher's nationalist resolve. In the famous 'Bruges speech' – delivered to the College of Europe in Bruges in 1988 – Thatcher once again enunciated her fundamental position: 'It is ironic that just when those countries, such as the Soviet Union, which have tried to run everything from the centre, are learning that success depends on dispersing power and decisions away from the centre, some in the Community seem to want to move in the opposite direction. We have not successfully rolled back the frontiers of the state in Britain only to see them re-imposed at the European level, with a European super-state exercising a new dominance from Brussels.'

The fall of the Berlin Wall in November 1989 – in itself an event to be cheered – poured more coal into the European locomotive, according to Thatcher, as it invited a too-rapid German reunification: 'Arriving prematurely as it did, a united Germany has tended to encourage three unwelcome developments: the rush to European federalism as a way of tying down Gulliver; the maintenance of a Franco-German bloc for the same purpose; and the gradual withdrawal of the US from Europe on the assumption that a German-led federal Europe will be both stable and capable of looking after its own defence.'

In reading her memoir, it is impossible to doubt the strength of Thatcher's convictions. After all, she had seen the success of her own Thatcher Revolution – the rebirth in Britain of 'an enterprise economy' and a decade of prosperity during which Britain's economic performance 'astonished the world.' As her years in office drew to a close, Thatcher remained determined 'to stake out a radically different position from the direction in which most of the Community seemed intent on going, to raise the flag of national sovereignty, free trade and free enterprise – and fight.'

Moreover, in the short term, at least, Britain has held to Thatcher's course. In December 1991, when the European summit leaders met in the Dutch market town of Maastricht to conclude a treaty on the creation of a single European currency (the euro) by 1999, Thatcher's successor, Prime Minister John Major, insisted that the treaty include an 'opt-out' clause, whereby Britain could reject the currency later on if it so wished. Furthermore, when, as a result of the economic havoc caused by German reunification, European currencies came under speculative attack and sterling fell below its agreed-upon 'floor rate,' Britain withdrew from sterling's participation in the ERM.

Yet events in the 1990s and in the first years of the 21st century suggest that Thatcher's long-range vision may not have been long enough. As she left office in 1990, she called the Delors-style European Union 'a Tower of Babel (built) on the uneven foundation of ancient nations, different languages and diverse economies,' and she goes on to say that 'work on that shaky construction is still proceeding.'[58] Indeed, with the introduction of the euro into general circulation in January 2002, the work to unify Europe economically still proceeds, and many in Britain are beginning to worry about being left behind.

Was Thatcher's fierce nationalism finally out of step with the times? According to a senior US official, quoted in *Newsweek* magazine at the time of the signing, 'Maastricht is one of those very rare things these days – a virtually unmixed blessing.' And Peter Jenkins, in *Mrs. Thatcher's Revolution*, writes that Thatcher's fulminations against European union were 'the most signal failure of her foreign policy.' Instead of spurning the union, says Jenkins, Thatcher should have been working 'to achieve a role of political leadership within it... to establish at the heart of the Community the political direction which could only flow from a triple alliance of Britain, France and Germany.'[59]

Of course, it may be that Thatcher felt uninvited to France and Germany's party. After all, it was Valery Giscard d'Estaing and Helmut Schmidt who, in 1978, negotiated the European Monetary System (EMS), which created the Exchange Rate Mechanism, tying the franc and several other currencies to the Deutsche Mark and allowing them to fluctuate only within agreed limits. And, as noted above, throughout the 1980s Thatcher watched the burgeoning German-French alliance with increasing concern. It is likely that by the time the European Economic Community (EEC), or so-called Common Market, evolved into the European Community (EC) in 1987, Thatcher suspected that the French-German coalition had been organized primarily to minimize Britain's strength within a European federation.

In any event, Thatcher saw European federalism as an example of 'the establishment of tight blocs of countries which stood in the way of a wider internationalism. I said (to the cabinet) that we must build on the American proposals for strengthening the political aspects of NATO, by suggesting a trade dimension to the alliance, which would join Europe to a North American (US and Canada) Free Trade Area. I saw this as a way of averting the dangerous prospect of a world divided into three protectionist trade blocs, based on the European Community, Japan and the US, which over time could become seriously unstable.'[60]

Needless to say, Thatcher's vision of a world divided into three dominant trade blocs is proving quite accurate – with Britain in the role of the exception that proves the rule. It is universally recognized that while Thatcher's relations with her European neighbors chilled, she cultivated extremely close ties with philosophically like-minded US president Ronald Reagan. The US would clearly be a beneficial economic ally for Britain, and Thatcher encouraged massive US investment into the country. Increasingly, the 23-mile-wide English Channel became more difficult for her to cross than the 3,000-mile-wide Atlantic Ocean.

Moreover, as the 2003 war in Iraq shows, Britain under Tony Blair continues to look westward toward the US rather than eastward toward the European continent. From the American perspective, once again, 'The British are coming! The British are coming!'

Other Problems for the Union

It is a radical experiment, actually. We have to keep in mind that the European Union consists of 15 nations – going on 25 – each with its own history, culture, personality, and ethnicity. Economic necessity will wash out many differences, but in the meantime we can expect to see a lot of squabbling.

The tremendous contention between Britain and the rest of the European Union is the most obvious problem, and it only becomes more obvious as Britain continues to resist adopting the euro. Tony Blair, perhaps already feeling alienated enough from Germany and France, would like to see the currency adopted, but he is opposed not only by the Chancellor of the Exchequer, Gordon Brown, but also by two-thirds of his citizens. Many Britons, no doubt, recall the good times under Margaret Thatcher, along with her bitter opposition to relinquishing the pound sterling.

This quarrel spills over into others on the microeconomic level. For example, British telecommunications company Vodaphone, after purchasing the US firm AirTouch in 1999, wanted to buy the German firm Mannesmann, a gas company that had diversified into wireless. Mannesmann wanted to get out of telecommunications, but didn't want to sell to Vodaphone, so the British company threatened a hostile takeover. Mannesmann chief executive Klaus Esser vowed to keep the company independent, and German chancellor Gerhard Schroeder, who bitterly denounced the deal, vigorously supported him. He simply didn't want to see a British invasion into German corporate territory. It's interesting: unlike relations between Germany and France, German-British tensions have never completely dissipated since World War II. (Britain eventually won this battle, however, with the 2000 acquisition of Mannesmann's telecommunications division.)

These merger/acquisition arguments don't always pit Britain against the rest of Europe, however. Germany has recently found itself at odds with the rest of the EU in its determination to protect Volkswagen (VW). The European Commission is calling into question the so-called 'VW' law, which prevents any shareholder in the company from exercising more than 20 percent of voting rights, effectively blocking a hostile takeover. In the face of the Commission's review of this law, Schroeder has declared, 'Any efforts by the commission in Brussels to smash the VW culture will meet the resistance of the federal government as long as we are in power.'[61]

And then there are the smaller squabbles. Since the process of becoming a union involves thousands of agreements, compromises, and conditions, everybody's toes get stepped on. Take the banana wars, for example.

While most of the world's bananas come from Central America's original 'banana republics,' France and Britain – among others – prefer to import theirs from their past or present colonies in the West Indies. To protect these island producers, France and Britain have traditionally imposed quotas against the 'dollar bananas' of Central America. Germany, on the other hand, without any West Indian colonies, had been happily importing the cheaper bananas from the Americas and roared in protest when the European Commission tried to impose a pan-European import quota against them.

Similarly, in the rush toward standardization, the European Community proposed new guidelines on manufacture of cheese. Much to the dismay of French gourmets, these guidelines would have banned some traditional French cheeses, including Camembert. Meanwhile, back in England, the time-honored breakfast sausage known as 'the banger' got caught up in the proliferation of guidelines. Because of its relatively low-meat, high-cereal content, the banger was not going to meet the original EC minimum standards for any product labeled 'sausage.' But you don't ask a Brit to change his breakfast routine any more than you ask a Frenchman to give up his cheese.[62]

Such problems seem petty, but they persist. At a European Union gathering in 2002, all the attendees stood for the anthem, Beethoven's 'Ode to Joy,' adopted in 1986. But, of course, nobody sang. There are no lyrics. Christoph Leitl, the head of Eurochambers, an umbrella organization for Europe's 1,600 regional and local chambers of commerce, is sure there should be some. But who is going to write them, and, more important, in which language? This dilemma may not prove the Union's undoing, but it's one of hundreds of problems that resist an easy solution.[63]

And, finally, a much larger problem – one that will grow thornier as the EU expands. In addition to its economic ties, should the European Union also be a 'political union,' speaking with one voice on matters of foreign and defense policy? EU commissioner Gunther Verheugen believes so, and also believes that his native Germany, like France, is committed to a vision of Europe as 'a strong partner but also a counterweight to the US.' The problem is, the new members coming aboard – notably Poland, the Czech Republic, and Hungary – feel quite differently about the US and have incurred the outrage of French president Jacques Chiraq by openly supporting the US position on Iraq. This doesn't bode well for the European Union's political convergence.[64]

Will Europe ever be truly integrated? History suggests that only a common enemy – or an empire-minded conqueror – has ever been able to unite the states of Europe.

But perhaps a common enemy is what we have today. Or, two enemies: America and Asia. The difference is that this time around the conflict will be economic rather than military.

CHAPTER 4

ANSWERING THE CHALLENGE: THE AMERICAS

When Ronald Reagan initiated a free-trade agreement with Canada at the end of his second term, he was looking towards America's future. The 12 members of the European Community had already signed the Single European Act, committing themselves to creating a single internal market by 1992. On the other side of the world, Japan and China were beginning to rediscover each other. When Bill Clinton brought Mexico into the North American Free Trade Agreement, he, like Reagan, knew that the real goal had not yet been reached. The end of the journey, the realization of the destiny of the Americas, may be left to George W. Bush, or perhaps to his successor. The signing of the Free Trade Agreement of the Americas, a historic economic partnership among the 34 nations of the Western Hemisphere, would constitute a significant part of the legacy of the president who makes it a reality.

Let us take a look at the milestones along this remarkable journey.

With his approval rating bottoming out at 25 percent, President Jimmy Carter returned from the Tokyo energy summit, in 1979, to hear chief domestic policy advisor Stuart Eizenstat lament, 'In many respects, this would appear to be the worst of times.'[65] It was true: hard times had fallen on the greatest nation in the free world.

The inflation rate during 1979 climbed to 13 percent. Unemployment, which had been reduced to 5.8 percent, was on the rise again and would hit 7.2 percent in 1980. The growth rate of the output per worker – which ultimately determines the standard of living – had been declining for six straight years. In other words, Carter was still struggling against the phenomenon of 'stagflation,' which had first arrived on the world economic scene after the first oil crisis of 1973. As economist Herbert Stein describes the situation, 'By 1979... we were at the end of two decades in which government spending, government taxes, government deficits, government regulation and government expansion of the money supply had all increased rapidly. And at the end of those two decades the inflation rate was high, real economic growth was slow and our 'normal' unemployment rate – the rate we experienced in good times – was higher than ever.'[66]

With a reelection campaign looming, something had to be done. Carter shuffled his cabinet, shifting William Miller into the position of Treasury secretary and naming Paul Volcker to the chairmanship of the Federal Reserve Board. Volcker's clear mission was to solve the most visible and troublesome of the various economic woes: high inflation. His tight money-policy proved to be the right weapon, but the results weren't evident until well after Carter's departure. The immediate effects of his policy for Carter's administration were an upsurge in the inflation rate to an unheard-of 20 percent, and a further contraction of the economy. Unfortunately for Carter, this handed Ronald Reagan a remarkably effective campaign theme. 'Just ask yourselves,' Reagan advised voters, 'whether you are better off today than you were four years ago.'

These problems – inflation, unemployment and stagnant growth – were immediate, 'pocketbook' issues, and they certainly played a key role in Carter's 1980 defeat. But another problem – even more deeply pervasive – marked Carter's final years in office and no doubt contributed to what he himself called the national 'malaise.' This was the deterioration of US' global competitiveness.

For the first time ever, it was possible to describe the US as *losing* on the economic battlefield. The US was losing to the OPEC cartel, which not only forced Americans to pay more at the gas pump but also brought home the fact of their energy dependency. President Carter's suggestion that Americans lower their thermostats and put on sweaters provided very little consolation.

In consumer electronics, US companies were losing to Japan, a nation the US had helped to rebuild just a few decades earlier. The 'retreat into oblivion' by US companies in this sector is vividly demonstrated in the production of radios. In 1955, 96 percent of the radios sold in the US were made there. By 1975, that percentage had dropped to virtually zero. The huge television industry tells a similar story. By the late 1980s, the US had only one manufacturer, Zenith, left in the field.[67]

Perhaps even more dramatic was how the Japanese were beating the US in the automobile industry. Thanks to the new 'energy consciousness' generated by the oil crises of the 1970s, American highways were suddenly chock full of Toyotas, Hondas, and Datsuns (Nissans). In fact, demands for protection by US auto manufacturers led to the first 'voluntary export restraint' agreement between Japan and the US in 1981. Less visibly, at the high end of the auto sector, the US was getting beat by Europe, whose BMWs, Mercedes-Benzes, and Jaguars enjoyed a cachet unmatched by US luxury carmakers.

A number of factors led to the particular plight that President Carter found himself in toward the end of his presidency – and to the more general condition of the US economy at that time. One was a momentous decision from the Nixon White House: the closing of the 'gold window' in 1971. According to Stein, who was chairman of Nixon's Council of Economic Advisors at the time, there was little choice. Because the US had been running deficits in its balance of payments – spending more dollars abroad than it was raking in from exports – foreign treasuries had accumulated more dollars than there was gold to redeem them. Stein and his fellow economists liked the idea of removing the dollar from the gold standard, allowing it to decline and float freely against other currencies. 'A free exchange rate,' he writes, 'seemed to be a necessary condition for freedom in other international economic transactions.' Of course, it was understood that the dollar's decline would be inflationary in the US, because it would raise the dollar price of imports. This is why, at a time when the nation was already in the grip of spiraling wages and prices, the closing of the gold window was announced at the same time (August 1971) as the imposition of the infamous 'wage and price freeze.'

Ultimately, Nixon's wage and price controls – particularly when he re-imposed the freeze in 1973 – proved disastrous, and the declining value of the dollar provided further impetus to the rise in inflation. When Gerald Ford took office in 1974, the inflation rate had hit 12 percent, and the new administration responded with the creation of the WIN (Whip Inflation Now) buttons, which, as Stein recalls, 'became an object of ridicule and a symbol of vacuity in economic policy.'[68] As we have seen, the inability to 'whip' inflation helped bring down Carter's administration as well. (As an interesting comparison, we might note that in 2003, when inflation poses no serious threat, a 'weak' dollar was being promoted as a way to make US exports more attractive to foreign consumers.)

Another factor contributing to the economic distress of the late 1970s was the burden of government regulation of business and industry. Nixon's wage and price controls are a spectacular example, of course; but America's 'regulatory capitalism' has a longer history. The Interstate Commerce Commission, created to oversee the railroads, dates from the nineteenth century, and the Federal Trade Commission, intended to police 'big business' and 'unfair' trade practices, was created during Woodrow Wilson's administration. To pull the nation out of the Great Depression – and to try to prevent another 1929-style crash – Roosevelt put a number of regulatory agencies in place: the Securities and Exchange Commission, Federal Communications Commission, Civil Aeronautics Board, and the National Labor Relations Board, among others. As Daniel Yergin points out, this was roughly the same time (1936) at which John Maynard Keynes' *The General Theory* made its appearance, and Keynes' ideas speedily crossed the Atlantic and found a welcome home in the Harvard economics department.[69]

Needless to say, the liberal Kennedy and Johnson administrations did little to curb the appetite for regulation; but, surprisingly, even the 'conservative' Richard Nixon added to the regulatory roll call. During his tenure, the Environmental Protection Agency, the Occupational Safety and Health Administration, and the Equal Employment Opportunity Commission all came into existence. Moreover, outside of his wage and price freeze, Nixon tried to combat the oil crisis with pricing and allocation systems that failed miserably and 'managed to produce a shortage of energy in the richest country in the world.' As Stein writes, 'An immense Rube Goldberg structure of controls was erected simply to deal with the problems created by unwillingness to let the prices of oil rise to a free market level, and the structure was dismantled only when Ronald Reagan freed oil prices.'[70]

In addition, several ingrained structural problems impeded American business and industry and significantly weakened US competitiveness in the global economy. These are illustrated by the strategic planning initiative created by Reginald Jones, Jack Welch's predecessor as CEO of General Electric. His initiative concluded that after the energy crisis, the US suddenly found itself in an increasingly fierce economic battle in which competitive advantage no longer fell automatically to the American side. When Jones's strategic planners investigated the problem, they concluded that they were competitive in raw materials, and in labor, and in automation. Where they lost the edge was in non-operating costs. One of these was the dividend paid to the shareholders, money that perhaps should be plowed back into the business for capital improvements or research and development. Another was cost of capital: the American industry was paying 10 and 12 percent interest on money borrowed for capital investment, while the Japanese government, with immense reserves available in the postal savings system, intervened to make capital readily available to favored enterprises. However, the biggest source of US competitive disadvantage was corporate income tax. Some US corporations were being taxed at rates approaching 50 percent, whereas their competitors in Europe and Japan were paying less than 10 percent.

Events seemed to conspire against President Jimmy Carter. The toppling of the Shah of Iran in 1979 caused a second oil shock, and, if that wasn't bad enough, the Iranian hostage crisis in 1980 – and the failed rescue mission – sealed the fate of his re-election bid. Before his one term was over, however, Carter did begin the process of dismantling the regulatory structure that was proving so cumbersome to US industry. In 1978 he reformed the Civil Aeronautics Board and deregulated the airlines, allowing carriers to set fares competitively for the first time in decades. This return to the market continued with the truck industry and the railroads – which had been regulated out of business for all practical purposes. Carter also signed the Public Utility Regulatory Policies Act in 1978, which allowed entrepreneurs to build power plants and sell power to a local utility – the first step in deregulating electricity.[71]

Tax reform was left to Ronald Reagan. According to Martin Anderson, one of the White House economists who helped him formulate it, Reagan's tax dogma was as follows: 'The level of taxation in the US has now become so high that it is stifling the incentive for individuals to earn, save, and invest. We must have a program – of at least three years' duration – of across-the-board tax cuts. The personal income tax rate must be cut by a specific percentage every year for three years, especially the higher, incentive-destroying marginal rates. The capital gains tax, and the corporate income tax must be cut a commensurate amount. Tax rates that are too high destroy incentives to earn, cripple prosperity, lead to deficit financing and inflation, and create unemployment.'[72]

Coincidentally, the movement to reduce the tax burden was bolstered by the work of Arthur Laffer, who had joined the increasingly influential University of Chicago economics faculty in 1967. Laffer's lasting fame is attributable to his having sketched a simple curve to demonstrate how government tax revenue changed as the tax rate went from 0 percent to 100 percent. The significance of 'Laffer's Curve' was its persuasive suggestion that, as tax rates continued to climb, government revenue would actually begin to decline at a certain point. This potent argument for tax-cuts added to the growing body of 'supply-side' economic thought that underpinned Reagan's tax proposals.

But the tax cuts carried out during his first term in office were not the end of Reagan's tax initiatives. In 1984 he campaigned on a promise of top-to-bottom tax reform, a promise realized in the Tax Reform Act of 1986 – hailed by Reagan biographer Lou Cannon as 'arguably the most important domestic accomplishment of Reagan's second term.'[73] At the heart of this program were lower rates and closed loopholes. Specifically, the burdensome top corporate rate of 46 percent was reduced to 34 percent. Moreover, while this reduction was to some extent offset by the repeal of the investment tax credit, wholesale collapsing of tax shelters immensely benefited American business. Billions of dollars of private money were transferred out of wasteful tax-avoidance schemes into legitimate, economically productive investments.

Reagan also tried to keep his promise to 'get government off our backs' by easing regulation on business and industry. Despite Carter's best efforts, between 1970 and 1980 the social regulatory agencies of the federal government grew from twelve to eighteen and their budgets increased from $1.4 billion to $7.5 billion. Moreover, Murray Weidenbaum, Reagan's first chairman of the Council of Economic Advisers, estimated that government regulations were costing US businesses as much as $100 billion annually; slowing economic growth and pushing up the costs of goods and services.[74] Consequently, shortly after being sworn in, Reagan named Vice President George Bush to chair the Presidential Task Force on Regulatory Relief. According to Martin Anderson, one of its seven members, the task force tore into the job with zeal. 'Only three months after we began,' he writes, 'the task force had taken action on 181 federal regulations in 13 departments and agencies. The estimated savings were as much as $18 billion the first year, with annual savings thereafter of $6 billion.' Anderson also reports that the work was extremely tedious and that it was difficult to keep up the momentum. In fact, more important than its work on existing legislation, says Anderson, was 'the effect the task force had in choking off a blizzard of new, even more onerous regulations.'[75]

Another aspect of US economic competitiveness Reagan sought to bolster was in terms of the basic size of US corporations. It was becoming clear that competitiveness depended on global reach, on being the dominant player, on taking advantage of economies of scale. Japan had learned this lesson, as illustrated by their dominance of the machine tool industry, as well as consumer electronics. In America, antitrust laws had hampered the ability of industry to grow through merger and acquisition, but under Reagan's influence the bias against bigness began to dissipate, and while antitrust enforcement didn't altogether disappear, a corporation's size or dominance was no longer an antitrust criterion. As a result, according to Lou Cannon, during the Reagan administration American business engaged in a record wave of 25,000 mergers, takeovers, and restructurings. 'Reagan's belief was that government should get out of the way,' writes Cannon, 'and government did.'[76]

Reagan's basic domestic economic policy had three points: reducing taxes, increasing military spending, and balancing the federal budget. As most analysts now agree, his success on the first two points led to failure on the third, with the result that under Reagan's watch the national debt nearly tripled, to $2.684 trillion. But this was the price the US paid for the largest, most sustained, peacetime economic expansion in its history. When Carter left office, inflation stood at 12.5 percent and unemployment at 7.1 percent. In the last year of Reagan's presidency, inflation was 4.4 percent and unemployment was at 5.5 percent. The gross national product had nearly doubled, and the stock market had recovered from its 1987 crash to soar again.

But as Martin Anderson points out, as the Reagan era came to a close, some economic problems persisted – especially on the international front. The trade deficit remained high, and calls for protectionism were growing louder. The bright spot here, says Anderson, was the 'historic' trade agreement between the US and Canada – 'a stunning step in the right direction.'[77] Biographer Lou Cannon writes that a 'North American accord' between the US and Canada had long been a dream of Reagan's, that he had touted the idea even in his 1979 campaign. While the idea of free trade between the US and Canada had long been just that – an idea – Reagan and Canadian Prime Minister Brian Mulroney 'overcame protectionist objections on both sides of the border' and signed the Canada-US Free Trade Agreement on January 2, 1988. Cannon also notes that it was Reagan who took the next step toward a North American common market by approving a 'framework agreement' with Mexico, paving the way for the North American Free Trade Agreement.[78]

To appreciate the importance of eliminating trade barriers as a spur to economic growth, let us take a brief look at the 1988 Canada-US Free Trade Agreement, then proceed to take a fuller look at the expanded North America Free Trade Agreement, negotiated by President George Bush and finally signed by President Bill Clinton, Canada's Brian Mulroney and Mexico's Carlos Salinas in 1993. Finally, to complete our overview of the development of the pan-American trade bloc, we will look ahead to the issues surrounding the ultimate expansion of NAFTA into the 34-nation accord currently called the Free Trade Agreement of the Americas.

The Canada-US Free Trade Agreement (CUFTA)

In achieving this historic agreement, there were protectionist measures to be overcome, along with larger issues of national identity. In fact, John Turner, the Liberal Party candidate opposing Mulroney in Canada's 1988 election, ran on a promise to maintain 'economic nationalism' and to repudiate the trade agreement, scheduled to go into effect on the first day of 1989. 'I'm not going to allow him to sell out our birthright as a nation,' said Turner of the incumbent Mulroney. Turner pledged not to let Canada become 'an economic colony' of the US, and his rhetoric clearly found sympathetic listeners. As the election neared, Turner erased a 10-point deficit in the polls to take a narrow lead. On the other hand, possibility that Turner's isolationist views might actually prevail on the day of election caused the Toronto stock market to plunge 75 points.[79]

Behind the nationalist rhetoric, however, were thornier issues. One of the most troublesome – and interesting – evolved from the Auto Pact of 1965, which Nels Ackerson, writing in the *Wall Street Journal,* described as a 'dormant volcano in Canada-US relations... now threatening to erupt.' Under the terms of the accord, signed by President Lyndon Johnson in simpler times, America's Big Three auto makers agreed to make at least one vehicle in Canada for every one sold there, in return for duty-free importing and exporting. It was a good deal for both sides at the time. Two decades later, however, the pact was attracting offshore manufacturers to assemble cars in Canada and enabling them to use Canada as a conduit for duty-free importation of vehicles originating in Asia in the US. The result: by 1985 there was a $3.6 billion US trade deficit in the auto sector – along with howls from the US auto industry that no Canada-US Free Trade Agreement could be contemplated without scrapping – or rewriting – the Auto Pact.

The Canadian Auto Workers, who continued to benefit from the pact, were just as strenuously opposed to any revision of the agreement, and the province of Ontario, where Canada's auto industry is based, announced that it would reject any free trade agreement that altered the Auto Pact. As the argument heated up, American negotiator Peter Murphy demanded that the Auto Pact be put on the Free Trade Agreement agenda, and Canadian negotiator Simon Reisman retorted that Murphy was either 'foolish' or 'a knave' for making such a demand. Meanwhile, Prime Minister Mulroney assured the Canadian Parliament that he could keep the Auto Pact off the table.[80] And he succeeded in doing so.

Mulroney won the election and signed the trade agreement; even the nay-sayers must concede that it has proven an economic boon for both countries. Three years after the agreement – and despite the fact that both the US and Canadian economies had slipped into recession in 1990–91 – the statistical evidence was overwhelming.

CUFTA's key provision was the elimination of all tariffs on North American goods traded between the two countries by 1998 – with some tariffs abolished immediately and others phased out over five or 10 years. As a direct result of the agreement, trade flows between Canada and the US have grown steadily. The total trade figure for 1991 was $176.2 billion, a 35 percent increase since 1987. Even in spite of the recession, the 1991 figure was $1.1 billion higher than the previous year.

Perhaps more important to the US side, the 42 percent gain in exports to Canada between 1987 and 1991 significantly reduced the long-standing American trade deficit with its northern neighbor. The $6 billion deficit in 1991 was almost 50 percent lower than it had been in 1987. More good news for the American economy was a Department of Commerce estimate that US exports to Canada might have accounted for as many as two million jobs in 1991, including 28,000 new jobs created between 1990 and 1991, softening the impact of the recession at that time.

Canadian exports to the US were also rising steadily, up 28 percent from 1987 to 1991. Falling tariffs have spectacularly benefited a number of specific Canadian industries. Canadian whiskey, for example, suddenly found itself competitive in the American market, and aviation firms like Canadair and Bombardier won lucrative contracts on the south side of the border.

Each country's direct investment in the other was also rising significantly thanks to CUFTA. Canadian investment in the US jumped 16 percent in just the first two years of the agreement – while US investment in Canada was up 18 percent – to $68.4 billion by 1990. Moreover, foreign investment in Canada – from countries other than the US – totaled $3.7 billion in 1990, marking the first net inflow of foreign investment into Canada in 16 years. Swedish multinational Ericsson, for instance, committed $176 million to build a high-tech research and development center in Montreal – and cited the positive environment created by CUFTA as one of the reasons for its choice of location.

As journalist Jeffrey Hawkins noted in assessing the impact of the agreement, benefits would also accrue in less concrete ways. The newly created free market area encompassing 276 million consumers allowed Canadian and US industries to take advantage of economies of scale, to rationalize production, and to be more competitive in the global marketplace. Furthermore, the enhanced atmosphere for trade would encourage heretofore domestic companies to expand across now-friendly borders, in the process increasing competition and lowering costs and prices. Finally, the agreement fostered cross-border alliances, such as the one between Canada's largest food processor, Maple Leaf Foods, and America's agricultural giant, ConAgra, which gave Maple Leaf access to ConAgra's low-cost grain and gave ConAgra its first manufacturing foothold in Canada.[81]

But did the signing of CUFTA in 1988 constitute the first step in the gradual loss of Canada's identity as a sovereign nation? Peter C. Newman, for one, believes that it may have. Writing in *Maclean's* in 2001, just before 34 Western Hemisphere leaders were to meet in Quebec City to draft a treaty for a Free Trade Area of the Americas, Newman worried that free trade areas tend to evolve into customs unions, then into common markets with a common currency, and ultimately into economic and political unions. His fears are not without merit, and we will return to consider this issue in more detail. Now, though, it is enough to note that even Newman conceded that thanks to CUFTA, Canada's exports to the US 'exploded' from $112.5 billion in 1988 to $384.4 billion in 2001 and that without this windfall 'our economy would be relegated to backwoods status.'[82]

Indeed, CUFTA seems to exemplify free trade doing what it does best: growing the total pie.

The North American Free Trade Agreement (NAFTA)

Other than the occasional small brush fire, the Canada-US Free Trade Agreement incited virtually no protest in America. Not so NAFTA, which provoked a legislative battle that was not resolved until the eleventh hour. Opponents of the pact raised two nettlesome issues; in fact, ten years after the signing of the agreement, these same issues continue to confound trade negotiations. They are jobs and the environment.

The chief mouthpiece for the jobs issue was Texas billionaire H. Ross Perot, who made his battle against NAFTA the central plank in his unsuccessful bid to be president in 1992. It was during that campaign that he warned America to listen for the 'giant sucking sound' as US jobs disappeared south of the border. After the presidential election was over, Perot's campaign against NAFTA steamed ahead with his prediction that three million American jobs would be lost as US industry succumbed to the lure of low wages in Mexico. Perot even went to the trouble of publishing *Save Your Job, Save Our Country: Why NAFTA Must Be Stopped Now!*, A book about the trade pact released on Labor Day 1993, two and a half months before the legislature was to vote on the issue. Debating against Vice President Al Gore in the days before the House vote, Perot discredited himself with patronizing remarks about Mexicans ('People who can't make anything can't buy anything'), but the jobs issue struck a chord in middle-class America. A *Wall Street Journal*/NBC News poll found that 65 percent of all adults believed the treaty would cost the US jobs.[83]

Obviously sensitive to the jobs issue, labor leaders and labor unions were staunchly opposed to the trade pact, as were politicians with labor constituencies. A prime example was Democratic Whip David Bonoir of Michigan, No. 3 Democrat in the House, who, in the final weeks, promised to use all the available staff and resources to defeat the pact. Since his job as whip was to round-up votes on the Democratic side of the House, his opposition to NAFTA was especially significant.[84]

While Perot and the labor contingent continued to hammer away at the job-loss issue, pro-NAFTA forces were suddenly stopped cold by the other opposition camp. In the middle of the summer, Federal District Court Judge Charles Richey ruled that the Clinton administration had to file an environmental-impact statement evaluating the effects of the trade agreement – a process that could take months or years. The Sierra Club, Public Citizen, and Friends of the Earth filed the suit, and Judge Richey found it meritorious. He cited a Bush administration study that concluded the trade pact could worsen environmental problems already existing along the US-Mexico border, and he ordered that

Clinton would therefore have to prepare a statement before submitting NAFTA for congressional approval.

For NAFTA backers, who were already having difficulty generating momentum for the agreement, the ruling came as a devastating setback. 'It would be the death of NAFTA,' said trade negotiator Julius Katz, who went on to point out that the requirement was so onerous that 'it would take the US out of the business of negotiating trade agreements.' Of course, the administration immediately appealed the ruling, on the grounds that it represented an unconstitutional interference with the president's authority.[85]

The ruling also pushed President Clinton into fiercer negotiations on behalf of NAFTA's so-called 'side agreements' about labor and the environment. Hoping to quiet the opposition at home, Clinton insisted on supplemental agreements that would ease fears of job-loss and establish environmental safeguards. To protect the environment, US negotiators proposed tough, commercial sanctions against polluters enforced by a trilateral commission. This was a sticking point for Canada and, especially, Mexico. They argued that sanctions imposed by a supranational commission would violate their sovereignty. The agreement ultimately reached, that each nation could impose its own fines or sanctions, was not as strong a measure as Clinton had hoped to present to Congress. And time was running out.[86]

In what was already a game of strange bedfellows (with a higher percentage of Republicans than Democrats lining up to support the president), Ronald Reagan came to bat for Clinton in the waning hours. In an open letter to the *Wall Street Journal*, the former president not only reminded the country that free trade within the Americas had long been his own dream, he also offered a shrewd assessment of the global reality: 'I might suggest NAFTA to you for another convincing reason: because virtually every other region in the world is doing it. A major objective of NAFTA is similar to what is being adopted by the European Community now. There's also talk afoot of creating an Asian free trade zone, including booming economies like Japan, Korea, Hong Kong and Singapore, as well as the Chinese giant. If NAFTA fails to be approved by Congress, America runs the risk of being left on the sidelines, while our Asian competitors and the European coalitions may become economically self-sufficient and the demand for US goods would be dramatically reduced.... The future of the world economy is in these mega-alliances, and NAFTA is an investment in America's future.[87]

Coincidentally, a couple of weeks later, in October, Prime Minister Goh Chok Tong of Singapore sounded a similar theme. He encouraged the passage of NAFTA – as well as expanded trade across the Pacific – as a counterweight to Europe's fortress mentality. 'We see Europe becoming more and more of a fortress despite what the Germans and the French may claim,' said Goh. 'I think some European governments, especially the French, may succumb to electoral pressure to implement protectionist measures.' Looking across the Pacific, Goh added, 'If NAFTA can reach out to countries in Asia through the Asia Pacific Economic Cooperation forum (APEC), then there is a possibility for a Pacific-American Free Trade Agreement (PAFTA)... a bigger group which will be able to counter protectionist developments in Europe.' Ironically, Clinton responded by looking at the other side of the NAFTA-Asia coin. Two weeks before the House vote, he played global politics by raising the troubling possibility that if NAFTA failed to win approval, Japan would very likely strike its own trade deal with Mexico and shut the US out. 'If Congress votes this down on the 17th of November,' he said in a speech disseminated by the US Chamber of Commerce, 'I would, if I were the Prime Minister of Japan, have my finance minister in to see the president of Mexico on the 18th of November.'[88]

Then the wheeling and dealing began in earnest. In the days before the vote, Clinton's negotiators struck a series of deals with the Mexican side designed to sway the votes of as many as 20 members of Congress. Mexico agreed to concessions that would protect US growers of sugar, citrus fruits and vegetables from too sudden a surge in imports. Mexico also agreed to hasten tariff reductions on flat glass, wine and appliances. Special agreements were also underway to aid Georgia peanut growers, along with the apparel and textile industries of the Southeast.

Nevertheless, two days before the November 17 vote, the outcome was still too close to call. David Bonoir, the Democratic whip from Michigan, declared that he had just enough votes to defeat the measure, but Majority Leader Richard Gephardt, also a Democrat, declined to predict the outcome. Meanwhile Vice President Gore maintained, 'The undecided members of Congress still hold the balance.'

In the end, it wasn't that close. The House approved the North American Free Trade Agreement 234-200. Its major provisions were as follows:

- *Tariffs and quotas:* US and Mexican tariffs and quotas would be phased out, many in the next few years, others over 15 years. Tariffs could be reimposed temporarily to slow a surge in exports.
- *Rules of Origin:* Goods made with materials or labor from outside North America would qualify for NAFTA treatment only if they undergo 'substantial transformation' within the US, Mexico or Canada.
- *Autos*: Tariffs would be eliminated after eight years for autos only if 62.5 percent of the cost represents North American materials or labor. After 10 years, US producers would no longer have to produce in Mexico to sell there.
- *Textiles and Apparel*: Strict rules would eliminate tariffs only for goods made from North American-spun yarn or from fabric made from North American fibers. Quotas could be re-imposed temporarily if imports caused 'serious damage' to industry.
- *Agriculture*: About half of existing tariffs and quotas would be eliminated immediately, but those on politically sensitive crops – such as US corn sold to Mexico, or Mexican peanuts or orange juice sold to the US – would be lifted over 15 years.
- *Trucking*: Limits on truckers driving cargo across the border would be lifted by the end of 1999. US companies could buy majority stakes in Mexican truckers in 2000, and own entirely in 2003.

- *Government Procurement*: Major purchases would be open to companies from all three nations, with a 10-year phase-out of Mexican restrictions for purchases by its government-owned energy industry.
- *Foreign Investment*: Foreign investors generally would be treated no less favorably than domestic investors, with exceptions and varying phase-out periods. Limits remained in place on Mexico's energy and railroad industries and land ownership, US airlines and radio communications, and Canada's cultural industry.

As for the 'side agreements' on labor and the environment, an agency would be established in Canada to investigate environmental abuses in any of the three countries, and another agency would be established in Washington to investigate labor abuses if two of the three nations agreed. Moreover, the US and Mexican governments would contribute funds to the creation of a new North American Development Bank, which could subsequently borrow money for environmental clean-up or community development projects.

Restrictions and stipulations notwithstanding, the implementation of NAFTA on January 1, 1994, created the world's largest free-trade zone. The worldwide trend of toppling barriers would continue. Among the old-line Democrats who spurned the traditional pleas of the labor unions and other liberal constituencies, perhaps none was more eloquent than Rep. Carrie Meek, who represented some of Miami's poorest voters. 'The old solutions to unemployment have not worked,' she said. 'The time has come to take a bold step forward.... International trade is the key to revitalizing our economy.'[89]

Not everyone was cheering. Nor had the concerns of environmentalists, labor leaders, and consumer advocates been laid to rest. The left-leaning journal, *The Nation,* was quick to take up the gauntlet. Writing in the December 6 issue, Jeremy Brecher inveighed against the 'devastating' implications of the transformation from a system of national economies toward an integrated global economy. The massive resistance to NAFTA, Brecher hoped, was a sign of changing consciousness. 'Poor and working people in large numbers have recognized that NAFTA is not primarily about trade; it is about the ability of capital to move without regard to national borders. Capital mobility, not trade, is bringing about the "giant sucking sound" of jobs going south.'

Interestingly, Brecher found no relief from either right or left: 'The right offers racism and nationalism. Conventional protectionism offers no solution. Globalization has also intellectually disarmed the left and rendered national left programs counterproductive. Jimmy Carter's sharp turn to the right in 1978; Francois Mitterrand's rapid abandonment of his radical program; the acceptance of deregulation, privatization and trade liberalization by poor countries from India to Mexico; and even the decision of Eastern European elites to abandon Communism – all reflect in part the failure of national left policies.' The 'worldwide attack of the haves on the have-nots' launched by the 'unregulated globalization of capital' must be met, said Brecher, by transnational grassroots organizations that seek to raise environmental, labor and social standards in developing countries. Programs like 'A Just and Sustainable Trade and Development Initiative for North America,' proposed by representatives from environmental, labor, religious, consumer and farm groups in the US, Canada and Mexico, can effectively thwart 'the race to the bottom.'[90]

In Mexico, unfortunately, opposition to NAFTA went beyond words and took the form of armed rebellion. On January 1, the day the agreement was signed, several hundred guerrillas of the Zapatista National Liberation Army (ZNLA) seized towns in the impoverished southern state of Chiapas, a protest against NAFTA's 'death sentence' on Mexico's Indians. The rebellion was quelled after four days of fighting, during which approximately 150 people – mostly guerrillas – were killed. This was the worst political violence in Mexico for two decades.

The Zapatistas take their name from Emiliano Zapata, the hero of Mexico's revolution of 1910–17, who fought to recover communal land seized by rich landowners. Mexican president Salinas, who signed the NAFTA accord, was also behind the generally popular decision to change the constitution so as to halt land distribution and allow the communal farmers to sell their plots. But many in Chiapas had never enjoyed the fruits of land reform and remained without property in a region of large estates. With NAFTA inspiring additional fears that the gap between the prosperous north and the destitute south would only widen, the guerrillas rose up to accuse the Salinas government of cheating them of their land, denying them basic services, and eradicating their culture. As *The Economist* observed, it was a powerful reminder that 'the benefits of economic reform must be shared out to those who need them the most.'[91]

But if the purpose of NAFTA was to lower barriers and increase trade, evidence of the agreement's success was immediate and overwhelming. By the end of 1994 – after one year – US exports to Mexico were averaging $1 billion per week, a 22 percent increase over a year earlier, and imports from Mexico were up 23 percent. Moreover, the US export boom was led by high-value products like automobiles (up 500 percent!), machine tools (up 33 percent), and consumer goods (up 20 percent). What this meant was that any low-wage job losses to Mexico were more than compensated for by an upsurge in production. According to a Commerce Department estimate, without the increased exports to Mexico, there would have been 130,000 fewer jobs in the US at the end of 1994. Trade with Canada also continued to grow steadily in 1995. Exports were up 11 percent over a year earlier and imports from Canada were up slightly more. Altogether, US trade with its NAFTA partners grew twice as fast as its trade with the rest of the world.[92]

Even so, according to a wry editorial in *The Economist*, NAFTA's opponents, who noted only 'that imports from Mexico are expanding slightly faster than exports to Mexico, and conclude that this is costing America jobs', were ignoring such statistics. These critics 'not only pass over the boon to consumers as imports bring down prices. They also tend to be oblivious to the fact that imports as well as exports help create jobs, by freeing resources at home.'

This astute observation returns us once more to the principles of David Ricardo, and to the fundamental virtue of outsourcing. *The Economist* went on to observe that while such criticisms are 'senseless,' they do point to the problem inherent in the 'politics' of NAFTA and other trade-liberalizing efforts: 'The benefits are to be counted mainly at the broad, macroeconomic level (and, over time, the effect is on the quality of jobs, not their quantity). The costs, on the other hand, are painfully visible in laid-off workers and factory closures.'[93]

These same NAFTA critics were given additional ammunition in 1995. During that year, US exports to Mexico totaled $46.3 billion, down $4.5 billion – nearly 9 percent – from the record-setting $50.8 billion in 1994. As a result, the US ran a $15 billion merchandise trade deficit with its southern neighbor. If more imports than exports mean job losses in the US, and if job losses constitute NAFTA's failure, than NAFTA had to be a disaster.

The real story was far different. The truth is that Mexico's economy plunged into the tank in 1995, and NAFTA played a huge role in reviving it. US exports to Mexico were down from the year before because Mexico's gross domestic product contracted by almost 7 percent in 1995, the country's deepest recession since 1932. Yet US exports to Mexico were still $4.7 billion higher than they were the year before NAFTA – and export totals in 1996 were already rebounding. Compare this situation to Mexico's sharp decline in 1982. That year, Mexico's response was to close off its markets, raise import duties to 100 percent, impose import licenses, and nationalize parts of its economy. US exports were cut in half and took six years to recover. This time, instead of retreating into protectionism, Mexico honored its NAFTA commitments and implemented a third round of tariff cuts on January 1, 1996. As a result, US exports in the first quarter had jumped 16 percent over the same period in 1995. 'The substantial increase in US exports to Mexico engendered by NAFTA's negotiated trade barrier reductions is testament to its substantive economic benefits.'[94] An editorial in *Business Week*, addressing the same issue, made the broader point: 'NAFTA bashers will no doubt take advantage of the trade numbers to try to stop the expansion of NAFTA. That would be a serious mistake. In a truly free market, such as NAFTA, trade surpluses and deficits rise and fall, but over time, everyone benefits.'[95]

Of course, the larger public interest – as represented by NAFTA and free trade generally – can sometimes be held hostage by local politics. The ongoing issue of trans-border trucking between Mexico and the US graphically illustrates this truth. Before NAFTA, the situation was complicated and frustrating. Long lines at inspection stations and hefty fees demanded by customs brokers were just part of the story. The real problem was that once truckers crossed the border, they had to unload their cargo within a designated 20-mile-wide strip, turn around and go home. They were not allowed to deliver to their final destination. The first step to alleviating this border impasse was to be taken on January 1, 1995, when, according to NAFTA provisions, truckers would be allowed full access throughout the ten states – four in the US and six in Mexico – that make up the border region.

That didn't happen. As *The Economist* observed, 'the American truckers would have none of it. Mexican trucks, they said, were dirty, dangerous and exceeded weight limits. President Clinton, eager for trucker support just before the election, therefore delayed implementation of that part of the trade agreement.' Mexico's trade minister, Herminio Blanco, was incensed. 'We simply cannot afford to have this archaic, inefficient system at the border holding up our multi-billion dollar trade,' he said. US border governors, equally frustrated, wrote to Clinton: 'The only factor limiting our ability to enjoy the benefits of NAFTA is the current delay imposed by the federal government.'[96]

According to the provisions of NAFTA, on January 1, 2000, all restrictions on cross-border trucking were to be lifted, giving truckers full intercontinental access. But Clinton, still arguing that Mexican trucks were unsafe, had not yet implemented even the 1995 expansion of access throughout the border-states. Truckers were still unloading or handing off their cargo just on the other side of the border. As *Newsweek* reported in February 2000, 'the Teamsters Union has yet to hand out its presidential endorsement, and the Clinton administration's move is widely seen as a way to shore it up for Al Gore. The union frets that an opening would cost US truckers their jobs.' The Mexican government sued the US under NAFTA's dispute-resolution process, but of course no one expected any resolution before the November elections. [97]

President George W. Bush, less beholden to the Teamsters, sought to settle the issue and uphold the NAFTA provisions. When the dispute-resolution panel unanimously ruled that the US was in violation of the trade pact, Bush agreed that the highways should be open and promised to end all restrictions by January 2002. But the battle wasn't over after all. In July 2001, at the Teamsters' urging, the House of Representatives voted to continue the ban – and to keep Mexican trucks confined to that same pre-NAFTA 20-mile strip along the border. Bush has vowed to fight the House on the issue, but no end is in sight. According to Mexican economy minister Luis Ernesto Derbez, the restrictions have cost his country $2 billion since 1994.[98]

In 1995, President Clinton started the process of bringing Chile into NAFTA membership by meeting with the leaders of Canada, Mexico, and Chile. In a statement released by the White House, Clinton expressed how 'proud' he was to be 'welcoming Chile to the NAFTA partnership.' This is a country, he continued, 'that has benefited from disciplined and responsible economic leadership... has high economic growth and low inflation, [and] has virtually extinguished its foreign debt.... So Chile is an ideal partner.'[99]

But this was another free-trade initiative thwarted by political pressures. Two years after the 'welcome' speech to Chile's president Eduardo Frei, Congress had still not authorized 'fast-track' status to US-Chile trade talks. Impeding progress was the same old stumbling block – how to handle the issues of labor rights and the environment in 'fast-track' legislation. And Clinton, perhaps tired of alienating the liberal constituencies who had elected him, apparently had quit pushing. Meanwhile, according to *Business Week*, Caterpillar was considering shifting South American production – and thousands of jobs – to a plant in Brazil. The rationale? Caterpillar sells $100 million worth of its earthmovers to Chile every year. If those machines were built in Brazil, they could be sold to Chile duty-free, but coming from the US they face an 11 percent tariff. In 1997, the US Chamber of Commerce estimated that the tariff-related loss of US exports to Chile was $480 million a year and growing.[100]

Of the government's refusal to put Chile on the fast track, Thomas Friedman writes, 'Think of how stupid this was: The US Congress appropriated $18 billion to replenish the International Monetary Fund, so that it could do more bailouts of countries struggling with globalization, but the Congress would not accept expansion of the NAFTA free trade zone to Chile. What is the logic of that? It could only be: 'We support aid, not trade.'[101]

President Bush, too, has seen first-hand how political pressure puts the squeeze on trade issues. On behalf of US farmers, in May 2002 he signed a 10-year, $182 billion farm bill. Mexico's president Vicente Fox quickly responded with a promise to 'armor plate' Mexico's farm sector against a flood of cheap imports from the US. Europe is sure to retaliate as well, as rich nations continue their long tradition of protecting the politically important food-producing industry. US farmers, on average, receive one fifth of their income from government subsidies. European subsidies average 31 percent, and 59 percent of Japanese farmers' income comes from the government. In total, industrialized nations spend $311 billion a year in agricultural subsidies, twice the amount of total farm exports from the developing world. The result is overproduction, and artificially low prices. The only thing poor nations can do is raise tariffs on food imports – which they have done, to 17 percent on average, compared to 6.4 percent for the industrialized world.

President Bush talks about the necessity of lowering food subsidies worldwide. In the meantime, to protect domestic steel-makers, he is levying tariffs of up to 30 percent on foreign steel.[102] And so it goes.

International trade is complicated, and bound to be fraught with problems of 'fairness' – since no two nations are likely to agree on what is fair. But the inevitable disputes that arise cannot diminish the overwhelming conclusion: for all three nations involved, NAFTA has been a tremendous success.

As for Mexico, by 2000 – the sixth year of the agreement – its annual exports had nearly tripled, from $52 billion a year to $137 billion, and annual foreign investment had doubled, to $12 billion annually. Moreover, Mexico gave its ultimate endorsement to NAFTA when in 2000 it signed a similar trade agreement with the European Union. Like NAFTA, the deal between Mexico and the EU will give Mexico easier access to a huge market, it will likely mean a new surge in foreign investment, and it will reduce the country's dependence on the US (to which, prior to the deal, it sent 87 percent of its exports). Benefits to both parties are exemplified in the auto sector. Under the agreement, European carmakers with operations in Mexico can now (as of 2003) export cars back to Europe duty-free, so long as local content stipulations are met. Volkswagen, for example, planned to satisfy that stipulation – and therefore avoid the 7 percent tariff on the Beetles it makes in Mexico – by having dozens of its suppliers set up shop in Mexico. For Mexico, of course, that means more jobs and more foreign investment.[103]

As for the projected NAFTA-related job drain from the US to Mexico, most analysts agree that it just hasn't happened. Even in the textile and apparel industries, where jobs have disappeared since 1993, NAFTA is not the culprit. According to Gary L. Shoesmith, director of Wake Forest University's Center for Economic and Banking Studies, an 11 percent increase in textile shipments from the US shows that increased automation and productivity are responsible for job losses, not trade. As Shoesmith says, 'NAFTA has resulted in lower prices for US consumers and created many export opportunities for US companies, all the while being mistakenly blamed for hundreds of thousands of American job losses.'[104]

In the year of its tenth anniversary, NAFTA draws nearly unanimous cheers. It is a trade pact, after all, and the increase in volume of trade among the three partners has exceeded even the most optimistic predictions. The staggering increase in US-Mexican trade has already been cited. As for Canada, suffice it to say that total trade volume between that country and the US now exceeds $1 billion daily – roughly 60 percent more than in 1993.

But NAFTA's uniqueness – and what sets it apart from the European Union – is that it is an agreement between two industrialized nations and one developing one, and NAFTA's ultimate evaluation will depend on its effects upon its southern partner. Of course, this will also be the central issue in the discussions about the Free Trade Area of the Americas. Would such a trade pact be good – ultimately – for the nations of Central and South America, or will it simply be a matter of the US extending its hegemony and, in effect, a return to colonialism? So, before we turn to a consideration of the FTAA, let's consider post-NAFTA Mexico – aside from trade statistics.

In fact, NAFTA has forced Mexico into healthy economic *and* political reform. We have already noted how, because of NAFTA-mandated provisions, Mexico was in effect prohibited from turning protectionist in response to its 1995–96 recession and how, consequently, the repercussions of that downturn were immeasurably milder than the effects of the 1982 debt crisis. Perhaps even more profound, it's no coincidence that in the year 2000, with the liberalizing influence of NAFTA rippling outward for more than half a decade, the Institutional Revolutionary Party (PRI), which had held uncontested power for more than 70 years, was swept out by the election of Vicente Fox and his progressive National Action Party (PAN). Fox is leading Mexico into the complicated world of the global economy, and there's no doubt his plate will be full. But his eyes are on the future, and his vision is exciting: 'Today we have democracies in Latin America, we have new leaderships. I dream of putting together these four machines of Chile, Argentina, Brazil, and Mexico, working for a purpose of growth in Latin America. Those four machines will move the rest of Latin America.'[105]

The Free Trade Area of the Americas (FTAA)

In recent years, there has been much discussion as to if, when, and how a free trade agreement can be negotiated between the 34 nations and island states of the Western Hemisphere. Preliminary talks have already taken place – indeed, have been going on for several years. In 2003, a free trade agreement between the US and Chile was finally signed, adding to FTAA's momentum. Further impetus to shore up the pan-American bloc is provided by the European Union, which has extended membership to 15 Central and Eastern European nations, as well as by ever-closer ties among the potent economies of Asia.

However, before we consider the shape that debate is likely to take, let's provide some backdrop to put it into context.

In 2003, 125 executives in New York City gathered for an event called the Strategic Outsourcing Conference. It was an opportunity for business consultants like Chris Disher to explain how companies can lower costs as much as 80 percent by shifting tasks such as computer programming, accounting and procurement to India, the Philippines, China, Malaysia, and elsewhere in the developing world. Fisher told the group that there was just no place left to squeeze costs in the US. 'We need to look to other areas.'

Meanwhile, outside the Waldorf-Astoria, dozens of high-tech workers with advanced degrees but no jobs marched in protest, carrying signs with slogans like 'Outsourcing Is Stealing Billion$ From America.' Their spokesman was John Bauman, president of the Organization for the Rights of American Workers, who declared, 'The bottomline is there are no jobs out there – they are all being taken by foreign workers.'

Marilyn Geewax, covering the event for the *Atlanta Journal-Constitution*, made the point that, according to recent studies, by 2015, 3.36 million jobs, worth about $136 billion annually in wages, will have moved offshore as US employers trim salary costs and office rents. Congressman Donald Manzullo (R-Ill.), chair of the panel investigating the phenomenon, voiced his concern: 'The US economy is growing and creating jobs,' he says; 'it's just not Americans filling those jobs. They've been moved overseas, where foreigners will work for a lot less.'

For example, reported Geewax, a beginning computer programmer in the US might earn $60,000 a year, while the same job in India pays about $6,000. This is a pretty attractive salary because India alone is estimated to have more than a half-million computer engineers. Moreover, all over the developing world, students are racing to become accountants, engineers, and tech specialists – looking to work for companies based in the US, Europe and Japan.[106]

The future for white-collared US jobseekers looks pretty grim. Or does it? Doesn't outsourcing lower costs, enhance competitiveness, fuel research and development, and promote the business growth that produces more jobs across all sectors? And just as important, doesn't outsourcing create good jobs in poor countries, and raise the distinct possibility that those countries one day – like Japan now – will be expanding their businesses into America and bringing jobs here?

At the other end of the wage scale, many of the jobs that do remain in the US are being filled not by US citizens but by illegal immigrants – mostly from Mexico. This situation, too, is a source of controversy and protest – though not from the people who create the jobs.

In 1986, President Reagan, whose administration had for the most part tried to ignore the problem, finally signed the Immigration Reform and Control Act (IRCA). But not until powerful West Coast farmers were granted concessions on two key points of the legislation: first, a Special Agricultural Worker provision allowed illegal farm workers who had worked at least 90 days the previous year to apply for legal status – the so-called 'amnesty' program; and, second, employer sanctions against farmers who hired illegal workers were deferred for a year longer than sanctions against employers in other sectors.

Nevertheless, Big Agriculture, according to the *Wall Street Journal*, still fretted over the effects of the legislation, and in early 1987 growers in California, Oregon, and Washington threatened that 'spot shortages' of workers posed the risk that billions of dollars worth of produce would be rotting on vines, bushes, and trees by mid-summer. These dire predictions forced the INS to relax its procedures for allowing migrant farm workers into the US, waiving the restriction that migrants had to prove that they had picked perishable crops the year before. In a snowball effect, these first-time workers would then be able to use this year's employment to apply the following year for legal status. Subsequently, the Federation for American Immigration Reform charged that there was never going to be any shortage of workers, and that the growers had manipulated a gullible press into spreading the labor-shortage scare.[107]

Not surprisingly, by 1993, a report by the Commission on Agricultural Workers concluded that IRCA had largely failed to stem the flow of illegal aliens into the US. It also offered the same three standard measures to correct the problem: tighter border control, more effective enforcement of employer sanctions, and fraud-proof identification for immigrant workers. But the real problem, according to an editorial in *The Economist*, is the 2,000-mile-long border and the fundamental economic fact: wages in Mexico are, on average, 60 percent lower than they are north of the border. Until this discrepancy is addressed – the ultimate goal of free trade agreements such as NAFTA – the tide of illegal immigration will continue to flow in.[108]

To those who protest the loss of jobs at either end of the pay spectrum, another point can be made – harsh though this may sound. Business owners, large or small, are under no legal obligation to provide jobs to anybody. Nor is the right to a good job guaranteed under the Bill of Rights. A business's only obligation is the self-imposed mandate to prosper, to stay in business. It doesn't take an MBA to figure out that if a business fails in that single obligation, then it won't be hiring anybody anywhere.

This is a truth that America was weaned on. After all, the US was once a colony. It was part of the developing world. The British outsourced manufacturing to the US. Ultimately, the US prospered, and raised the level of the world's prosperity along with it. Why can't the same phenomenon occur in India, in China, in South America?

Dinesh D'Souza, in his popular book *What's So Great About America*, offers an interesting perspective on the US, its past, and its place in the world. Because he was born and raised in India, his enthusiasm for America is both clear-eyed and refreshing. He tells the story of a friend from Bombay who had been trying to immigrate to the US for nearly a decade. When D'Souza asked why the man was so eager to move to America, he answered, 'Because I really want to live in a country where the poor people are fat.'

D'Souza uses this amusing anecdote to make the serious point that 'the US is a country where the ordinary guy has a good life. This is what distinguishes America from so many other countries.... The moral triumph of America is that it has extended the benefits of comfort and affluence, traditionally enjoyed by very few, to a large segment of society.'

The ultimate fruit of free trade – and of its handmaiden, outsourcing – is that it extends this rising standard of living to other nations. To reiterate, it grows the total pie. Contrarians cry, *No! It just subjugates the developing world to the manipulations of multinational corporations.* But the people in the poor countries don't seem to see it that way. Nobody is forcing them to take the jobs that outsourcing brings them. As D'Souza writes, 'The very concept of "underdeveloped" nations, of nations seeking "development," shows that the poor countries of the world are unanimous about wanting to get richer. Until we can find cultures that prefer hunger rather than plenty, disease rather than health, and short lives rather than long ones, we have to acknowledge that material improvement is a universal objective.'

To the radical anthropologists who argue that indigenous cultures are tainted and ultimately destroyed by the 'westernizing' influence of global trade and outsourcing, D'Souza offers the example of Claude Levi-Strauss, the most radical cultural relativist of them all until he made the 'alarming discovery [that] the people in those remote cultures don't want to stay in those cultures.' D'Souza quotes Levi-Strauss's ultimate insight: 'The dogma of cultural relativism is challenged by the very people for whose moral benefit the anthropologists established it in the first place. The complaint that the underdeveloped countries advance is not that they are being Westernized, but that there is too much delay in giving them the means to Westernize themselves.'

Free enterprise – in the most literal sense of the two words

– has an American sound to it, the sound of people working to better their circumstances. As D'Souza puts it, 'In most parts of the world your identity and your fate are to a large extend handed to you; in America you determine them for yourself.... This notion of you being the architect of your own destiny is the incredibly powerful idea that is behind the worldwide appeal of America.' Finally, D'Souza reminds us of Jeane Kirkpatrick's wry observation: 'Americans need to face the truth about themselves, no matter how pleasant it is.'[109]

Even as he was working to finalize the Canada-US Free Trade Agreement, Ronald Reagan was already dreaming of a pan-American trade pact that would stretch from northern Canada to the tip of South America. Reagan understood that, as the European Union flexed its muscle and as Japan and China began to unleash the huge power of the Asian economies, a Western Hemisphere alliance would be imperative to meet the global challenge. The fact that every US president since the Reagan era has endorsed the idea underscores its fundamental appeal and urgency.

The journey has been slow, sometimes halting, but ultimately steady. As we have seen, Clinton was able to consummate NAFTA and began immediately to talk about its expansion southward. But Congress balked, momentum slowed, and finally even his overtures to Chile remained unfulfilled. President George W. Bush has now signed the free trade agreement with Chile and has sought to revive FTAA's momentum. However, the attention of his administration has been almost entirely consumed by the 'war against terror' initiated in the wake of 9/11. The relative neglect of the administration toward its potential partners in the Western Hemisphere (hardly any of whom supported the US-led war in Iraq) has led to a drifting apart of viewpoints on the urgency of the need to achieve greater regional economic integration.

Progress toward FTAA has several other obstacles to overcome. One is the kind of generic anti-regionalism expressed by *Newsweek* on the eve of the Summit of the Americas in the spring of 2001. As the 34 Western Hemisphere leaders prepared to meet in Quebec City, writer Tony Emerson proclaimed that 'the free-trade world is breaking up,' and that trade now 'flowed increasingly within and not between Europe, Asia and the Americas.'

Calling the WTO 'rudderless' since the Seattle disruptions in 1999, Emerson wrote that globalization had come to a standstill. 'Instead, regional blocs led by the European Union are quietly widening their free-trade zones by cutting exclusive deals country by country and continent by continent' – with 'growing animosity' among the regional blocs.

Emerson is correct, of course, in his diagnosis of the phenomenon. It is also true, as one of his expert sources suggests, that 'Washington's focus on the Americas will stir up "economic conflict on two fronts," by provoking Europe and Asia to tighten their own alliances.' What we may question, however, is his implication that the FTAA, because it exemplifies and extends this regionalism, should be derailed.

Clearly, the 'economic conflict on two fronts' is already upon us. As Emerson pointed out, the European Union already has 'a growing roster of preferential trade agreements with 27 countries,' compared to only three for the US (four counting Chile), and he correctly noted that the Bush administration has had to accept this trade bloc competition as 'a fact of life' and feels pressed to 'get in the game more aggressively.' Moreover, he quotes a senior trade official to the effect that all these deals will produce 'a competition for liberalization on the global level.'[110]

Perhaps the trade official's view is too optimistic. Perhaps Emerson's view that 'this is not a race to liberalize the trading world (but rather) a duel to cut exclusive deals' is too pessimistic. In either case, the alignment of the global trading world into the three major blocs is a very real development that the US is in no position to ignore. If America is to lead the way toward the ultimate goal of barrier-free global trade, it must first consolidate its hand in its own back yard.

Like NAFTA before it, FTAA must also answer the vocal attack from the left, whose position is articulated by Claudio Katz in the *NACLA Report on the Americas*. Katz begins with a fundamental economic truth against which there is no argument. 'The immediate objective of the US,' he writes, 'is to find external trade outlets to compensate for the US economic slowdown. Unlike Asia and Europe, Latin America represents a possible new export niche for North American companies.' That trade must provide the engine of growth for the economic engines of the world's industrialized nations has, of course, been this book's guiding thesis.

Katz continues, somewhat more stridently, that 'FTAA's introduction has been accompanied by a major marketing campaign that seeks to recreate the fantasies that surrounded privatization plans in the 1990s. But, as with everything neo-liberal, the predicted prosperity is a promise for the future, while sacrifices are immediately required for implementation.' Even with this we do not entirely disagree. The opening of closed markets, the toppling of barriers to trade and enterprise, tend inevitably toward an elevation in the world's standard of living. It is a slow process, but a sure process. Look what has happened in China over the last 25 years.

The roster of specific denunciations is predictable – that the US will use FTAA as a vehicle for increasing exports but continuing to limit imports; that the huge subsidies used to protect American farmers will not even get to the table in FTAA negotiations; that FTAA will authorize the US to continue violating environmental protection agreements. We take a closer look at some of these, later in this discussion. Let us now move to Katz's conclusion: 'The differences between the EC and the FTAA are obvious. The EC is constituted as a power bloc seeking to challenge the US, while the FTAA is a pawn of US supremacy used to confront such a challenge. It is therefore appropriate to define this initiative as an imperialist, neocolonialist project for Latin America.'[111]

Who knows? The way things are, maybe Latin America could use an infusion – at least temporary – of imperialism and neocolonialism. Of course, that's overstating the case, but it's interesting that in late 2002, just a few months after the *NACLA*

Report, Jeffrey Garten of *Business Week* was taking the Bush administration to task for failing to pay attention while Latin American economies plunged into the tank.

Garten reported that Brazil's $290 billion public debt was 'an astronomical 60 percent of gross domestic product,' and that foreign bank lending and investment in the Brazilian stock markets were 'seizing up.' The possibility of a debt default, said Garten, was 'bad news for some major US banks. Citigroup's exposure to Brazil is 13.5 percent of its equity.'

Garten turned next to Argentina, which was struggling with political as well as economic chaos: 'Its economy will shrink this year by at least 11 percent, and it has defaulted on more than $100 billion of debt to commercial banks and on $800 million to one of its lenders of last resort, the World Bank.' Venezuela's troubles included violent strikes and a deepening recession, according to Garten, and Colombia was being torn apart by narco-guerrilla gangs spreading from the countryside to the cities.

An important step to solving Latin America's painful problems would be to get FTAA negotiations moving forward more quickly. And the way to do this, according to Garten, is not by imperialism, actually, but by the sorts of concessions that would be of material help to struggling Latin economies. President Bush should not only cultivate ties with Brazilian president Lula, says Garten, but he should also 'signal his willingness to address US trade barriers to Brazilian exports such as steel, citrus, and sugar.'[112]

Of course, the actual trade negotiations between the US and the major nations of Latin America constitute the final stumbling block for FTAA. And at times these negotiations sound quite acrimonious. In May 2003, for example, at a meeting in Rio de Janeiro between US trade representative Robert Zoellick and Brazil foreign minister Celso Amorim, plenty of differences went unresolved.

Brazil suggested that negotiations begin on a trade deal between the US and Mercosur (Argentina, Brazil, Paraguay, and Uruguay) – the so-called 'four plus one.' Zoellick said no: the US priority was the hemisphere-wide FTAA.

But Brazil, led by left-leaning Lula, has been strengthening its alliance with its Mercosur partners, and his embrace appears to be welcomed by recently elected Nestor Kirchner in Argentina and Nicanor Duarte Frutos in Paraguay, both of whom seem to support Brazil's bid for South American trade and political integration. In fact, Duarte, on a visit to Brasilia shortly after his election, said 'the priority is to strengthen Mercosur' and that the bloc should 'think twice, three times' before signing on to FTAA.

At the end of Zoellick's visit to Brazil, among the important points of discord remaining were:

- *Farm Subsidies*: Brazil wants to negotiate subsidy cuts within the FTAA. The US would prefer to negotiate this matter within the WTO, and only if the EU and Japan also reduce farm subsidies.
- *Anti-Dumping Rules*: Brazil wants to include them in the FTAA because they represent a major US barrier. The US says this also is a matter for the WTO.
- *Tariff Cuts*: Brazil says they should be the same for all countries in the FTAA. The US has proposed different levels for different regions, with the Caribbean and Central America benefiting most, and a more gradual approach for Mercosur.
- *Mercosur*: Brazil wants to maintain the bloc's identity and deepen its integration. The US aims to subsume regional agreements under the FTAA.[113]

Integral to the art of negotiation is to bring everything to the table, and what we see here is a perfect example of both sides doing so. But the negotiations will succeed because, ultimately, everyone stands to gain from the implementation of FTAA. And the nations of South America – including Brazil and Argentina – understand this very well.

What we shall see in FTAA is, once again, the fruits of David Ricardo's theory of comparative advantage. Consider the following sectors in which the US is dominant and should remain dominant: knowledge (higher education and specialized training); health care;

technology (especially IT – computer chips, software, etc); services in general, and especially financial services; and travel and transportation, particularly airlines. The fact is that the US is so far out in front in these industries that it makes no economic sense for Latin American countries – through subsidies, protections, government controls, and the whole program of 'import substitution' – to try and catch up. What *does* make sense is for the US to serve the Latin American markets in such industries as these – to take over the local companies through mergers and acquisitions, so that the individual economies, and local industries, are not bleeding money in no-win situations.

A perfect example is Citigroup's buyout of Mexico's major bank, Banacci, in 2001. (First, it must be pointed out that the deal would have never happened if it were not for NAFTA, which like the FTAA will, has the wonderful side benefit of stabilizing developing economies and encouraging foreign investment.) The price tag was $12.5 billion, the largest-ever investment in Mexico and equal to all of the foreign direct investment in the country in the entire previous year. More important than the dollars, however, were the deal's implications. With Citigroup and two Spanish firms having now bought most of the country's banks, Mexico no longer has a nationally owned banking sector. As *Newsweek's* Fareed Zakaria writes in describing the deal, 'Foreign ownership of banks is one of the best things that can happen to countries like Mexico.'

Why? Because, says Zakaria, 'Bad banking systems have been the silent killer of emerging-market growth over the past two decades.' Not only in Mexico, but also in Argentina and Brazil, financial systems that were protected, or closed, or corrupt, or incompetent, or all of the above contributed to the economic crises in the mid-1990s. Zakaria's conclusion bears upon the present discussion: 'Once upon a time countries believed that domestic ownership of key industries was a crucial symbol of national independence. In most cases they have realized that this attitude is both expensive and often a cover for cronyism. Steel, automobiles, telephones and airlines are all now getting ownership that is efficient and responsible, whatever its nationality.'[114]

Similarly, lured by a 70 percent plunge in the value of the peso in 2002, leading US high-tech firms like Microsoft, Oracle, IBM and Sun Microsystems are expanding their operations in Argentina. Motorola led the way when in 2000 it set up a center to develop software for its handsets and wireless technology in Cordoba City. These moves may not presage a US takeover of Argentina's high-tech industry. After all, the country has abundant bandwidth – thousands of miles of fiber-optic cable laid throughout Argentina after deregulation of its telecommunications industry in 2000 – along with the highest level of post-secondary education in Latin America, and the government is working on programs to develop its own globally competitive tech industry. Regardless, US firms are welcome because they bring badly needed jobs. In fact, to win the Motorola contract and a promise of 500 jobs within five years, the government offered a 7 percent subsidy on salaries, payroll-tax exemptions, and several years worth of rent-free property.[115]

The interesting question is: What industries will the US give up; where will the other nations of the FTAA dominate?

First, let us consider agriculture. Brazil, whose rich natural resources and land mass larger than the continental US constitute a major competitive advantage, is now the world's largest exporter of raw sugar, second-largest exporter of soybeans and third-largest exporter of beef. Remarkably, Brazil's farmers operate without the huge subsidies enjoyed by US and European farmers; instead, relying on vast scale and the latest agricultural technology. And still Brazilian agriculture, its 'green anchor,' is profitable, as measured by the nation's $23 billion agricultural trade surplus in 2003.[116] Meanwhile, that same year, US agricultural subsidies doubled from the year before to $21.3 billion under the provisions of the farm bill signed by President Bush in 2003. Isn't there something wrong with that picture?

Sugar producers in Hawaii, soybean farmers in Illinois and Texas cattlemen are not going to want to give up those industries to Latin America, and they may not have to – entirely. The eventual elimination of subsidies for US agriculture, in combination with the force of simple economic logic, will certainly effect profound changes in the American food-producing industry. Similarly, there is no viable economic justification for Wisconsin to be 'America's dairyland.' It may have made some sense in the 19th and early 20th centuries, before the University of Wisconsin at Madison became a premier American university and before Milwaukee evolved from a beer capital into an important US city, but it makes no sense *for the future.* (In fact, Wisconsin may be coming to that realization, since dairy products are now merely the state's third-largest industry based on output in dollars – and only half the size of the transportation equipment construction industry.)

Or consider the steel industry. Interestingly, Brazil's CiaVale do Rio Doce is the largest producer of iron ore in the world, and the company is growing. CVRD enjoyed a 29 percent surge in first-quarter profit in 2003 based on a 17 percent increase in sales. The ore goes into Brazil's huge steel-making industry, which, along with agriculture, is one of the country's most important sectors.[117] In fact, thanks to its vast ore resources, it's quite likely that Brazil will supplant Pittsburgh as the steel maker of the Americas. Why not? In the same way, Cemex, in Mexico, has become the third largest cement producer in the world.

It is in these labor-intensive industries – such as steel and cement that the US has ceased to be competitive. It should let them go. In fact, it is already letting them go – through outsourcing, and the ultimate consequence of outsourcing is that local companies will buy out the Americans and take over these heavy industries for themselves. Already, we see this in India where the local company, Mittal Steel, has bought out one of the largest steel makers in the US and has become the largest steel company in the world. Automobile manufacturing has already started to leave Detroit to set up shop in Mexico. We can expect it to continue its southward migration to Brazil.

Moreover, if Brazil does indeed become the steel-maker for the Americas, then perhaps Argentina will resume its dominance as one of the world's leading beef producers – even though Brazil has recently outstripped its neighbor in this industry. This is what the smaller customs unions like Mercosur are all about. When

Robert Zoellick says he hopes that Mercosur will be washed away in the rising tide of the FTAA, we can assume he is playing the negotiation game. The fact is that the US will benefit from having trade unions like Mercosur, the Andean Pact, and the Caribbean Community in place. By hammering out agreements among themselves, these nations simply pave the way for FTAA. If the US knows that it will be getting its beer from Mexico, its steel from Brazil and its beef and wine from Argentina, then its negotiations are just that much simpler. In our discussion of the European Union we have already described this phenomenon, where it was agreed that Germany would rule in automotive manufacturing and France would take the lead in aerospace.

Mercosur and the Andean Pact are, after all, small steps toward trade liberalization, the ultimate goal of the FTAA. The US is prudent to encourage these steps, by which the nations of Latin America begin to open up their markets and dismantle trade barriers. We will see the FTAA moving on several fronts at the same time, as the US negotiates with individual countries (like Chile) or with nation groups as the need arises. Nobody understands this better than Brazilian president Lula, whose politics are leftist but whose vision is realist. Lula supports a strong Mercosur but also understands that the FTAA is Latin America's destiny. At a visit to the White House in June 2003, Lula emerged from a meeting with President Bush to declare that Brazilian-American relations would 'surprise the world.'[118]

One free trade agreement encourages the next one. We can see the process at work by looking briefly at the Caribbean Community (CARICOM). The 15 members of the community have been working since 1989 toward the implementation of their 'single market and economy' (CSME). Derailed by economic upheaval as well as by the drop in tourism following September 11, 2001, the agreement is now scheduled to take effect in 2005. It will require a 'massive undertaking to harmonize policies and laws,' said Barbados Prime Minister Owen Arthur, but it is a good idea whose time has finally come. As Trinidad and Tobago Prime Minister Patrick Manning put it, 'The present global economic liberalization and the proliferation of regional economic and trade blocs demand that we implement the CSME as a matter of urgent priority.'[119]

How can 'harmonized policies and laws' among the Caribbean nations be anything but beneficial for US trade initiatives with the region? At the same time the CARICOM nations enjoy preferential trade status with Central America, an arrangement that is promoted by the so-called Caribbean Basin Initiative, through which the US is able to negotiate trade matters with the entire region.

Which brings us to CAFTA, now being negotiated between the US and five nations of Central America (Guatemala, El Salvador, Nicaragua, Honduras, and Costa Rica). Trade between the two sides is already substantial – $9 billion in exports from the US, $12 billion in imports from Central America – but should escalate dramatically when the agreement dismantles the sizeable barriers that now exist. El Salvador's Partex apparel group, for example, sells $20 million worth of athletic wear each year to the US each year, despite the 33 percent tariff on all garments not made with US yarn. To avoid the penalty, the company buys American yarn, has it woven into fabric in Florida and shipped to El Salvador – where it is stitched into the finished product. The Partex CEO notes that without these inefficiencies in the supply chain, he and other manufacturers in the Americas would have 'a fighting chance against Asian suppliers.'

Similarly, US products sold in Central America – machinery, chemicals, and farm products – also face heavy tariffs, including a duty on US wheat that ranges anywhere from 15 to 80 percent. The chance of such barriers coming down is good, thanks in part to liberalization efforts Central America has already made. As El Salvador's economics minister explains, 'We see CAFTA the same way we see the other trade agreements (we've made), such as the Caribbean Basin Initiative, but on a much larger scale.' Echoing David Ricardo, former US Secretary of Labor Robert Reich put the agreement in broader perspective: 'Free trade enables nations to specialize in what they do best, thereby improving living standards.'[120]

While CAFTA represents a step toward the FTAA in Central America, the recently signed trade agreement with Chile represents progress in South America. (As we have seen, though, politics can always interfere: the deal with Chile would have been consummated months earlier except that Chile earned a reprimand for failing to support the war on Iraq.) To the advantage of both partners, the agreement will immediately eliminate tariffs on 85 percent of goods traded between them, while providing protections for US intellectual property exports such as software and pharmaceuticals. Together, CAFTA and the Chile accord provide 'an incentive for others to move ahead' with the FTAA, says Deputy US Trade Representative Peter Allgeier.

Interestingly, Chile provides another example of how one trade deal paves the way for others. Prior to the new agreement with the US, Chile had already negotiated free trade accords with Canada, Mexico, the European Union, and South Korea. As a result of these initiatives, Chile has doubled the size of its economy and halved the number of its poor. As Chilean Foreign Minister Maria Soledad Alvear observes, 'Some believe it's perilous for developing countries to sign commercial agreements with industrial countries, but we are proof that it's not.'[121]

It seems clear, then, that the FTAA is the destiny of the Americas, and our prediction is that it will stay on track for implementation – perhaps as early as 2010. The question now, in fact, is not whether the FTAA will become a reality, but where it will be headquartered. Atlanta has been campaigning to become the FTAA's host city, and a number of factors make it an attractive choice. It is an international city, with one of the world's busiest airports. (It even has a slogan now: 'Atlanta: America's Gateway.) A friendly and welcoming city, Atlanta is proud of itself without being arrogant. There is a positive reaction to the city by the international visitors who go there; they feel good about Atlanta.

Miami, Florida, Pueblo, Mexico, and Panama City, Panama, are also vying to become FTAA headquarters. It is rather like competing for the Olympics but, unlike the Olympics, there is no established process in place. So the rules are being made along the way. Our bet is on Atlanta, but the outcome is not absolutely certain.

What is certain, however, is that the FTAA is coming. It is the right course of action for the economies of the Americas, and – with Europe to the east and Asia to the west – it is an imperative strategy for the global competition that lies ahead.

Chapter 5

Pacific Power Play

The European Union recently expanded to 25 member nations, as economic necessity unites Western Europe with formerly Communist-bloc nations in Central and Eastern Europe. We expect that the free-trade area now encompassing North America will answer the European challenge with the implementation of the Free Trade Area of the Americas, embracing all 34 nations of the Western Hemisphere. Now let us imagine the third pillar of the emerging triad – an East Asian free trade area that unites North Asia (China, Japan and South Korea), and the ten nations that comprise ASEAN (the Association of Southeast Asian Nations).

Can it happen? Can Japan and China – bitter enemies just a few decades ago – form an economic alliance? Can ASEAN – formed largely as a buffer against the spread of communism in Southeast Asia – align itself with the world's last major Communist nation?

It is happening already. Let us take a closer look at how this third (and largest) economic alignment is taking shape.

Japan's Miracle

Those of us who were alive in the years before and immediately after World War II remember well what the tag 'made in Japan' implied. Stamped or sewed on to a wide range of manufactured products – toys, textiles, and electronic gadgets – the phrase was universally understood to mean 'low price, inferior quality.' Fifty years later, products from Japan are rated No. 1 in quality worldwide. What happened?

Given the economic rivalry that exists today, it's ironic that the US had much to do with Japan's remarkable transformation. In the first place there was the MacArthur vice-regency, which prevented a Soviet presence in Japan, presided over the writing of the postwar liberal constitution, and insisted on preserving enough of the old industrial oligarchies – the *zaibatsu* – to allow economic reconstruction. Under MacArthur there was Joseph Dodge and his nine-point 'Dodge Line,' a program to balance Japan's budget, end subsidies to inefficient companies, and devalue the yen in order to stimulate exports and discourage imports.[122]

Moreover, while Dodge's plan was reshaping Japan into an export economy, it was also pressuring Japanese manufacturers to upgrade the quality of their exports. 'If you are serious about selling to us,' the US was saying in effect, 'then get out of the low-price/low-quality market.' Keep prices low, but improve quality: in that quadrant you will find the bulk of the consumer market.

The US not only offered this advice; it dispatched experts to Japan to provide specific instruction on quality control. One of these was W. Edwards Deming, whose 1950 book, *Some Theory of Sampling*, taught the basics of quality inspection to manufacturers in Japan. Such was his effect on manufacturing practices that Deming, a little known statistician in America, is still revered in Japan today. The country's prestigious 'Deming Award' is named in his honor, as is a street in Tokyo's business quarter.

Beyond this, America's participation in Japan's economic revival was perhaps inadvertent. While it is true that, as Robert Sobel says, the treaty between Japan and the US in 1952 'permitted

Japan a free hand in its own affairs,' the US also maintained a hand in Japan's affairs. As we saw in the previous chapter, where the US favors following the Ricardo model of specialization in South America, in Japan, similarly, the US moved to control a handful of industries where Japan was too far behind to catch up. In sectors like computers (IBM), soft drinks (Coca Cola), and pharmaceuticals, the US moved into a dominant position. The theory made sense: 'You don't have the money to import, nor the technology to catch up, so we will make these things here in your country.'

One result of this program was that it sowed the seeds of Japan's resentment of the US, resentment that has been growing steadily in recent decades. Even today, Japanese business leaders and students are quick to point out to us that there are quite a few industries in Japan where the companies ranked No. 1 and No. 2 remain American. How can Americans complain, they ask, when Japanese products win market share in the US?

A more important result of this program was that it encouraged Japan to compete aggressively in the sectors where the US chose to import rather than invest. Here is what happened. Following the British model – and, again, Ricardo's theory of specialization – Japan pursued a program of 'vacating markets,' or giving up industries in which it was no longer competitive. It would specialize in three industries at a time, gain dominance in those three, and then move on to industries of higher value.

Japan focused first on textiles, steel, and shipbuilding and, in each case, developed an improved technology that would accelerate its push for dominance. In textiles (where the US had lost interest with the end of slavery and the move away from family farms), Japan developed synthetic fabrics and soon became the world's No. 1 producer. In steel, Japan was in the forefront of blast-furnace technology and by the late 1970s was producing as much as the US. By 1978, 14 of the world's 22 largest modern blast furnaces were in Japan. Not a single one was in America. As a result of this technological edge, Japanese steel was out-competing US steel in American as well as in foreign markets.

In shipbuilding, Japan replaced bolting technology with lower-cost, high-efficiency riveting and quickly moved to dominance in this industry. In the late 1970s, when Japanese ships were undercutting the price of European ones by 20 to 30 percent, the Europeans were forced to restrict imports artificially. These measures, especially in conjunction with the oil crisis, forced Japanese shipbuilders to operate at much less than capacity, but even then they were still producing 50 percent of the world's shipping tonnage, beating Europe and America combined. As Asia specialist Ezra Vogel writes in *Japan as Number One*, 'Making good use of its comparative advantage first in labor costs, then in economies of scale, modern technology, and organization, Japan built up highly competitive industries in field after field.'[123]

With dominance established in these three relatively low-tech industries, it was now time for Japan to move to the next tier: consumer electronics, automobiles, and machine tools. Robert Sobel has clearly elucidated the four steps by which Japan has successfully invaded the US markets in these critical product categories – and others as well.

In the first step, the Japanese come to the US to study know-how, uncover weaknesses, and develop marketing strategies. Second, they return home to train the workforce and gear up for production. At the same time they enter into licensing agreements where these are available; where they are not, the Japanese may simply imitate without permission. This learning-curve phase is carried out in the domestic markets, which also allows for the development of economies of scale. Tariffs or other less formal barriers are likely to be erected to protect the fledgling industries from the predations of foreign producers.

Third, with the assistance of MITI, the invasion begins. The Japanese enter the US market with superior goods priced as low as possible – but not so low as to provoke valid charges of dumping or protectionist retaliation. When US producers protest against these 'unfair' practices, the Japanese appeal and delay, retreating slowly while consolidating their power over US consumers. At the same time, they subsidize their low-cost exports by keeping domestic prices as high as Japanese consumers will tolerate – keeping out lower-cost imports by means of tariffs and quotas.

Once market share is established, it is time for Step Four: upgrading quality and increasing price and profit margin. The auto sector provides spectacular examples: the steady progress from the Toyota Tercel to the Lexus, for example, or from the Honda Civic to the Acura, or from the early Datsuns to today's Infiniti.

Japan's decimation of America's consumer electronics industry illustrates the entire process. Consider television as a single example. This industry was utterly dominated by the Americans through the 1940s and early 1950s, a time of intense research and development and keen competition among US firms. RCA and CBS were head-to-head in the development of color TV, until in 1953 the Federal Trade Commission approved the RCA version. Granted this competitive advantage, RCA grew fat and slow. Research and development faltered. Why not? The domestic market was huge and unsaturated. Money went into advertising rather than technology.

Japan, passing through Steps One and Two, had learned the technology and developed its domestic market. It was time to invade the US, which, unaware that Japan was even capable of such an attack, felt no need for tariffs or quotas. With MITI's blessing, Japan's leading manufacturers came together to form the Television Export Council, a body that could coordinate the effort and monitor prices to keep them just above 'dump' level. Sony launched its first sortie in the early 1960s. Its sets cost a third less than comparably sized TVs from RCA, Zenith, and Motorola, and they were better built as well.

Still, prejudice in favor of 'home-made' prevailed until 1963, when Sears, Roebuck tried to buy black-and-white sets from RCA and Zenith to use as its 'house brand,' meaning that they would carry Sears' label. When the two cocky American firms rejected the deal, Sanyo sent representatives to Sears with an offer too good to refuse. They would supply all the sets Sears wanted, meet Sears' specifications, and undercut the price of RCA and Zenith. Sears took the deal, providing Japan its first critical foothold in the US

TV market. Over the next 14 years, Sears purchased and marketed 6.5 million Japanese television sets.

The move into the higher end came in 1968 with the introduction of the Sony Trinitron, the best color TV on the market. Selling at premium prices, these sets were devoured by American consumers, and the battle was as good as won. By 1971, Japan had half the American market, and 10 US manufacturers had left the field in defeat, taking with them 100,000 jobs in the industry. The Japanese consolidated their victory by purchasing American factories and, in the case of Motorola's Quasar, an entire company – bought by Matsushita for $100 million.[124]

In addition to having a plan, Japan also has had some systemic advantages, which it exploited to the fullest during its remarkable surge through the 1960s, 1970s, and into the 1980s. Chief of these was money. The Bank of Japan supplied capital to all of the *zaibatsu* corporations, doling out the dollars (or yen) at interest rates against which companies in the US and Europe could not compete.

The sources of this money were, first, the surplus created by Japan's economic engine during the post-World War II growth years and, second, the US$2 trillion (it is now US$3 trillion) that had been amassed in the Postal Savings System. This was the instrument into which Japanese workers poured whatever money they could afford to save. Without any other safety net supplied by the government or the corporations, Japanese workers needed the security of the safest possible investment. These funds would be needed for medical care, for daughters' marriages, and for old age care. In the meantime, this huge fund lay in the control of the Ministry of Finance, which generously loaned it to the *zaibatsu* corporations in their pursuit of a global economic edge. As we noted in an earlier chapter, Japanese corporations also enjoyed other financial incentives – low income tax rates, and no dividend payments to shareholders – which combined with their low cost of capital to create a huge competitive advantage. Yet there was one more. The *zaibatsu* not only were able to borrow money cheaply; they could also leverage it four times. In other words, if you had $100, you could borrow $400, while businesses in the US were discouraged from having more than a one-for-one debt-to-equity ratio.

A brushstroke of cultural anthropology helps fill in this picture. Japanese business – like Asian business generally – has its roots in trade, a line of enterprise with historically thin margins. By contrast, business titans in the US and Europe typically established themselves in manufacturing, with the high margins that flow from the new idea, invention, and patent rights. In trade, though, profit comes from volume. And for such business to prosper, low-cost capital is essential.

Another advantage of Japan's system has been its relatively closed nature. *Zaibatsu* means, literally, 'financial clique,' and each of these venerable groups (Mitsui, Mitsubishi, Sumitomi, etc.) owns sizable stakes in a large number of subsidiaries, sometimes as many as 200. These constitute the *zaibatsu's* suppliers, and the effect is that the big corporations hold their suppliers captive.

This arrangement gave the Japanese an advantage in the cost of raw materials. With their suppliers locked in, the *zaibatsu* dictate price. And for suppliers who balk, the consequence is often bankruptcy. In Japan's two-tiered economy, the big corporations hold all the power, and the small businesses of the lower tier are subservient. No rules, no regulations, and no union protect the mom-and-pop suppliers. When they need working capital, they go to the *zaibatsu*-affiliated bank (the Mitsubishi Bank, for example), borrow money at a premium and on 90-day terms. If the supplier causes any problems – in terms of performance, or even attitude – he may find himself talking through a teller's window at the bank manager, who can threaten to call in the loan. This is the so-called 'window guidance' system.

Adding to this image of Japanese business as rigidly self-contained is the legendary 'loyalty' of the Japanese employee. In Japan the established practice is to go to work for one company and remain there for life. 'Head-hunting' and 'job-hopping,' so familiar in American business, are alien concepts. Indeed, Japan's hierarchical social philosophy – that the individual's worth is measured in terms of his contribution to the group – would seem antithetical to the Western mind. To the larger purpose, this submission was widely understood – and accepted – as the price the Japanese would pay to restore their nation to prominence.

By the 1980s, no one could fail to notice that Japan's return to prominence had been accomplished. In fact, in 1981, when Japan overtook America as the world's leading manufacturer of automobiles, alarm bells were beginning to ring. The US suggested the first of its 'voluntary export quotas' on Japanese cars. Japan complied, reducing exports by 1984 from 2 million cars to 1.8 million. But as Sobel wryly notes, this was a perfect illustration of Japan's plan: though fewer in number, the cars were now more expensive. The US had paid $8.2 billion for the 2 million cars it imported from Japan in 1980. The 1.8 million cars cost $12.4 billion.[125]

President Reagan began to pressure Japan to open up its financial sector so that US investment bankers could do business there. After all, the Japanese had become major investors in the American economy. For example, they were the largest holders of treasury bonds, which gave them a measure of influence over the American banking system. Reagan understood that this was a potential threat, which – if all these holdings were cashed in the Federal Reserve – might have to intervene. Reagan also wanted to see a rise in the price of the yen, which would make Japan's exports more expensive and imports from the US more affordable. However, the Bank of Japan, under the Ministry of Finance, politely refused to accede to these suggestions, adding more strain to relations between the two nations.

As it turns out, US pressure was not needed to slow down Japan's juggernaut. By the late 1980s, the system that had abetted Japan's resurgence began to show its weaknesses. What had been Japan's biggest advantage – the financial system that made all that low-cost capital available – was beginning to look like an Achilles heel. Imagine this scenario: Mitsubishi's Division A uses equity of $100 million to borrow $400 million from the Mitsubishi Bank. Division A now has $500 million, of which $200 million is allocated to Mitsubishi's troubled Division B. Of course, Division B can then use this $200 million equity to borrow $800 million. The system – basically a pyramid scheme – is supported by Mitsubishi

Bank's unlimited credit at the Bank of Japan, as well as by the unwritten understanding that Mitsubishi, one of the *zaibatsu*, must not be allowed to go under.

Eventually, this hollowness at the core of the banking system was exposed. The huge problems that ensued – exacerbated by Japan's unwillingness to open up the system for reform – remain unresolved more than a decade later. As Yergin and Stanislaw write, 'It was no secret that many banks were insolvent because of loans that had gone very sour. But they were also regarded as too big to be allowed to fail. Too many interests were engaged. Yet, at the same time, there was no concerted plan to restructure the banking sector, with its immense inventory of bad loans. This became a huge drag on the whole economy – a drag that more than offset the world competitiveness of Japan's export-oriented manufacturing sector.'[126]

Similarly, while Japan's distinctive socio-cultural profile – strong work ethic, intense identification with the firm, deep-grained national identity – contributed to the country's remarkable explosion, now it too is revealing its dubious side-effects. In the first place, out of ethnic pride, Japan has metaphorically insulated its bloodstream from international infusion. No one who is not of Japanese heritage can become a citizen of Japan. Even more remarkably, no foreigner is allowed to become a full professor in a Japanese university. Surely this is a terrible mistake. It is our contention that countries remain vital when they allow two resources constantly to flow in: money and people. This is a lesson Japan should learn from the US. People come to America and become American – which is completely to the benefit of the US.

As global competition heats up in the 21st century, Japan may come to rue its insularity. As Lester Thurow notes, 'If winning requires absolutely first-rate foreign managers, Japanese firms will have a problem. To hire the very best foreign managers, these foreigners must have a chance to get to the top, but such a chance cannot be provided in the closed Japanese corporate culture.'[127]

Moreover, the sense of national mission which so effectively bonded the Japanese people in the decades after World War II may now be dissipating – perhaps an inevitable result of the national success. As Vogel observes, '(The Japanese system) worked when there was a high internal consensus about growth, but this consensus is now drawing to a close. Ordinary citizens are now more interested in social benefits than economic growth, and the new generation of youth reared in affluence have very little interest in economic growth at all.'[128]

Finally, even though Japan rebuffed Reagan's demands, it must be said that Japan's slowdown does have at least something to do with its changing relationship to the US. The most obvious point here is that America no longer constitutes a wide-open, barrier-free, and insatiable market for Japanese products. Mutual well-wishing has been replaced by mutual distrust and resentment. Americans are resentful that the Japanese have 'come over here and bought up everything' (Rockefeller Center and the Exxon Building in New York, two major studios in Hollywood, and 40 percent of the real estate in Hawaii, among the notable examples). Meanwhile, Japanese resentment of America – no doubt always there in lingering bitterness over World War II but sublimated during the booming 1960s and 1970s – has had ample reason to resurface during the global tensions of the last decade. In the first place, given the unsettled political situation in the world today, and the enormous Communist neighbor next door, Japan surely resents having been prohibited by Clause IX of its post-war constitution from developing a military industry. In the second place, the US trade and investment dollars that used to pour into Japan now pour into that same Communist neighbor next door – China.

So Japan today is in something of a mid-life crisis: What should it do with the rest of its life? A divorce from one-time partner America seems likely. The European Union is even less alluring. What then? Can Japan pull itself out if the quagmire in which it has wallowed for more than a decade and continue its push for global economic dominance?

Quite possibly. No one can say that Japan has lost the zeal that enabled it to out-compete the rest of the world for three decades. Japanese schoolchildren may not be studying English, but they are studying – sixty days more per year, on average, than their American counterparts. And Japanese workers remain among the most productive in the world. Former MITI director Masahisa Naitoh is quick to remind critics that Japan still has 'a clearer vision and a common target,' that it has 'the vitality and the capability... and the technological expertise.'[129]

As evidence of the latter, consider how Japan is attacking the tremendously complex problem of its aging population. The Japanese age at home. Rather than being shunted into retirement facilities, they typically move back in with their children. This is a burden the children have traditionally accepted, but a burden nonetheless – especially when regular medical care is required. How is the aged parent supposed to get back and forth from the doctor's office two or three times a week? Answering this challenge, the Japanese have become the world leader in the development of the 'smart toilet.' During every visit to the bathroom, the elderly person's vital signs are recorded and sent by computer to the local medical center. 'Telemedicine' provides the latest example of Japan's continuing ability to take existing technology a step further, create a world standard, and then dominate the market.

The 25-year boom may be over. Emerging markets with lower labor costs may be able to undersell Japan in a broad variety of products – just as Japan once did. Continuing its long-range plan, Japan will move on to the next tier of products – high technology and services – in the face of stiffer American competition and in the expectation of slower growth. Nevertheless, assuming that Prime Minister Koizumi holds to his pledge of 'reform with no sacred cows,' steady growth will return to Japan. 'The fact is that the Japanese are likely to remain extraordinarily competitive in the world markets for a long time,' wrote Ezra Vogel in 1978. 'What they reluctantly give up in labor-intensive industries like textiles and low-level electronics can more than be replaced by their rapidly growing capacity in new high-technology fields such as copiers, computers, and telecommunication equipment – a capacity that already threatens to weaken some of America's few remaining areas of competitive strength.'[130]

In relatively few short years, Japan went 'from worst to first' in product quality. Emerging from the rubble of World War II, Japan became the world's No. 2 economy. We may be sure that it is not going to disappear from the globe. But Japan is at the crossroads. One road leads to Europe and the US; but it is an old highway, worn out with broken pavement and potholes. The other leads west and southwest to Korea, Taiwan, Singapore, Malaysia, and Indonesia; ultimately it leads to China. Along this road Japan will find new friends, old family ties, and its future.

South Korea

When Korea was partitioned at the end of World War II, the South had little. When the Korean War ended in 1953, it had even less. Two-thirds of its already meager industrial capacity had been destroyed, and the threat from the North remained constant.

The nation's survival depended on economic development, fast – which was well understood by General Park Chung Hee, who came to power by means of a military coup in 1961. Ironically, given the Koreans' lingering resentment over Japan's relatively recent occupation of their country, Korea closely followed the Japanese model for economic recovery. After all, General Park simply had to glance across the Sea of Japan to see how well it was working.

Exactly like Japan's *zaibatsu*, Korea promoted – and protected – its own chosen industrial conglomerates, the *chaebols*. A company was picked in each of six critical industries – steel, petrochemicals, nonferrous metals, shipbuilding, electronics, and machinery – and, just as in Japan, the six companies were favored with low-interest loans and other incentives to rapid growth. Moreover, Korea was the beneficiary of Japan's system of vacating markets. As Japan moved beyond low-value manufactures, Korea took them up and followed the pattern.

The system worked brilliantly in Korea, like it had in Japan. By 1997, Korea had the world's eleventh-largest economy. But the financial crisis of that year not only hit Korea hard; it also exposed the weaknesses of a system dependent on the symbiotic relationship among the government, the banks and the *chaebols*. Foreign reserves poured out of the country at the rate of $1 billion a day, necessitating a massive bailout by the IMF. The crisis also brought a new government into power, led by President Kim Dae-jung, who promised an overhaul of the *chaebol* structure. The new government's resolve passed its first stern test: it allowed Daewoo (one of the major *chaebols*) to collapse under the weight of $80 billion in debt. Strong medicine: but necessary for long-term recovery.[131]

Still, South Korea's relations with its neighbors remain strained by history. The Korean people's virtual subjugation by the Japanese has left scars. It has also left an over-zealous determination to out-compete, out-grow, out-do its former master. Japan senses this rivalry, and it is a source of tension.

As for China, which aligned with the North during the Korean War, memories surely linger there too. Seoul and Beijing exchanged ambassadors in 1992, and South Korea is now a heavy investor in China.

As we have seen, economic considerations ultimately drive all else, and the prospect of Korea's inclusion in free trade arrangements with Japan, China, and ASEAN is a compelling incentive to lick wounds and forget the past.

ASEAN

To understand the evolution of the Association of the Southeast Asian Nations (ASEAN), we must look to Singapore. And to understand Singapore, we must know the story of Lee Kuan Yew.

In 1959, Lee Kuan Yew became the first Prime Minister of the self-governing state of Singapore, which until that time had been a British colony and also – situated at the southern tip of the Malay Peninsula – an important trade and distribution hub. Lee foresaw a single country comprising both Singapore and Malaysia, which had gained its independence in 1957, and this vision was realized in 1963. Two years later, however, the union dissolved. The fact was that the educated and industrious Chinese, who constituted a large majority of Singapore's population, were perceived as a threat to the Malay ruling majority in Kuala Lumpur.

As a result, says Lee in his memoir, *From Third World to First*, 'All of a sudden, on 9 August 1965, we were out on our own as an independent nation. We had been asked to leave Malaysia and go our own way with no signposts to our next destination.'[132]

As Henry Kissinger writes in the foreword to Lee's book, 'Circumstances could not have been less favorable. Located on a sandbar with nary a natural resource, (and) by far the smallest country in Southeast Asia, Singapore seemed destined to become a client state of more powerful neighbors, if indeed it could preserve its independence at all.' Unemployment was Singapore's most pressing problem, one that would be exacerbated when the British began to dismantle their naval installation in 1968. The British military expenditure, says Lee, 'was some 20 percent of our GDP, providing over 30,000 jobs in direct employment and another 40,000 in support services.' Lee's response to this loss typified his determination to lift his nation into true independence. He tells of having visited Malta in 1967 to see how it had survived the removal of British forces: 'I was astounded. The Suez Canal had been closed as a result of the Arab-Israeli Six-Day War three months earlier, in June. The dockyard in Malta was closed because ships were no longer going through the Canal, but dockworkers on full-pay were playing water polo in the dry dock that they had filled with water! I was shaken by their aid dependency, banking on continuing charity from the British.'

The only aid Lee wanted from the British was the expeditious handover of the real estate and facilities they would be vacating, so that Singapore could quickly convert them to civilian industrial use. 'The world does not owe us a living,' he told his people. 'We cannot live by the begging bowl.' Thanks to Lee's guidance, the potential catastrophe was averted. The 30,000 retrenched workers were absorbed by industries Singapore invited from abroad to set up shop on the former military grounds. At the end of the withdrawal in 1971, says Lee 'our people were quietly confident. There was no (increase in) unemployment, and no land or building was left idle or derelict.'[133]

A long-range plan, however, was more difficult to formulate. Singapore was still ostracized by its immediate neighbors, Malaysia and Indonesia, and the Taiwanese and Hong Kong entrepreneurs, as Lee recalls, came in with only low technology such as textile and toy manufacturing. They represented jobs, but not the kind of jobs that would propel Singapore into the world economy. An expert from the United Nations Development Program, who reminded Lee of Israel's experience, gave direction to his thinking. The Israelis 'had found a way around their difficulties by leaping over their Arab neighbors who boycotted them, to trade with Europe and America.' Singapore would have to do likewise: 'link up with the developed world – America, Europe, Japan – and attract their manufacturers to produce in Singapore and export their products to the developed countries.'

Interestingly, Lee says he was well aware of the 'dependency school' of economists who argued that multi-national corporations (MNCs) were interested only in cheap land, labor, and raw materials, and that these companies continued the colonial pattern of exploitation and left the developing nations worse off than they found them. 'Third World leaders believed this theory of neocolonialist exploitation,' writes Lee, 'but (finance minister) Keng Swee and I were not impressed. We had a real-life problem to solve and could not afford to be conscribed by any theory or dogma.... Our duty was to create a livelihood for 2 million Singaporeans. If MNCs could give our workers employment and teach them technical and engineering skills and management know-how, we should bring in the MNCs.'

The second part of Lee's strategy was 'to create a First World oasis in a Third World region.' If Singapore could establish First World standards in public and personal security, health, education, telecommunications, transportation, and services, Lee foresaw that it would become 'a base camp for entrepreneurs, engineers, managers, and other professionals who had business to do in the region.' It would mean a massive retraining of his people, but Lee believed it was possible: 'If the Communists in China could eradicate all flies and sparrows, surely we could get our people to change their Third World habits.'

Still, plans are one thing; realizing them is another. The 9,000-acre Jurong industrial park, a massive infrastructure development that by 1960 had already been fully outfitted with roads, sewers, drainage, power, and water, still lay virtually empty when Singapore and Malaysia severed relations in 1965. It was called 'Goh's Folly,' ridiculing the dream of Goh Keng Swee. Lee's efforts to attract MNCs began to pay off in 1968, when Texas Instruments came to Singapore to set up a plant to assemble semiconductors. National Semiconductor and Hewlett-Packard quickly followed suit, and the game was on. It helped that during this period China was 'in the mad throes of Mao's Cultural Revolution.' As a result, many investors decided that, by being further away, Singapore was a safer location than Taiwan or Hong Kong. 'We welcomed everyone,' says Lee.

At the same time Singapore's evolution into a 'First World oasis' was moving forward, and, as Lee predicted, this also brought business. He made sure that when the visiting CEOs came into the country, 'the roads from the airport to their hotel and to my office were neat and spruce, lined with trees and shrubs.' The heart of the city was indeed 'a green oasis, 90 acres of immaculate rolling lawns and woodland, and nestling between them a nine-hole golf course.' Thus would visitors understand immediately that Singaporeans were 'competent, disciplined, and reliable, a people who would learn the skills they required soon enough.' Lee's prescience was again confirmed; American manufacturing investments quickly overtook those of the British, Dutch, and Japanese.

A brief anecdote illustrates Lee's – and Singapore's – commitment to an open-market economy. When one of his Economic Development Board officers asked how much longer they had to maintain protective tariffs for the car assembly plant owned by a local company, the finance director for Mercedes-Benz haughtily answered, 'Forever,' implying that Singapore workers were not as efficient as Germans. But this was in the mid-1970s, when Singapore had recovered from the oil crisis of 1973, and Lee saw that it was no longer necessary – or prudent – to protect weak industries. 'We did not hesitate to remove the tariffs and allow the plant to close down,' he writes. 'Soon afterward we also phased out protection for the assembly of refrigerators, air conditioners, television sets, radios, and other consumer electrical and electronic products.'

If Japan could move their factories into Singapore and produce electronics of higher quality and at lower cost than the locals, then so be it. In fact, according to Lee, by the mid-1980s, Japan had largely relocated their middle-technology factories to Taiwan, Korea, Hong Kong, and Singapore and quickly discovered that their investments in Asia yielded much higher returns than those in America and Europe. By mid-1990s, in fact, Japan had become the largest investor in manufacturing in Asia.

Lee saw clearly that such investment would ultimately be for Singapore's – and its neighbors' – benefit. 'It was the British, Dutch, and French,' he writes, 'who first came and incorporated these countries into the world economies through their empires. These former imperial powers, however, were slow to adjust to the new trade and investment patterns of the postcolonial era, and left the fields they had ploughed to be sown by the Americans and the Japanese.'[134]

What was going on in the other four Southeast Asia nations, which would join Singapore to form ASEAN in 1967, while Singapore was industriously writing its economic success story?

Malaysia, for the most part, was dealing with its 'Chinese problem' – the dominating influence of the Chinese on Malaysian economic activity. We may pause to note that the Chinese, with their gift for trade and commerce, have a long history of leaving the mainland to become the engines of local economies throughout Asia. Lee Kuan Yew records that his own great-grandfather migrated to Singapore from Guangdong province in southeast China to escape the turmoil of the disintegrating Qing dynasty. More recently, a large Chinese diaspora was created by Mao's final victory over Chiang Kai-shek in 1949. The Communist victory – and the institution of state control – drove China's coastal traders and merchants away *en masse*, naturally, since their livelihood had suddenly disappeared. Often the destination of these migrants was Singapore, Malaysia, and Indonesia (a point we will return to in our following discussion on China).

Malaysia proved inhospitable. We have already seen that Singapore's heavily Chinese population was the cause of its forced departure from the union with Malaysia. Moreover, four years later, in 1969, a strong showing by the Chinese in local elections led to widespread anti-Chinese riots in Kuala Lumpur, which, in turn, resulted in the suspension of democracy and the formation of a 'New Economic Policy.' As Daniel Yergin notes, this policy was actually 'a massive program of affirmative action, quotas, and favoritism that was meant to lift the majority *bumiputras* – the sons of the soil, that is, indigenous Malays – out of poverty and into schools and universities and then into the middle class.'[135]

Actually, because of its huge investment in education and enticement of foreign investment, the program did considerable good. The nation moved into a high-growth phase – close to 8 percent a year during the 1970s – and enjoyed both prosperity and national unity. However, the program's high degree of state control began to show at the end of the decade. The government's large investment in heavy industry was not panning out, inefficiencies multiplied, public enterprises increasingly ran deficits, and growth faltered. It wasn't until Mahathir Mohamad became Prime Minister in 1981 that the Malaysian economy made the necessary shift to the market.

With 200 million people spread over 17 thousand islands, Indonesia had its own problems. Chief among them was political instability. In 1965, the same year Singapore was divorced from Malaysia, Indonesia's military leader General Suharto violently suppressed an attempted coup by the Communists. In the aftermath, he gradually removed President Sukarno from power and installed himself as head of state – a position he would maintain for more than 30 years. Actually, Suharto immediately ended the 'Confrontation' that had been Indonesia's policy toward its close neighbors Malaysia and Singapore, and thus paved the way for the formation of ASEAN. Indonesia's hostility, according to Lee Kuan Yew, was replaced by a 'big-brother attitude' that forestalled any real economic cooperation among the key ASEAN nations.[136] In 1975, by which time Indonesia had finally accepted Singapore as an economic equal – or superior – Suharto invaded and occupied East Timor, again thwarting economic progress by political disruption.

Thailand's concern was survival. It was the only Southeast Asian nation never to have been colonized, but, as the US efforts in Vietnam faltered in the late 1960s, it pondered the consequences of the 'domino theory.' Only Cambodia stood between Vietnam and Thailand, and a Communist insurgency would threaten the long and relatively stable reign of King Bhumibol Adulyadej. Thailand's political future in the region became all the more precarious when it was clear that they had picked the losing side in the Vietnam War. It had not only supported the US but had also made available the air bases from which the Americans had bombed North Vietnam. Now it had to fear retaliation. In April 1975, the Khmer Rouge captured Phnom Penh, and two weeks later Saigon fell to the North Vietnamese. Clearly, what Thailand looked for in ASEAN was a united front against the spread of communism.

The Philippines were mired in the quagmire of corruption that flowed from their longtime dictator, Ferdinand Marcos. As Yergin points out, social inequalities were extreme, with virtually the entire wealth of the nation in the hands of the landed elite. Moreover, unlike other authoritarian leaders of the region, 'Marcos rarely channeled his ill-gotten wealth back into the local economy. Instead, he and his cronies stashed it in Swiss banks and spent it overseas.'[137] His wife's shoes (thousands of pairs) became the best-known symbol of the Marcos's profligacy, but Lee Kuan Yew recalls an even more egregious one. Then, when Ferdinand and Imelda came to Singapore on their way to the ASEAN summit in Bali in 1976, they arrived in two DC8s: his and hers.

To Lee, the Philippines seemed 'a world apart from us, running a different style of politics and government under an American military umbrella.' Lee did not visit Manila until 1974, and nothing of substance occurred even then. 'There was no friction and little trade. We played golf, talked about the future of ASEAN, and promised to keep in touch.' Nevertheless, at that 1976 summit in Bali, it was Marcos who pushed for greater economic cooperation among the ASEAN nations. 'To set the pace,' recalls

Lee, 'Marcos and I agreed to implement a bilateral Philippines-Singapore across-the-board 10 percent reduction of existing tariffs on all products and to promote intra-ASEAN trade.' Unfortunately, Lee discovered that, for Marcos, 'the communiqué was the accomplishment itself; its implementation was secondary.' Soon enough, Marcos would become preoccupied solely with his deteriorating position in his own country.[138]

Given the widely varying circumstances of the five signatory nations, it is not surprising that Lee's first efforts at creating economic goals for ASEAN were not successful – as he himself admits. Typically frustrating was a bilateral meeting with Suharto in Bali, a few months before that first ASEAN summit in February 1976. 'I tried to persuade him to agree to set economic targets for ASEAN... to go for a trade liberalization policy, starting with a 10 percent reduction of tariffs on selected items by member countries and leading eventually to a free trade area. I thought he was sympathetic.' It was Suharto's technocrats who changed his mind, recalls Lee; free trade, for them, conjured fears of free-for-all competition in which Indonesia would become a dumping ground for the goods of the other ASEAN nations.

Nor is it surprising, given the keen interest of both the Soviet Union and Communist China in the region, that for almost the first 20 years of its existence ASEAN devoted its energies to political matters. While the group had 'lofty aims' – to accelerate economic growth, social progress, and cultural development; to promote peace and stability; to collaborate in agriculture and industry and expand trade – Lee writes that 'its 'unspoken objective was to gain strength through solidarity ahead of the power vacuum that would come with an impending British, and later a possible US, withdrawal.' Lee concedes that the five nations 'were banding together more for political objectives, stability, and security'... and that the fall of Saigon in 1975 'increased our sense of the danger from subversion and insurgency.' Vietnam's occupation of Cambodia absorbed a tremendous amount of the group's attention during the late 1970s and through much of the 1980s. The Communist threat to Thailand – and thence to the rest of

Southeast Asia – was exactly the kind of aggression that the group had formed to prevent.

In the meantime, for Lee, any true economic partnership among the nations had been a tough sell. 'Singapore had long urged a greater emphasis on economic cooperation to supplement political cooperation. Our efforts had not been successful. Suggestions from Singapore for greater economic cooperation were regarded with suspicion by other ASEAN countries. As we had a more advanced economy, open to the world and almost totally free of both tariff and nontariff barriers, they feared that we would benefit disproportionately.' The change began to come in the mid-1980s, says Lee, when ASEAN began to unleash its economic potential. 'By opening up their economies to trade and foreign investments as recommended by the World Bank and the International Monetary Fund, the countries of ASEAN achieved 6 to 8 percent economic growth yearly for more than a decade. Their economic dynamism made them attractive as economic and political partners.'

Moreover, as the threat of Communist insurgency finally abated with the fall of the Berlin Wall in 1989, the group needed a new common objective to consolidate their union. At their fourth summit in 1992, says Lee, 'the ASEAN countries were ready to promote a free trade area.' Spearheading the effort was Thai Prime Minister Anand Panyarachun, who had been a successful businessman and who 'understood the economics of trade and investment in an interdependent world.' To avoid lingering suspicions about Singapore's motives, recalls Lee, he advised his successor, Prime Minister Goh, to persuade Anand to take the lead in the negotiations. Anand's efforts were successful, and the ASEAN summit in Singapore agreed to establish AFTA by 2008 – a target date later moved forward to 2003. For Lee, 'AFTA marked a major milestone in ASEAN's evolution.'[139]

This assessment is confirmed by Asian economics expert Professor Lim Chong Yah, who notes that the diminished threat of communism 'rendered one of the two major reasons for forming ASEAN insignificant. ASEAN has since evolved into a more economic-oriented organization. When ASEAN was established in 1967, the amount of intra-regional trade was a mere 12 percent... In 1997, the amount of intra-regional trade increased to 21 percent.' Total intra-ASEAN merchandise trade, adds Professor Lim, increased six-fold between 1985 and 1997.[140]

Trade with nations outside the group has exploded as well, as all of the original ASEAN members have worked to develop their export economies. According to figures released by the World Bank (and cited by Professor Lim), exports (as a percentage of GDP) have more than doubled in the Philippines, from 12 percent in 1960 to 27 percent in the 1990s; have almost doubled in Thailand, from 20 percent to 34 percent; have surged in Malaysia, from 53 percent to 81 percent; and have increased in Indonesia from 25 percent to 30 percent. In Singapore the increase was less pronounced, but only because Singapore was always – thanks to Lee Kuan Yew – an overwhelmingly export-driven economy. Here exports (as a percentage of GDP) grew from 127 percent to 134 percent.

As we have seen throughout this study, an open-trade environment tends to create an additional economic boon: it invites foreign investment. Since the mid-1980s, foreign direct investment in the five original ASEAN nations has been nothing short of spectacular. In gross numbers, Singapore again leads the way, with a ten-fold increase from $810 million in 1985 to $8.6 billion in 1997. Malaysia's growth was almost as staggering: from $695 million to $5.1 billion. In Indonesia, direct investment also surged more than 1,000 percent, from $310 million in 1985 to $4.6 billion in 1997. Thailand's $3.7 billion in 1997 was a whopping 23 times more than the 1985 level. And the Philippines rate of growth from $49 million to $1.1 billion was almost identical to Thailand's.[141]

Of course, this was all part of the economic boom, which the World Bank named 'East Asian Miracle' in 1993. The term refers specifically to the almost three decades during which the countries of East Asia enjoyed steady and rapid growth rates – often double-digit – unmatched by any other region, including the developed economies. As we know, this growth came to a screeching halt in 1997 when a sudden financial crisis turned into a widespread and prolonged contagion.

Daniel Yergin's version of the story is the generally accepted one: that in July 1997, Thailand's baht collapsed, triggering a crisis that swept through East Asia and rippled outward as far as Russia and Brazil. The problem was that the baht was overvalued against the US dollar, tempting local banks and finance companies to borrow huge amounts of short-term ('hot') money at market rates from international lenders, then lend it out again at higher rates to domestic borrowers, 'fueling a fiendishly speculative construction boom.' The boom was unsustainable, and when it became clear to money managers that the baht would have to be devalued, the sell-off began. Thailand spent $23 billion in defense of the baht, to no avail. The government did devalue, surrendering the baht's peg to the US dollar, immediately bursting the bubble and exposing the weakness of local banks and financial institutions. As the baht sank in value, repayment obligations became impossible to meet. Nobody could get his money out of Thailand fast enough. As the contagion spread, currencies in Malaysia, Indonesia, and the Philippines also plummeted in value.[142]

Interestingly, Lee Kuan Yew points to another trigger point, six months earlier than the baht meltdown. 'In January 1997,' he writes, 'Hanbo, a South Korean *chaebol*, went bankrupt in a major corruption scandal involving President Kim Young Sam's son. Many other banks and *chaebols* were believed to be in similar straits and the value of the South Korean won dropped. The Korean central bank defended its currency until it ran out of reserves in November and sought IMF help. In the next few weeks, the whole of East Asia, including Hong Kong, Singapore, and Taiwan, was swept up in a financial typhoon.'[143] Lee and others have noted that Malaysian Prime Minister Mahathir didn't help matters when, at an IMF/World Bank meeting in Hong Kong at the height of the crisis in September, he denounced currency trading as 'totally immoral' and argued that it should be made illegal. As Lee recalls, 'Another sellout of all ASEAN currencies and stocks followed.'[144]

Whatever its precise origin, Yergin agrees that when the crisis hit Korea, the world's eleventh-largest economy, its global implications became frightening. The $55 billion package Korea negotiated with the IMF looked like it was not going to be enough. Banks that had loaned money to Korea were not willing to roll over their loans, so Korea's reserves continued to pour out of the country. 'I think that the world may have been very close – far closer than almost anybody realized – to a very severe crisis in the last week of December of 1997,' said Robert Rubin, secretary of the Treasury at the time. 'There was a very real chance you could have had a default in Korea.' No bailout was going to be effective without the cooperation of the bankers, who had to be persuaded to extend their loans. It was up to Rubin and other financial policy makers to get that message across, and they ultimately succeeded. On Christmas Eve 1997, the IMF released a statement reassuring the financial world that, first, rescue funds to Korea would continue, and, second, the international banks had agreed to roll over their loans. The gravest moment of the crisis had passed.[145]

But its repercussions would be felt for some time, especially in the East Asian nations whose currencies hit bottom during 1998. Professor Lim offers these startling figures for the eight 'crisis' nations (the five original ASEAN countries plus Japan, Taiwan, and Korea). The Indonesian rupiah lost an astounding 83 percent of its value, causing widespread civil unrest and ultimately forcing the resignation of Suharto. Next in severity was the Thai baht, which fell 53 percent. The South Korean won, the Malaysian ringgit, and the Philippine peso plummeted 47 percent, 42 percent, and 40 percent respectively. Less severely damaged were the Japanese yen, at 21 percent, and the New Taiwan dollar, at 20 percent. Singapore's dollars were devalued by 19 percent, the smallest drop among the eight. Perhaps not surprisingly, Singapore's economy also pulled out of recession more quickly than any of the others – after only two quarters as compared to Thailand's six.[146]

What made Singapore relatively immune to the crisis? As Lee explains, 'The Singapore dollar... was not tied to the US dollar but was managed against a basket of currencies of our major trading partners. It had steadily appreciated against the US dollar until the mid-1990s. Singapore dollar interest rates were much lower than US dollar rates. 'Singapore companies had little US dollar debt because it was unattractive for Singapore companies to borrow US dollars.'[147]

Almost as surprising as the sudden Asian collapse, however, was the speed of the recovery. As Professor Lim points out, with the exception of Japan (whose growth problems preceded the crisis), all of the affected East Asian economies were already reporting positive growth rates in the second, third, and fourth quarters of 1999. The speedy recovery was to a considerable extent explained by the fact that devaluation had made these countries more competitive by making their exports more affordable in world markets.[148]

Over the longer haul, if growth continues among the ASEAN nations, it will be attributable to the kind of restructuring and reform forced upon Indonesia and Thailand (as well as Korea) by the terms of the IMF bail-out. It will be because the kind of transparency that has always characterized Singapore's government-business relationship will begin to shine its light on the other ASEAN economies. And even then, says Daniel Yergin, growth is likely to be slow, in the face of the recent global downturn. At the beginning of the 21st century,' he observes, 'the Asian countries... faced a new crisis – not a financial contagion, but a worldwide economic slump. It would be a new test for a region that had found its destiny not in dominoes, but in the global economy.'[149]

Lee Kuan Yew's post-crisis prognosis for ASEAN is more hopeful: 'ASEAN leaders will learn from this setback to build stronger financial and banking systems, with sound regulations and rigorous supervision. Investors will return because the factors for high growth will remain for another 10 to 20 years. Cronyism and corruption will be difficult to erase completely, but with adequate laws and supervision, excesses can be checked. Another meltdown is unlikely as long as the pain and misery of this crisis are not forgotten. Within a decade, the original five ASEAN countries will resume their growth, and from a leaner base new leaders will emerge who will gain stature and respect.'[150]

In fact, as the 20th century neared its end, ASEAN's problems centered less on economic growth than on the growth of its own membership. Oil-rich Brunei had joined the organization in 1984, and Vietnam became the seventh member in 1995. That left three Southeast Asian countries still outside the fold: Myanmar, Laos, and Cambodia. These last three had expected to be invited to join in July 1997, when ASEAN celebrated its 30th anniversary in Kuala Lumpur. However, the inclusion of these countries posed serious difficulties. As *The Economist* noted at the time, 'The applicants' keenness (to join) is understandable: this is a successful club. But it is less obvious why the present members are in such a hurry to welcome them.'[151]

Myanmar's invitation was particularly controversial. The brutal military junta that had ruled the country since the late 1980s, further alienated the West in 1990 when it chose to ignore the results of democratic elections overwhelmingly won by the National League for Democracy, the party led by the hugely popular Aung San Suu Kyi. Miss Suu Kyi was subsequently placed under 'house arrest,' then released in 1995. The junta's flagrant abuses of power had already earned economic sanctions from the US and Europe, and ASEAN's embrace of Myanmar would obviously render such sanctions less effective.

Typical of Asian pragmatism, however, the policy of ASEAN's members had always been one of mutual non-interference. As an editorial in *The Economist* explained it, 'The group already spans a variety of political systems, from Thailand's 'newish' democracy to Vietnam's one-party state. The only way to keep such a diverse bunch together is to insist that each country's internal affairs are its own business. As ASEAN sees it, to break this principle over Myanmar would be inconsistent, even dangerous.'[152] Thus Myanmar's entry into the organization proceeded on schedule.

But the non-interference policy was strained to breaking point just when the celebratory conference in Kuala Lumpur was to get under way. *Asiaweek* reported that 'the first meeting of the long-heralded ASEAN Ten turned into a conclave of the ASEAN Nine – plus one non-member. The odd man out was, of course, Cambodia. On July 5, that country's co-Prime Minister Hun Sen dispatched his partner, Norodom Ranariddh, in a violent putsch.' The nine foreign ministers met behind closed doors and made a hasty – and difficult – political decision. Cambodia's entry was postponed.

The magazine was betting that the blackball would not last long. Economic considerations would prevail – especially the considerable foreign investment in Cambodia that would give Hun Sen the leverage to say, 'Deal with me or your investments go down the tube.' Malaysia alone had an investment of $2 billion in Cambodia. Japan, an ASEAN dialogue partner and a huge aid donor to Cambodia, set the tone. Said a senior Japanese official: 'Our policy is realistic. We're committed to Cambodia; our interests are at stake. So our aid will continue. We don't condone or reward Hun Sen, but we have to deal with the people in charge.'[153] In fact, Cambodia was formally admitted to the organization in 1999.

Recently, ASEAN's non-interference policy seems finally to have been thrown out the window. In May 2003, Aung San Suu Kyi was arrested again, after junta forces in northern Myanmar attacked a convoy of her supporters. After a two-day meeting in Phnom Penh, ASEAN foreign ministers issued a statement that they 'looked forward to the early lifting of restrictions placed on Aung San Suu Kyi.' *The Economist* editorialized that if this seemed like a feeble response, 'by ASEAN's standards it was a tough one. It was the first time ASEAN had rebuked a member state.'[154] The *New York Times* also noted with approval that Myanmar's junta was finally reaping the 'international opprobrium' it had long deserved. 'The Association of Southeast Asia Nations yesterday broke with its dubious tradition of not criticizing member governments and urged Myanmar to release Mrs. Aung San Suu Kyi.'[155]

Political intrigue aside, in the first years of the new century – with the financial crisis of 1997–98 receding into history – the ASEAN nations had reason to look ahead with some confidence. The year 2002 saw new – and apparently moderate – leaders installed in three of the five original nations: Thaksin Shinawatra in Thailand, Gloria Macapagal Arroyo in the Philippines, and Megawati Sukarnoputri in Indonesia. Economic integration and attracting foreign investment appear to have returned to the top of the organization's agenda – particularly with the implementation of the ASEAN Free Trade Agreement.

At the AFTA 2002 Symposium in Jakarta, ASEAN secretary-general Rodolfo Severino expounded on the significance of the new accord. He recalled that at their fourth summit in 1992, ASEAN leaders had acknowledged the importance of economic integration by agreeing to sign a free trade agreement that would reduce most tariffs within the region to 0-5 percent by 2008. 'Before long,' said Severino, 'ASEAN found fifteen years to be too conservative. The world was not going to stand still for AFTA. So, in 1995 ASEAN moved the target year forward by five years, to 2003. Faced with the challenge of the financial crisis of 1997–98, the ASEAN leaders decided to advance the target further, to the beginning of 2002.' The results of the agreement are already spectacular, said Severino: The first six signatories to the AFTA agreement have dropped tariffs according to schedule, and the reductions have brought on 'a massive expansion of intra-regional trade' – from US$44.2 billion in 1993 to US$97.8 billion in 2000. The average tariff on intra-ASEAN trade, added Severino, is now down to 3.2 percent.

Severino's remarks underscored AFTA's critical importance not only for its own members, but also for the economic strength and stability of the whole Asian realm. 'AFTA is the centerpiece of ASEAN's work toward regional economic integration, and integration gives Southeast Asia the strength to more deeply engage its neighbors – China, Japan, Korea, and Australia and New Zealand – as it is doing now for the benefit of all.... ASEAN's leaders clearly recognize the fact that the impact of regional economic integration goes beyond economics; it has everything to do with peace and stability in Southeast Asia.'[156]

Moreover, ASEAN has been busily negotiating free trade deals with its neighbors in the region. *The Economist* reported that at their November 2002 summit in Phnom Penh, ASEAN leaders were working on a trade agreement with China to be implemented by 2013, as well as exploring ways to strengthen trade with Japan and India. In analyzing the proposed deal with China, the magazine enumerated the ways in which such an agreement would be in ASEAN's best interests: 'trade with China has grown threefold over the past decade, with ASEAN running a healthy surplus. This boom is helping to lessen Southeast Asia's dependence on exports to America, Europe, and Japan, which are stuck in the doldrums. The prospect of duty-free exports to China will doubtlessly persuade some of those flighty investors (who left during the crisis) to return to ASEAN. The proposed free-trade area, after all, would be the world's biggest, with some 1.7 billion consumers.'[157]

There's a fundamental truth to be grasped here: today, *everybody* wants a piece of China. We will take up this point shortly and explore it at some length. Before we leave ASEAN, let's return to our starting point – Singapore – and the miracle performed by Lee Kuan Yew.

When Lee became the leader of Singapore in 1959, per capita income was $400. By the time he left office in 1990, it exceeded $12,000. By 1999, the figure was at $24,000, and the most recent statistics put the number at a remarkable $35,000. This spectacular rise accompanied the development of the region's best infrastructure – roads, port, airport and communications – along with the development of Asia's best health and education systems.

Lee explains that it was either succeed or perish. 'We had to make ourselves competitive, even before we knew the word. We had to remake ourselves and become relevant to the world. Being relevant to the world – and as the world changes being relevant in spite of those changes – is the business of living. The countries that make themselves relevant become better off. Their people become better off. Those who opt out, suffer.'[158]

Now, here is the salient point: while Lee Kuan Yew was working his miracle in Singapore, Deng Xiaoping was watching very carefully.

Dragon Ascendant

If Japan's rise 'from worst to first' in the quality of its manufactures seems like an impressive transformation, consider China's evolution in roughly those same five post-war decades.

Japan may have been devastated by the war, but at least its market was open. China had no market, no private enterprise, no private property. Mao Zedong's program entailed the abolition of capitalists and landlords at home and complete withdrawal from commerce with the West. Even its business with the Soviet Union was curtailed when the two Communist nations fell out in 1960. Meanwhile, the US embargo on trade with China lasted from 1950 to 1971. In other words, when Deng Xiaoping came to power in 1978, China was standing on Square One.

The door had been opened in February 1972 with the Mao-Nixon summit that initiated diplomacy between the two countries. Six years later, at the Third Plenum of the eleventh Chinese Communist Party Congress held in December 1978, the Party announced its historic shift away from class struggle and in the direction of economic development. The results have been remarkable, to say the least: over the next two and a half decades, China's GDP per capita rose at an annual average of 8 percent, and per capita income doubled once and then doubled again, lifting 300 million people out of poverty. Out of nowhere, China had overtaken Japan to become the world's second largest economy (as measured in PPP – purchasing power parity).

How did China do it? As we have observed, Deng was watching Lee Kuan Yew, and in Singapore he found a model for his own nation's economic transformation. As Jonathan Story describes it: 'The formula is straightforward enough: modernization transforms economic structures, social classes and state tasks. If the process is to be mastered and breakdown avoided, then a balance must be kept between political development and economic modernization. This requires strong government, guided by elite who would act as masters of the market (for instance, Lee and his cadre of ministers). As populations move away from traditional occupations, and become more educated, democratic development evolves alongside the extension of the rule of law, and the developmental state gradually withdraws – in favor of the decentralized market decisions of citizens.'[159]

Of course, China first had to begin to build a market system.

This process began with Deng's special brainchild – his Special Economic Zones (SEZ). They were initially developed opposite Hong Kong in Guangdong province, and opposite Taiwan in Fujian province. Deng hoped to attract investment from ethnic Chinese businesspeople in Hong Kong and Taiwan by offering to shield their operations from the heavy state regulations that impeded business on the mainland. The experiment was so successful that additional zones were soon located up and down China's eastern seaboard; and when all this coastal activity opened up a noticeable wealth gap between the coast and China's interior, Beijing created more special zones in five inland provinces. From out of these zones emerged the critical component of China's transformation: a mainland Chinese business class.

The evolution continued in 1984, when the former 'commune and brigade enterprises' were renamed 'town and village enterprises (TVEs)' and business in the countryside was effectively liberalized. The number of these enterprises grew exponentially: from 1.4 million in 1983 to 6.4 million in 1984, to 24.5 million in 1993. What this meant was faster reform, more goods in the shops, more jobs being created, and greater incentives for Party members to become entrepreneurs.

The next step was state approval of private enterprise. As Story documents, 'The shift in official attitudes was confirmed at the fifteenth Party Congress held in September 1997, when private enterprise was recognized as an important component of the economy. The forum also emphasized the rule of law and its key role in a modern market economy. Private ownership and the rule of law were incorporated into the Chinese Constitution in March 1999. By the late 1990s, private enterprises were the main source of new employment, were more efficient in the use of resources, and were present in all sectors. (Today) well over 90 percent of retail outlets and restaurants are in private hands, as is well over 50 percent of the wholesale trade.'[160]

By this time, however, the financial crisis of 1997–98 had washed over the shores of East Asia, exposing economic vulnerability, and China began to expand its search for a model on which to build. It looked all the way across the North Pacific

Ocean and saw America, which two hundred years earlier had been something like China in the 1970s – a vast, rugged land, rich in resources, but without the first spark of economic life. Yet it had soon become the world's greatest economic power, beating out the long-entrenched Europeans. How had America done it?

China identified a few things America did right.

First, invest in infrastructure: China is doing this now on a massive scale, as exemplified by the 300,000 miles of highways laid in the past five years. Every year China deploys 15 million new telephone lines – roughly the size of one of the original seven US 'Baby Bells' – and it now has more telephone users, 425 million, than any other country in the world. There are also more cell phones in China now than anywhere else, but penetration is still only 25 percent – compared to 60 percent in the US. Such is the vast size of the market.

But forget cell phones and pipelines. In order to accommodate the massive migration from agricultural to industrial labor, China is building entire cities. One of these is Pudong, right across the Huang Pu River from Shanghai. Interviewed on US National Public Radio in 1995, Shanghai's planning commission director reported that his city had built 29 million square meters of new housing in that year alone, but Shanghai would nevertheless be overwhelmed if it weren't for the new city across the river. As for Pudong, its population had grown from 130,000 to 1.4 million in five years, necessitating the building of tunnels, ring roads, sewage systems, and industrial parks, not to mention three new suspension bridges spanning the river.

But Pudong's 1.4 million is a tiny fraction of the estimated 120 million former farm workers who have already shifted to the industrial sector. There will be millions more. To answer this challenge, says Song Shuway of the Beijing Academy of Social Sciences, by the middle of the 21st century China plans to build 1,000 medium-sized cities, each with 200,000 to 500,000 residents.[161]

Certainly the most widely publicized infrastructure project in China is the Three Gorges Dam project in Hubei province, ongoing since 1997. Corporations from eleven countries are involved, including global MNEs like Alstrom, Siemens, Mitsubishi, ABB, Caterpillar, and C.S. Johnson, as well as the US Army Corps of Engineers. Premier Zhu Rongji likes to remind investors that capital expenditure builds up wealth-creating assets for the future, and he has many people listening. That's why 300 business executives looking to do business in China's infrastructure development flocked to the US-China Business Council meeting in Washington, shortly after the Three Gorges project landed on the drawing board. There they met with 150 senior Chinese government and industry officials, including a delegation from the China Council for the Promotion of International Trade, who came prepared to negotiate deals on the spot.[162]

And that's why Cheung Kong Infrastructure, a conglomerate owned by high-powered Hong Kong entrepreneur Li Ka-shing, was massively oversubscribed when it was listed on the Hong Kong exchange in the late 1990s. According to an industry analyst touting the offering, 'CKI provides investors with one of the best exposures to China's rapidly expanding infrastructure industry.' In addition to running its two large cement subsidiaries, at the time of the listing CKI was working on infrastructure projects all over Southern China – toll roads, power plants, and bridges. As a Goldman-Sachs representative in Hong Kong put it, 'You aren't just buying cement. You are buying future earnings in China.'[163]

Second, attract capital: In 2002, foreign direct investment in China soared to $52.7 billion. With those figures, it finally pulled ahead of the US, Japan, and Germany as the world's No. 1 recipient of FDI, which rose further to $153 billion in 2004.

What began as a trickle of investment in the 1980s widened to a surging river in the 1990s, when slow growth in Japan, Europe and the US at the start of the decade motivated corporate expeditions to Mainland China. By the end of the 1990s, according to the *Wall Street Journal,* roughly 80 percent of investment in East Asia was going to China, while 20 percent was going to ASEAN – a complete reversal of the situation a decade earlier.[164]

Tax incentives, low wages, the business-friendly environment of the Special Economic Zones, and – of course – China's huge consumer market make China an attractive place to invest, and the appeal is felt both near and far.

While China openly woos investment from the West, says Jonathan Story, 'Deng's deeper message on foreign direct investment... was to the Chinese overseas diaspora, the more than fifty million Chinese people who had made their homes anywhere between British Columbia and California to Taiwan, Singapore and Southeast Asia.' The weight of Chinese business throughout the ASEAN region is immense. Story reports, for example, that in the Philippines the Chinese represent 1 percent of the population but hold 35 percent of the sales of domestically owned firms, and that in Indonesia ethnic Chinese account for 2 percent of the population but hold 70 percent of private capital. Overall, the Chinese diaspora's combined overseas liquid assets in 1990 have been calculated as equivalent to about two-thirds of Japanese bank deposits at the time. Moreover, of the $250 billion investment flooding into China over the decade of the 1990s, about half came from Taiwan, Singapore and Hong Kong.

'This is the heart of the formula for China's reunification,' writes Story, '– rich, overseas Chinese businessperson meets powerful, Mainland Chinese politico. A deal is done.' But for the overseas Chinese, the attraction to the mainland goes beyond economics. Ties of blood and kinship often lure these expatriates to invest in the provinces from which they came originally, notably Guangdong and Fujian. In addition, their success abroad has taught them the value of *guanxi* – relationships – and they can bet that this special kind of networking will be equally important back on the mainland.[165]

MNEs (multinational enterprises) in the US and Europe are also racing into China, but some are running into potholes on the road to riches. High operating costs, poor distribution networks, and harshly competitive domestic markets are among the unpleasant surprises that often confront new investors in China. Story lists Whirlpool, Procter & Gamble, Unilever and Nestle as examples of MNEs that 'strode into China only to see their markets eaten up by local brands and pirates.'[166] Or, as an analysis in *Newsweek* reports, 'China offers many multinationals an alluring market, but to survive there many have had to slash prices and compete on volume, to the point where many aren't turning a profit.'

Furthermore, *Newsweek* cites a recent Merrill Lynch study of MNEs in China that finds a pattern of excessive foreign investment leading to brutal price wars as multinationals hurry to set up shop in China. Amid the haste to get a foothold, says the report, 'there is little data on profits and margins' except for anecdotal evidence from big players like Coke and Dell who claim to be making money. 'Most multinationals are boosting production, admitting prices will fall and hoping that margins can be supported by cost cutting and scale economies.'

Still, the bet on China appears worth taking because 'no matter how competitive the market, the boom in demand is huge.' Honda executives see China as a perfect example of the emerging market pattern, where 'consumers start on two-wheelers and work their way to luxury cars.' Which is why Honda in 1999 took over a failed Peugeot plant in Guangdong and began making high-end sedans and minivans. The only surprise was that the company began turning a profit in just its second year. Now it predicts that by 2005 China will overtake Europe as its third largest market after the US and Japan.

Perhaps more important than the foreign direct investments themselves are the ripple effects they generate. For example, MNEs now account for more than half of all imports into China, as companies like Honda import steel to make their cars. According to Berkeley economist David Roland-Host, every dollar spent in China is re-spent many times not only within the country, but also throughout the region, magnifying the effect of 'a more liberal global trading environment.'[167]

Third, trade – with a strong export orientation: In 1978, China's trade was less than 1 percent of GDP, and the trade deficit was widening. By the turn of the millennium, however, China had risen from the No. 32 exporter to No. 6 in the world – behind the US, Germany, Japan, France and Britain but ahead of Canada, Italy, the Netherlands and Hong Kong. While exports grew at double-digit rates, their structure shifted from mostly primary goods (raw materials) in the 1980s to 90 percent of manufactured goods by the end of the century.[168] After just 25 years, China was poised to lay claim to the title 'factory to the world.'

China's trade evolved like Japan's had: promoting out and protecting in. But as trade pacts proliferate, barriers are falling, and trade continues to surge. Not surprisingly, China's efficacy as an export machine raises fears: factories and jobs everywhere else cannot compete, while the flood of cheap imports from China exposes the risk of global deflation. But these fears are laid to rest by the equally strong growth of domestic demand in China. In fact, during the first months of 2003, imports were growing faster than exports, and the Asian Development Bank issued a forecast that China would become the world's top importer by 2005 (and the world's top exporter five years later). Instead of worrying, China's neighbors in East Asia should be celebrating. The region's exports into China grew 35 percent in 2002, and the mainland will soon become their biggest customer, surpassing Japan and the US. Out of nowhere, China's middle class (household with assets worth $18,000 to $36,000) has grown to about 250 million, fueling a demand expansion that pulls the world along with it. American investor Wilbur Ross illustrates this point. He was willing to buy Bethlehem Steel because he sees China as a huge buyer, not just a cheap seller of steel. 'China is an engine,' says Ross.[169]

In fact, China is sounding downright Ricardian these days. In its move to join the World Trade Organization in 2001, China answered opponents in both Washington and Beijing with the argument that both sides would win. As it has grown into the region's new giant, it now uses 'win-win' rhetoric to calm the fears of its East Asian neighbors. 'We must look at areas of cooperation,' says Xu Changwen, a researcher at the China Academy of International Trade and Economic Cooperation in Beijing. On a visit to a Japanese factory that made bath towels, Xu asked why such an advanced economy still produced such simple household goods. It would be much more efficient, he pointed out, for China to supply Japan with cheap towels, while Japan could specialize in luxury towels to sell to China's rising middle class.

'China could be concerned that Japanese manufacturing products will damage our market, and Japan could worry about Chinese agricultural products, but then we'd never move or do anything,' says Xu, perfectly articulating the rationale behind the theory of comparative advantage.[170]

Fourth, exploit natural resources: China is a nation rich in natural resources, and, given its one billion-plus population, it needs to be. Let's consider just the energy sector.

The International Energy Agency estimates that China, which now consumes 9 percent of global energy, will raise its share to 20 percent by 2010. Moreover, China became a net oil importer in 1993 and its oil dependency continues to grow. Where will the oil come from?

Jonathan Story observes that instability in the Middle East – China's primary source – has forced China's leaders to look for an alternative source of oil and gas supply in Siberia, the Russian Far East and central Asia. 'Kazakhstan is the key state in terms of location and reserves,' writes Story. 'In 1997, China National Petroleum Corporation (CNPC) purchased a 60 percent stake in Kazakhstan's Aktobemunaigaz; and in September, then Premier Li Peng signed $9.5 billion in contracts for the oilfields in western and northern Kazakhstan, and to help fund pipelines through to China and Iran.'[171]

But Story overlooks the efforts going on within China's own boundaries, particularly in terms of natural gas exploration. According to *The China Business Review*, China is now pushing three natural gas core projects: the West-East gas pipeline, the Guangdong liquefied natural gas terminal, and East China Sea development and exploration, all exemplifying China's commitment to increasing the share of energy supplied by this plentiful natural resource. Moreover, thanks to successful public offerings, the three leading Chinese petroleum companies Kazakhstan PetroChina, China Petroleum and Chemical, and China National Offshore Oil – have the necessary incentive to move into this largely untapped resource and increase natural gas investment. The strategy will not only reduce the country's dependency on oil imports, but also on coal-generated power – which China has in abundance but which has environmental repercussions.[172]

Like the US in the early 19th century, China's rapid economic development since Deng's accession to power has taken place almost exclusively along the east coast. Only now is the financial and technological wherewithal becoming available to discover the location and size of China's oil and gas reserves. Recent exploration in the vast Tarim basin in Xinjiang, for example, is expected to uncover huge quantities of both these fuel sources. More to the point, current China policy reflects the country's urgency to tap its natural resource wealth. Similarly, open-market incentives are also now driving mineral exploration and land usage rights.

Fifth, create political stability: From the US example, China could see that wealth follows political stability. Investment looks for a safe haven. Nobody wants to put his money in a region of political crisis, upheaval, and revolution. Mao's regime, it had to be admitted, was an unmitigated economic disaster. Even European governments, with their various factions and coalitions, are messy. The US system, with its two parties, and three distinct branches, is sound. Especially attractive from the Chinese viewpoint is the considerable power vested in the executive branch. If President Bush wants to go to war, he goes to war. Europe, by contrast, is paralyzed – more so, when one considers the endless haggling that goes on at EU headquarters in Brussels.

Moreover, if America's two-party system was an improvement over Europe's coalition governments, then it was natural for China to conclude that one party would be even better. That was convenient, since Deng was certainly not looking to create competition for the Communist Party's rule in China, but it also made sense. After all, in Singapore, Lee Kuan Yew's one-party rule had produced an economic miracle. In any case, the point was stability, continuity, and peaceful succession from one leader to the next. America had set the example, and China could follow it.

Sixth, make the world welcome: Wisely, China is choosing to emulate the US here, rather than neighboring Japan. As we have noted, Japan – perhaps out of excessive ethnic pride – clings to an insular mentality and seems to resist the influence of foreign business and culture. China, by contrast, has laid down the welcome mat.

In business, for example, while Japan has resisted reform in its troubled banking sector, China acknowledges that reforms there cannot come fast enough. Horrendous customer service, outdated back office systems, and unsophisticated financial products are problems the Chinese are anxious to leave behind. Which is why, according to *Business Week*, Chinese officials are now encouraging deals to allow foreigners to buy stakes in mainland financial institutions. Citigroup is negotiating with Pudong Development Bank in Shanghai; J.P. Morgan Chase is talking to Shenzhen Development Bank. 'Everybody's talking about everything,' says R. Ralph Parks, Asia chairman for Chase, as China eagerly works to lift the financial sector out of the 19th century.[173]

China's openness to the West extends beyond the realm of business development. Evidence lies in the seven jazz clubs that have opened in Beijing since that city hosted the Goethe Institute-sponsored International Jazz Festival in 1993. More evidence can be found in Shanghai, where in the gleaming new Pudong International Airport it takes less than 20 minutes for passengers to deplane, clear passport control, baggage claim, and customs, and be outside at the taxi stand. On a recent tour of Shanghai, Japanese writer Aoki Tamotsu noted that the Chinese city's cultural warmth and sophistication put his own Tokyo to shame. Commenting on Singapore's efforts to raise its cosmopolitan profile, Tamotsu notes that China 'is well aware of this trend and is currently implementing a bold cultural policy, striving to raise its cultural level and its image abroad. In autumn 1997 Puccini's opera *Turandot* was performed in Beijing's Forbidden City by the Florence Opera, conducted by Zubin Mehta. The main sponsor was the Ministry of Culture. This sort of event was previously unimaginable.'

Tamotsu cites the blandishments of Shanghai as well, from the beautiful adornment of government buildings, to the spectacular illumination of the after-dark skyline, even to the delicious food served at the Tongji University cafeteria, a phenomenon he had never experienced at any school in Tokyo. 'Today,' Tamotsu concludes, 'most Japanese who visit Shanghai must ask themselves searching questions about Japan's future and what course their country should take.'[174]

It might be said that China is not arriving at world economic preeminence, but returning to it. After all, Chinese silk is the most ancient brand in the world, knowledge of which goes back at least to 650 BC. The Chinese invented paper, printing, gunpowder, and were a sufficiently enticing producer of fine goods to lure Marco Polo across the world in the 14th century.

If China fell from the world's radar screen for a century or two, it seems now more than ready to make up for its absence. The considerable advantages it enjoys today combine felicitously with Deng's policy of cautious pragmatism – embodied in the slogan 'feeling the stones as you cross the river.' Borrowing Fukuyama's notion of 'the end of history,' Jonathan Story outlines China's role in tomorrow's world: 'The age of tragedy, and therefore of heroes and tyrants on the scale of Mao, Stalin and Hitler, is a thing of the past. Large-scale conflicts are passing from the scene to be replaced by a United Nations of global governance, agreement on collective and individual rights and duties, the elaboration of common rules and regulations to govern trade, investment or the environment, and the guarantee of equal access for all to world markets. China's task is to be a full participant in this dull, rich, global village.'[175]

In Conclusion

It seems clear that China, Japan, Korea, and the Southeast Asian nations are on the verge of an alignment that will profoundly influence the global economic architecture.

We find evidence even in the changing protocol at the annual ASEAN conference. At the recent meeting in Singapore, with Prime Minister Goh presiding, ministers from China and Japan – mere 'dialogue partners' – were seated beside him, with the ministers from Malaysia and Indonesia further down the table. The acknowledgment is implicit: ASEAN wants economic integration with China and Japan.

And as for the trade bloc's two magnets, their alliance strengthens every day. In 2002, China for the first time became the largest exporter to Japan, and Japan-China trade increased 14 percent, posting an annual record high for the fourth straight year. In 2004, Japan – China trade rose nearly 27 percent to $168 billion. Companies like Toshiba and Nissan are investing heavily in China, and Japan is second only to the US in total investment there.

The inevitable tensions persist. Now that Japan runs a trade deficit with China, it feels some of the wariness that the US has felt toward Japan. Japan would also like to see some appreciation in the value of the Chinese yuan, to make China's exports a little less affordable on world markets. China likes the yuan where it is.[176]

And ancient animosities linger. In a visit to Beijing in 2003, Japanese foreign minister Yoriko Kawaguchi failed to make any headway in the effort to arrange a visit to China by Prime Minister Koizumi. The explanation from the Chinese was that Koizumi would not be invited to Beijing as long as he continued to visit Tokyo's Yasukuni Shrine, which honors Japanese war dead, including war criminals. The visits 'hurt the feelings of the Chinese people,' according to the Chinese foreign minister who hosted Kawaguchi. But hurt feelings are one thing, and economic destiny is another. While snubbing Koizumi, China prudently issued an invitation to Naoto Kan, leader of Japan's major opposition party.[177]

We may be certain that nothing will hinder the formation of the dynamic economic axis in East Asia.

CHAPTER 6

THE FINAL PIECES

Our historical journey through the world has almost come to an end. We have seen that the European Union will conjoin Western and Eastern Europe – a formerly unthinkable alliance between NATO and the Warsaw Pact nations. We believe that the Free Trade Area of the Americas will bring together the 34 nations of the Western Hemisphere. And the third member of the triad will be a potent Asian combination of China, Japan, South Korea, and ASEAN.

In this chapter let us consider how this global economic alignment will affect those nations – and continents – not yet accounted for in our discussion.

Cuba

More than all the other countries to be discussed in this section, Cuba's position in the world economic architecture was profoundly influenced by the collapse of the Soviet Union. Not only was the Soviet bloc Cuba's most important trade partner, Moscow also subsidized Castro's regime to the tune of $6 billion a year. When Yeltsin cut off that aid in the early 1990s, Cuba's economy plummeted into disaster.

According to a recent *Newsweek* report, jobs are nonexistent and the average income is $12 a month. Education is free, but university graduates can't make a decent living. 'As it was under the corrupt Batista regime that Castro overthrew,' writes James Pringle, 'Cuba has become the kingdom of the hustler and the *jinetera* (prostitute).' Outside of top government officials, only those in the tourist industry can support themselves, so engineers drive taxis, hoping for tips in US dollars. The young, says Pringle, are particularly disaffected. One young woman hopes to be a model, but in the meantime complains, 'We've got nothing to do, nothing to read, nothing to look forward to.' Another adds, 'It's not worth going to the university. You know even if you get a degree, you're only going to earn at most $20 a month, not enough to raise a family on.'[178] Not surprisingly, people are leaving in droves (if they can). Havana's National Office of Statistics reports that the island's population (approximately 11.2 million in 2002) shrank by 30,000 people in 2002 and by 33,000 the following year.[179]

Castro didn't help matters with his shocking crackdown on dissent in March and April 2003. Those who thought the 76-year-old dictator was mellowing were taken aback when he rounded up 78 independent journalists, human rights activists and political protesters, tried them in a kangaroo court, and handed down sentences of up to 28 years. Worse, just a few days later, three men who had commandeered a ferryboat and demanded that it sail to Florida were arrested and summarily executed in Havana.

Now Castro found himself to be a pariah and relations with neighbors worldwide – which had seemed to be thawing – were freezing over again. According to *Business Week*, this latest round of repression threatens to reinforce, rather than loosen, the US trade embargo with Cuba, and the Treasury Department has already announced new curbs on travel to Cuba by American executives and academics. The $200 million in US food exports to the impoverished nation (representing 25 percent of all food imports) may be the next casualty.[180]

Moreover, Castro's crackdown elicited loud criticism and diplomatic sanctions from the European Union, which Castro responded to in a self-defeating way. Cuba withdrew its request to join the Cotonou Agreement, through which the European Union extends aid and preferential trading conditions to former colonies in Africa, the Caribbean and the Pacific (ACP). Cuba is a participating member of ACP, and joining the Cotonou Agreement would have tripled the amount of its aid from the EU. Instead, according to a Cuban analyst who preferred to remain anonymous, 'Cuban-European relations are at their lowest point ever, and could get even worse.' The Cotonou Agreement would have been Cuba's best chance at 'institutionalizing' Havana's relations with the EU, its leading trade partner and biggest foreign investor.[181]

Anyone can see that Cuba cannot continue down this road to self-destruction. Castro knows this, and he sometimes offers evidence that he knows it. Witness the seeds of capitalism that he allowed to be sown in the tourist industry after the cut-off of Soviet aid. Witness the invitation he extended Pope John Paul II, whose visit to Havana in 1998 was a remarkable event. Less well publicized was the fact that in early 2003 a top Vatican official traveled to Havana to dedicate a new Brigittine convent requested by Castro, as a follow-up to the pope's visit. In 2002, Castro was able to look the other way while a grassroots movement called the Varela Project collected more than 11,000 signatures on a petition calling for a referendum on political reform.

We believe Castro also knows that Cuba's economic future lies in alignment with its neighbors in the Western Hemisphere, rather than with the EU. If relations with the US remain thorny, Cuba seems quite willing to deal with US strategic partner Canada. Canada is a major player in Cuba's tourist industry, both as a developer of resort property and as a source of touring visitors. During the winter, fifty flights a week bring Canadians to Veradero, Cuba's leading resort town, and at fast-growing Cayo Coco, along the northeast coast, several of the new hotels are owned by Canadian chains. A new international airport there, with the capacity to receive 1.2 million arrivals a year, will accommodate the increasing travel from Canada and Latin America.[182]

As for Mexico, the US' other NAFTA partner, its official – and almost always cordial – relationship with Cuba has lasted for a century. In fact, Mexico was the only Latin American nation that did not break diplomatic ties with Cuba as a consequence of Castro's revolution in 1959. The friendship has been strained recently – more fallout from Castro's 2003 crackdown – but the $300 million annual bilateral trade between the two nations is not in jeopardy.

Then there are the fifteen nations of the Caribbean Community (CARICOM). Back in 1972, four of these – Guyana, Jamaica, Trinidad and Tobago, and Barbados – refused to follow the example of the US' embargo against Cuba and signed documents breaking Cuba's hemispheric isolation. Since then, all other 11 CARICOM nations have established diplomatic relations with Cuba, and in 2002 Castro invited all the CARICOM leaders to Havana to show his enduring gratitude.[183]

It seems reasonable to conclude, then, that given its positive relations with Canada, Mexico and CARICOM, Cuba will understand that its best chance for revitalization and prosperity lies with its inclusion in the Free Trade Agreement of the Americas – when that agreement is implemented in 2005. Anti-US rhetoric has long been Castro's stock-in-trade, but Canada can provide the necessary buffer in negotiating Cuba into the agreement. Unfortunately, the recent alignment of Cuba with Venezuela's President Chavez may change all this.

Beyond that, Cuba's revitalization will depend on its continued development of three key resources.

The first of these, as we have mentioned, is the tourism industry. Although the global downturn, followed by the 9/11 attacks, dampened tourism all over the world, the growth of the industry in Cuba has been impressive during the 1990s. Tourism's contribution to the nation's income has risen from 4 percent in 1990 to 41 percent presently, eclipsing sugar as Cuba's greatest revenue producer. Until the slowdown in 2001, the industry was growing at 18 percent a year, and with hotel rooms growing at a rate of 3,000 a year, the tourism industry has created 200,000 badly needed new jobs over the course of the decade. Now with growth for the 2003–2004 season beginning to return to the industry, the goal of 2 million visitors a year could be within reach.[184]

Second is the sugar industry, long the mainstay of the Cuban economy. However, a worldwide glut has depressed international demand, and Cuba is developing a new strategy to cope with current market trends. Cuba's first step is the painful one: the closing down of nearly half of its 156 state-owned sugar mills in order to bring production levels down to demand. The second step is forward looking: the development of the sugar cane derivatives industry by opening it up to foreign investment and producing more value-added products for the international market. Bagasse, the cane fiber left after the juice has been extracted, serves as the raw material for 65 different products (including electric power), and this part of the industry will be much expanded.

Already, a dozen joint ventures in the by-products industry (with Spain, Mexico, Canada, Italy, and France) account for 8 percent of the sugar output. The new restructuring for the 2003-2004 season including an infusion of new technology along with foreign investment for the 2003–2004 season aims to increase that share to 20 or 25 percent.[185]

As we noted in chapter three, Brazil has recently become the world's largest sugar producer, and perhaps Cuba's drive to diversify its sugar industry acknowledges this competition from its Latin American neighbor. Assuming Cuba's inclusion in the FTAA, it will be interesting to watch how these two major sugar producers shake the industry out. Compared to Brazil, Cuba's relative economic impotence may force it to find another area of specialization and depart from the industry altogether.

Cuba's third key industry is healthcare, in which the socialist government takes justifiable pride. Cuba's life expectancy at birth is the same as that of the US. Cubans enjoy complete healthcare free of charge, and the healthcare industry in Cuba enjoys all the technological and scientific know-how of the world's richest countries. There is one doctor for every 167 inhabitants of Cuba, compared to one per 358 people in the US. Moreover, Cuba runs what is – basically – a medical training outreach program throughout Latin America and the Caribbean, offering thousands of scholarships every year to bring deserving students to Cuba for medical study. Cuban doctors and medical personnel also travel throughout the Caribbean to work alongside local doctors and provide superior care. As of 2003, Cuba's outreach even extended to the US, with the offer of 500 scholarships a year to low-income students who would be trained in Cuba and then return to practice in disadvantaged communities.[186]

Like the sugar industry, however, Cuba's health care system is in need of reorganization and restructuring. A plan to upgrade neighborhood clinics is on the drawing board, so they can offer the latest in such services as ultrasound, x-ray, electro-cardiology, and rehabilitation. As a result, the hospitals will be freed up to concentrate on only the most urgent and complex treatments. Once the overhaul is in place, perhaps Cuba will investigate the possibility of developing itself as a worldwide center for specialized care. The island has the potential to become a sort of health care spa, perhaps a place for wealthy patrons to find facilities and cures not available elsewhere. Perhaps such a niche market could become an area of specialization for Cuba's economic development in the 21st century.

Of course, Cuba's economic revival will be hindered as long as it has to struggle against the US trade embargo and restrictions on US travel to the island. Castro's intransigence doesn't help mollify Washington's hard line, but change may come nevertheless. Miami Cubans, for example, who for years would have settled for nothing short of Castro's demise, now look longingly at the potential $18 billion in trade with Cuba that is not being tapped. What's more, in a special deal brokered by the National Black Farmers Association and the NAACP, Cuba agreed to spend $20 million in 2003 on wheat, corn, soybeans, rice and chicken produced by black farmers in the US. Beleaguered black farmers were extremely grateful.[187]

Perhaps more significant, a growing number of US legislators, human rights groups, and influential Cuban-Americans are calling for an end to the prohibition on travel to Cuba. In 2002, the House of Representatives actually voted in favor of lifting the restrictions, but a similar measure died in the Senate. In 2003, both branches of Congress will take up the issue again. According to House member Jeff Flake (R-Arizona), 'Travel to Cuba is ultimately an issue of freedom' for Americans. No one supports Castro's recent crackdown, he says, but the travel ban is 'a failed policy.' The way to bring change to Cuba is to introduce US values. 'We have to export freedom to Cuba,' Flake declares. Bush is holding the line, possibly to win votes among hard-liners, but opinion may be mounting against him.

Behind official policy, a new consensus may be forming, one expressed by Jose Miguel Vivanco, executive director of the Americas Division of Human Rights Watch: 'A policy of allowing Americans to travel freely to Cuba would do more to encourage the cause of reform in that country than the current misguided policy of isolation.'[188]

Africa

In considering the evolution of Africa's economic alignment, it is useful to divide it into three zones: Northern, Southern, and Central Africa.

As for Northern Africa, above the Sahara, it is essentially connected – through simple geography – to both Southern Europe and to the Middle East, and it is our prediction that Morocco, Tunisia, Algeria, and Egypt will follow the Middle Eastern nations in the flight toward Europe – and away from America.

In fact, the EU is already doing its part to extend its influence into the region by offering Association Agreements to these North African nations. Tunisia and Morocco have long since signed on, with the goal of establishing a Euro-Mediterranean free-trade zone by 2010. Since 1995, when Tunisia signed the first of the agreements, the European Union has been working hard to convince these nations to lower tariffs in exchange for grants and credits to offset their lost revenues. The European Union's 'Mediterranean Assistance' (MEDA) program for 2000–2006 targets 5.35 billion euros to the region, to be matched by loans from the European Investment Bank totaling 7.4 billion euros.[189]

In the combined region of Tunisia, Morocco, and Algeria, Europe finds a tremendously attractive market of 70 million consumers, and it is steadily opening the door. Tunisia, which began dismantling its tariffs even before its Association Agreement was signed, has been particularly receptive. More than two thousand firms have received assistance through the MEDA program, under the terms of which they commit themselves to restructuring and modernization. According to Manfredo Fanti, head of the European Commission delegation there, Tunisia is the model to be emulated. 'For the EU,' he says, 'it is a reliable, stable, and rich partner. Here we can make business, invest money.' Morocco, meanwhile, is not far behind. For a measure of the European inroad there, consider that bilateral trade between Morocco and the EU in 2000 totaled $14 billion, 74 percent of Morocco's overseas trade.[190]

Moreover, unlike the European Union's expansion into Eastern Europe, North Africa is actually a developing, emerging market, with all that that implies in terms of growth opportunities for the industrialized world. And, as we have seen elsewhere, population pressures will add to Europe's zeal to develop the region. If Europe fails to create jobs there, through the development of industry and manufacturing, millions of North Africans are likely to move into Southern Europe.

Africa's southern zone is the most interesting piece of the puzzle. It has a moderate climate, incredible resources (diamonds, gold, copper), a developed manufacturing sector, and – of course – historic ties to Europe.

America's role in South Africa has been paradoxical. It, too, was a heavy investor in South Africa, up until the 1970s. But at that time, disillusioned by the Vietnam War and still struggling with the Civil Rights movement, the US began to express its humanitarian remorse with a wave of anti-imperialism. At the heart of this movement was an economic boycott of South America, as a protest of its apartheid policy. We all remember, for example, when heavily endowed American universities purged from their portfolios any investment in US corporations doing business in South Africa. Bowing to pressures from shareholders large and small, US companies did in fact participate in what became a very effective boycott – one which played a significant role in the creation of the Mandela phenomenon.

It was F. W. De Klerk who finally had the political courage to say, 'This isn't working any more. Change must come.' At a symposium aboard the *QE2* in 1990, one of us was part of a small group that had the pleasure of listening to De Klerk, then in his second year as South Africa's president, correctly predict that Nelson Mandela would eventually be freed from prison and become the nation's president. He said his party could adjust to that. (Of course, he couldn't have predicted that he and Mandela would share the 1993 Nobel Peace Prize, or that he would serve as Mandela's deputy for two years.) What De Klerk might have foreseen – though he certainly didn't say so – is what has happened since Mandela's retirement. Though his African National Congress is still nominally in power, with Thabo Mbeki as the current president, the economy is still largely controlled by the Dutch and German industrialists – and their conglomerates – who have been there for decades.

Here is the irony: America, pursuing its high-minded human rights agenda, effectively cut itself out of South Africa's economic life. The Europeans – not so conscience-stricken over Vietnam or civil rights – felt no such compunction and remained entrenched. So we see Dutch companies like Philips, Shell, and Unilever in the dominant position in South Africa, along with German automakers like Daimler-Benz and Volkswagen. In fact, according to *Global Information Network*, the auto industry is one of South Africa's biggest success stories since the advent of democracy in 1994. Daimler-Benz, Volkswagen, and BMW have a combined investment of R50 billion (nearly $6 billion) there already, with further investment on the drawing board.[191]

Such long-standing ties explain why the EU remains South Africa's principal trading partner, accounting for 40 percent of South Africa's imports and exports, as well as 70 percent of foreign direct investment flowing into South Africa. Moreover, the relationship was officially cemented in 2000 with the implementation of the EU-South Africa Trade Development and

Cooperation Agreement (TDCA). The most important piece of the wide-ranging bilateral accord is the establishment of a free trade area, fully WTO compatible, which will surely push trade volume even higher between the two partners.[192]

So our prediction is that longtime corporate investment and enduring trade ties will continue to pull South Africa into Europe's sphere of influence, and with South Africa will come the rest of the region – Namibia, Botswana, Zimbabwe.

It is quite fascinating to watch: despite the important US role in South Africa's regime change, it has now lost its position in the country. The political winds have shifted. Even Britain, America's ally, has lost its influence in Africa. As evidence, consider the fact that if you want to fly from Europe to Africa, you will no longer find yourself on British Airways – which used to be the standard – but on Air France or Swiss Air.

As we see it, the only part of Africa still in question is Central Africa – some 30 nations that stretch across the Saharan region from Senegal in the west to Somalia on Africa's horn. This is not an easy region in which to invest. Sudan, in recent years, has erupted in civil war; Ethiopia and Eritrea have been at war; and in Somalia and several other Central African nations conflicts have raged out of control, despite all efforts from foreign powers. Governments have failed, states have collapsed, and tens of millions of people have fled their homes, millions of them still unsettled.

When and if the leaders of these countries can create enough stability to initiate real market reform, industrial nations, searching for growth, may well rush in. Who will get there first, and how successfully, is difficult to predict. Perhaps the Scandinavian countries will invest in the considerable petroleum reserves in the region. Perhaps Russia, previously an arms merchant there, will return.

What seems clear, though, is that Africa will remain a sleeping giant for the next 30 years. Only in the second half of the century will Africa see the kind of transformation now taking place in China and India. It will happen, however, and it will add an interesting piece to the global economic architecture at mid-century. Also, it is more likely to be awakened by China and possibly by India. Both these rising economic powers are desperately in search of natural and industrial resources and Central Africa provides that opportunity, just as Brazil does in the western hemisphere.

The Middle East

As we suggested in chapter two, Russia will serve as the magnet that lures the Middle East toward the EU. We noted that, with Russia's huge reserves of natural gas and crude oil, such an alignment would create tremendous leverage in terms of world energy. We also noted Russia's recent attempts to strengthen its ties to the region: its help building a nuclear reactor in Iran; its meetings with OPEC ministers to agree on mutually profitable oil output levels; deals between Iraq and three different Russian oil companies right before the US' declaration of war in 2003.

In helping to establish and then continuing to defend Israel, the US has made few friends in the Arab world. The events of 1973 offer an extreme example. Egypt and Syria launched their massive attack on Israel, and in coming to Israel's defense, the US precipitated the oil embargo that forever shifted the fulcrum of the world economy.

The constant and ever-escalating tension since 1948 has been inevitable. In our opinion, creating a Jewish state in the middle of the Arab world was the worst mistake the Allies could have made after World War II. India's Mahatma Gandhi publicly pleaded against this decision. In any case, hindsight suggests that it has not worked, and the mistake has been compounded by the displacement of the Palestinians.

What was the assumption of the West? That the Palestinians wouldn't mind, or perhaps wouldn't notice? Or, that they were just poor tribesmen and farmers who would welcome a Jewish addition to the talent pool? What we know now is that the Palestinians were highly educated people. (Yasser Arafat, for example, had a degree in engineering.) Now we know that, as the Jews came in, many Palestinians departed – to Kuwait,

Saudi Arabia, Egypt, Lebanon, Iraq – where as bureaucrats and white-collar professionals they have become key players in the Middle East economy. Like the Jews, ironically, they are a displaced people who have become the intellectual class in neighboring countries. Among other things, this places them in an advantageous position to disseminate anti-American sentiment.

In a broader sense, the Middle East is simply an alien world from the American perspective. Americans cannot understand why Middle Easterners hate them. They don't understand the Middle Eastern contempt for the American way of life. It is not really that hard to understand. According to Dinesh D'Souza, two great ideas are in conflict. In America, the greatest value is freedom. In the Muslim world, the greatest value is virtue. The antipathy between the two is easier to see from the Muslim perspective, where the kind of personal liberty Americans cherish directly threatens the virtuous path of the Muslim believer, directly threatens the organizing principle of his life.[193] America is not merely a secular society; it cannot conceive of a society organized around religious teaching.

Middle East scholar Bernard Lewis elaborates upon this schism between the secular West and the theocratic Muslim world. He notes that, in 1798, General Napoleon Bonaparte arrived in Egypt and 'for the first time subjected one of the heartlands of Islam to the rule of a Western power and the direct impact of Western attitudes and ideas.' The spread of Western influence – especially as embodied in spirit of the French revolution – was a source of immediate alarm in Istanbul, and a proclamation was quickly prepared and distributed throughout the Ottoman lands. It begins: 'In the name of God, the merciful and the compassionate. O you who believe in the oneness of God, community of Muslims, know that the French nation (may God devastate their dwellings and abase their banners) are rebellious infidels and dissident evildoers. They do not believe in the oneness of the Lord of Heaven and Earth, nor in the mission of the intercessor on the Day of Judgment, but have abandoned all religions and denied the afterworld and its penalties. They do not believe in the Day of

Resurrection and pretend that only the passage of time destroys us and that beyond this there is no resurrection and no reckoning, no examination and no retribution, no question and no answer.'[194]

The world's greatest civilization in the centuries preceding the Renaissance, the Muslim world has been steadily losing ground to the West ever since – losing ground in scientific and technological advancement, in economic development, in living standards. The Muslim answer is to modernize, Lewis explains, but not to Westernize. To modernize means to accept 'and indeed to make the fullest use of modern technology, especially the technologies of warfare and propaganda...(even though) the methods and even the artifacts come from the West.' On the other hand, cultural change is Westernization. The materialism propounded through our media and entertainment culture is Westernization. Even the emancipation of women, writes Lewis, 'is Westernization; both for traditional conservatives and radical fundamentalists it is neither necessary nor useful but noxious, a betrayal of true Islamic values.'[195] The power of anti-Western sentiment is seen in the success of the Iranian revolution (Khomeini and his successors have been in power now for more than 20 years) and more generally in today's extreme fundamentalist movements.

If the enemy is 'the West,' then why, in our evolving global economy, will the Middle East be more likely to align with the western democracies of the European Union than with the US? There are three reasons. The first is geography: Turkey connects Europe to the Middle East, and across that land bridge many migrations have taken place, in both directions. The second is the understanding and affinity that come from centuries of a shared history. America, by contrast, has no historical perspective.

The third is Russia, which we have mentioned. America's defense of Israel in 1973 allowed Russia to cultivate ties not only with Egypt and Libya but also throughout the region – ties that remain. Now let us expand Russia to include the former Soviet republics of central Asia. Here is a route toward Europe through which Muslim populations already constitute a large majority. For example, in Turkmenistan (which lies along Iran's northern border) the population is 89 percent Muslim. In Uzbekistan, the figure is 88 percent. Even further to the north, in vast Kazakhstan, 47 percent of the people are Muslims, compared to the 44 percent who are Russian Orthodox. These countries' oil and gas reserves will add to global hegemony created by the Russia-Middle East energy axis.

Not that the US is likely to surrender the region without a fight. At a 2003 meeting of the World Economic Forum held in Jordan, US Trade Representative Robert Zoellick announced that the US is pushing to have a US-Middle East Free Trade Agreement in place by 2013. It would include up to 20 of the region's nations. Not surprisingly, given the current war in Iraq, Arab response to the initiative has not been entirely positive. 'This is to get Arab countries to swallow the occupation, the killings and the devastation in Iraq that the US caused,' wrote a columnist in a Jordanian daily. Ibrahim Alloush, a Jordanian activist and intellectual, was also unimpressed: 'The agreement uses conditions like 'fighting terrorism' and 'improving investment climate.' This means tailoring our local world to the tastes and whims of American companies and interests.' Still others see the proposed trade negotiations as a way to force the Arab world to do business with Israel 'despite the Jewish state's occupation of Arab land and its crackdown on Palestinians.'[196]

Moreover, while America is talking about a free trade agreement in the region, groups throughout the Middle East – especially in Egypt – are trying to foment a grassroots boycott of US products. An official Egyptian boycott of Israeli products is already in effect, but since trade between the two countries is miniscule anyway, the boycotters are turning their attention to America. Lists of American brand names – McDonald's, Coke, Marlboro – are circulating in Egypt and other Arab countries, and the pressure to give up these products in favor of local alternatives is growing.[197]

With American presence in Iraq becoming increasingly problematic, and with violence erupting again between Israel and the Palestinians, the US position in the Middle East looks unpromising.

Israel

But America still has an important friend, ally, and trading partner in Israel, right? Not necessarily. It is our prediction that Israel, too, will align economically with the European Union. We confess that this is a minority – even a radical – opinion. *New York Times* columnist Thomas Friedman, for example, wrote in September 2003 that 'Israel-US ties have never been tighter.' But let's examine that relationship.

True, the US cannot be faulted for lack of effort. Not only has it poured economic and military aid into the Jewish state, it helped create two great opportunities for peace between Israel and its neighbors. The first came when Egyptian president Anwar Sadat, despite having engineered the invasion of Israel in 1973, began to work for peace toward the end of the decade. With Jimmy Carter's prodding, Israeli Prime Minister Menachem Begin came to the peace table and signed what came to be known as the Camp David Accords. Few months later, in March 1979, Egypt and Israel formally signed a peace treaty, under the terms of which Israel returned the Sinai Peninsula in exchange for full diplomatic recognition. Of the two leaders, Sadat paid the heavier price for this compromise. His popularity plummeted among hardliners in his own country, and he was assassinated by Muslim extremists while reviewing a military parade in 1981. In 1982, Israel invaded Lebanon in an effort to drive the PLO out of its encampments there, and the peace in the region was over.

The second came in 1993, when Israeli Prime Minister Yitshak Rabin and PLO chairman Yasser Arafat came to Washington at the invitation of Bill Clinton and signed the Israel-PLO accords, in which Israel recognized the PLO and agreed to gradually implement limited self-rule for Palestinians in the West Bank and Gaza Strip. Despite escalating opposition on both sides, Arafat and Rabin, along with Israeli foreign minister Shimon Peres, again met Clinton in Washington in 1995 to provide for the expansion of Palestinian self-rule in the West Bank. This time the Israeli leader paid the price for his peace initiatives. Rabin was assassinated by a Jewish extremist while attending a peace rally in 1995.

Now as we know, the 'roadmap' to peace endorsed by the Bush administration, which looked so promising in the summer of 2003, was in tatters by the fall. Hopefully, with Arafat now gone, this roadmap may have a chance to succeed.

So while the US continues to talk about the importance of its relationship with Israel, the ongoing violence between Israel and Palestine, along with other pressures on Israel, are straining the relationship. The rift began under the administration of George Bush Sr., who – with his own recession to deal with – was the first US president to slash foreign aid to Israel. Moreover, when Israel requested $10 billion in loan guarantees to help absorb the wave of new immigrants from the then newly defunct Soviet Union, Bush Sr. made the aid contingent upon Israel's curtailing the construction of settlements in the occupied territories. This economic pressure was predictable. Said one member of the Israeli parliament, 'I knew it was coming.'[198]

Bush's stand was the first strong signal to the Israelis that the US could no longer afford to subsidize their nation – especially at an amount reported to be $24 billion annually. It also provided another example of how economics drives politics. Under the leadership of Rabin and Peres, Israel moderated its stand toward the Palestinians and paved the way for the 1993 meeting with Arafat in Washington (for which, ironically, Bill Clinton got the credit).

Still, loan guarantees aside, the US has continued to supply some $3 billion in aid to Israel annually, and despite the decades of border wars Israel's economy has flourished. In 1985 Israel became the first nation to sign a free trade agreement with the US, and over the next dozen years bilateral trade between the two nations tripled. On its 50th birthday in 1998, Israel's economy was 'one of the hottest in the world' according to a report in *Business America*. The article attributed the Israeli boom to, first, its success in making the desert bloom and, subsequently, its rapid development of a thriving high-tech sector – a spin-off of its defense industry.[199]

The economy took a downturn in 2003, thanks to the exorbitant costs of the war with Palestine combined with the effects of the global slowdown; Israel found itself in its worst recession since the state came into being in 1948. After 6.8 percent growth in 2000, the economy contracted in 2002 and had only 1 percent growth in 2003. Since that time the economic situation has improved and growth was up to 3.9 percent in 2004.

Still there are underlying problems with Israel's economy; let us briefly consider three key export industries for better understanding.

First, oranges. Thanks to the miraculous transformation of its arid land into an agricultural oasis, Israel gained international renown for its exports of oranges and other citrus fruits. Now that industry is teetering on collapse. According to the latest reports provided by the USDA, the 2001 citrus season was the worst in Israel's history. Deteriorating prices in 'new sheqel' terms, the ongoing political unrest, a continuing drought, and rising water prices added up to a catastrophic year for producers – down 18 percent from the year before. Moreover, the decline in profits combined with aging orchards and increasing water shortages, was expected to lead to the uprooting of 6,000 hectares (14,830 acres) of orchards by the end of 2001. In the third straight year of below-average rainfall, the government cut irrigation quotas in half and raised water prices, and, in such an environment, growers were reluctant to invest in replanting, re-grafting, or new irrigation systems. Meanwhile, better natural growing conditions, high-yield harvests, and lower production costs are increasing the citrus market share of countries like Morocco and Kenya.[200]

Second, diamonds. As recently as 1997, Israel was the world's largest manufacturer of polished diamonds, with approximately $6 billion worth exported into the international market. But, suddenly, Israel has been eclipsed by India. Helped into the sector by imports of rough diamonds from friendly Russia, India's low-wage cutting and polishing industry thrived. By the time diamond exports surged 32 percent in 1999, India was claiming to have a 'global stranglehold' on the industry. According to an article in *Business India,* India has captured an astounding 80 percent of the world diamond market in terms of total caratage, and 55 percent of the world market in terms of value. The chairman of India's Gems and Jewelry Export Promotion Council brags that nine of every 10 diamonds sold worldwide are processed in India.[201]

Third, weapons. We noted that Israel's successful high-tech sector had its origins in the development of its arms industry. The formula for Israel's military industry has been importing weaponry – including aircraft – from the US, upgrading it into a value-added product and then exporting it on the international market. The current status of this industry – as well as a source of friction between Israel and America – is illustrated in the recent diplomatic exchange concerning Israel's weapons sales to China. According to *Arms Control Today*, US protests over Israel's arms deals came to a head in 2000 when the US persuaded Israel to cancel the sale of the Phalcon, a high-tech, airborne early-warning system, to China. The issue resurfaced in early 2003 with a report in an Israeli newspaper that the US had asked Israel to halt all arms sales to China.

State Department spokesman Richard Boucher acknowledged the problem and offered a pointed reminder that 'suppliers of weaponry (need) to be considerate and concerned about the strategic situation in a region that's of great sensitivity and importance to us.' At the heart of the issue, of course, is Taiwan, caught in a tug-of-war between the US and China. China's reaction, published in the Associated Press, was predictable: 'No country has the right to interfere in the developing military trade cooperation between China and Israel.' A nongovernmental expert in Washington nicely encapsulated the contention: 'The US is seeking to curtail Israeli arms sales to China to the greatest extent possible, while Israel is seeking minimum restraint on its exports.'[202] With the US blocking access to one of the world's biggest markets, Israel's arms industry could face problems.

So Israel, like Japan, may see itself at crossroads now, wondering which route to take to the future. One may well ask, with its economy in poor health, won't the Jewish state lean even harder on the US, its longtime friend and benefactor, and do whatever is necessary to keep that alliance strong? Our answer is no – for several reasons.

First is simple history. The Jews in Israel predominantly came from Eastern Europe. Golda Meir was born in Russia. Yitzhak Shamir and Shimon Peres were both born in Poland. Menachem Begin was born in Belarus.

Second, again, is the Russian connection. After the collapse of communism, Russian Jews began migrating to Israel in vast numbers – sometimes as many as 300,000 people in a year. Finding jobs and housing for this population (much of it well educated) has brought another strain to Israel's economy, but it has also renewed old bonds – bonds that, through Russia, connected Jews to all of Europe. The historic banking center of Vienna, for example, has always been a gateway between old Russia and Western Europe, a gateway through which passed many Jewish traders and merchants. The Russian Jews fleeing from the Soviet Union are, in effect, bringing Europe to Israel.

Third, Israel's war with Palestine will end. It must, and Israel must deal with its neighbors in the Arab world. Begin knew this. Rabin knew it, which is why he tried so hard to push Israel to make peace with its Arab neighbors. Shimon Peres knows it; even Ariel Sharon knows it. When that happens, Israel's dependency on the US will naturally diminish, and it will follow the rest of the region into the economic camp of Europe.

Fourth, as noted, US aid to Israel has already been reduced significantly. The current package amounts to approximately $2.8 billion per year, most of which is funneled into Israel's defense budget. All civilian aid is to be phased out by 2006.[203]

And finally, Israel *already* falls within Europe's economic purview. It is remarkable, really. When you think of Israel, you naturally think of US aid – billions of dollars year after year. But the fact is that US companies in Israel have staked out a market share of only 20 percent, compared to 50 percent for the European Union.[204]

Australia

'The US is going to become more important, not less important to Australia,' declared Australian Prime Minister John Howard in the summer of 2003.

Don't believe that.

Howard's remarks came as he discussed the initiative that resulted in a free trade agreement with the US in January 2005. 'Our objective,' he explained, 'is to see if we can get an agreement which will get us access to the largest and most powerful economy in the world. If we can, it will make a huge contribution to underwriting our prosperity into the future.'

Among officials in Australia, the desire for a free-trade accord with the US was far from unanimous. One of Howard's most outspoken critics is his predecessor, former prime minister, Paul Keating, who considers a free-trade agreement with the US 'a fundamentally bad idea.' Such an agreement, says Keating, 'takes our focus off the place where our bread is really buttered' i.e. in closer economic ties with Asia. Moreover, the former Prime Minister explains, a bilateral agreement would benefit the US far more than it would Australia; it would open up vulnerable Australian sectors like film and broadcast media to brutal competition from US giants, while doing little or nothing to open the US market to Australian agricultural products.

'If we ask for the right to sell just one hamburger patty in the US,' Keating remarked in his typically acerbic style, 'we'll be struck down by the first xenophobic congressman we meet appealing to the farm lobby.'

Other experts – as well as trade statistics – seem to support Keating's contention that Australia's bread is buttered in Asia. A deal with Washington runs counter to the economic realities: two-thirds of Australia's international trade is with its Asian partners, whereas only 10 percent is with the US.

The prevailing opinion is that this is no time to let those Asian alliances weaken. According to Russ Garnaut, former Australian ambassador to China, the Howard government is in danger of missing the bus in Asia by forging closer ties with the US. If China and ASEAN conclude their proposed free-trade agreement – to the exclusion of Australia – Australian exports in the trade bloc will be badly hurt. Philippine sugar or Malaysian vegetable oil would compete in China's vast markets on better terms than Australian commodities, a crushing blow to Australia's export industries.[205]

Now let us backtrack to put this debate in perspective. In the early 1980s, Australia's economy was stagnant, many key industries were over-protected, and others were state-owned in whole or in part. The nation's economic system was ripe for reform. The healing began with the election of the Labor Party, and Prime Minister Robert Hawke, in 1983. Hawke appointed Paul Keating as his Treasurer and John Button as his Minister for Industry and Commerce. Both men were ardent reformers, and when Keating replaced Hawke as Prime Minister in 1991, Button stayed on for another term as minister. Keating was re-elected Prime Minister in 1993, but lost the election to John Howard's Liberal Party/National Party coalition in 1996. Thus ended 13 years of Labor Party rule.

Keating's agenda, as Treasurer and Prime Minister, focused on tariff reform and partnering with Asia. His first target was to open up a domestic manufacturing sector that had been insulated from competition by an average rate of assistance (including non-tariff barriers) as high as 35 percent. By 1990 Keating's program had reduced that rate to 17 percent with a projected goal of 5 percent. When the Hawke government took power in 1983, 49 percent of Australia's exports went to Asia. By the time Keating took over in 1991, that figure had already grown to 56 percent.

Not surprising then, Keating is credited for being 'the architect of the Labor government's drive to internationalize the Australian economy.' During his term as treasurer, trade with and investment in neighbors Malaysia, Taiwan, and China skyrocketed. Manufacturers like BTR Nylex began listing on the Kuala Lumpur Stock Exchange. BHP Steel established factories throughout Southeast Asia. And Pacific Dunlop, one of Australia's biggest conglomerates, transformed itself from a domestic manufacturer to a global marketer and product distributor. Meanwhile, China has become a major manufacturer of Pacific Dunlop's brand-name hosiery and footwear. It's another example of the win-win formula known as outsourcing. As a Pacific Dunlop spokesman explains, 'Socks are something that are labor intensive and cotton intensive, and China has lots of labor and cotton.'[206]

As prime minister, Keating continued the push into Asia, especially China. In 1993, he oversaw direct investment such as Carton United's brewery in Shanghai and Cadbury Schweppes' chocolate-making factory in Beijing, and the opening of Australia's first bank in Shanghai. On the home front, privatization efforts centered on the sale of Commonwealth Bank and Quantas Airlines.

As *Asiaweek* summed it up at the time of his defeat in 1996, Keating had succeeding in pushing through a series of major free-market reforms – floating the dollar, slashing tariffs, and partially selling off state enterprises. These initiatives – including his pro-Asia policy – were not blamed for his ouster. It seems that voters had become disenchanted with his style, not his substance. In fact, John Howard appealed to voters with a vision of a 'comfortable and relaxed Australia' and a promise of 'no change.'[207]

Will Howard, in fact, 'change' his predecessor's pro-Asia policy into a renewed courtship with America? No; not even if he wanted to. To see why not, let's look at two related issues: immigration and tourism.

In terms of immigration, Australia finally entered the 20th century in 1972 when it officially brought an end to the 'White Australia' policy of choosing immigrants on the basis of race. In 1979, Prime Minister Malcolm Fraser opened the doors to thousands of Vietnamese refugees, and the Hawke and Keating governments continued to welcome Asian immigrants. By the time Howard took office, approximately 50,000 Asians were immigrating to Australia annually, and the number has not been slowing.

Of course, not all Australians are happy about it. Shortly after Howard's election, new MP Pauline Hanson caused a furor in her first speech before Parliament with her remark that 'I believe we are in danger of being swamped by Asians.' Interestingly, Howard was widely criticized for failing to rebuke her. No doubt, he didn't want to antagonize the 70 percent of Australians – according to poll results – who agreed that immigration levels were too high. He certainly didn't want to antagonize the large conservative constituency in his own party who also feel that way.

Ultimately, it was Australia's business community that forced Howard to come out against Hanson's inflammatory remarks. Why: because of a threatened Asian tourism boycott. When the Tourism Task Force made it clear to the Prime Minister that such a boycott could seriously damage the economy, Howard – belatedly – stated that he supported Asian immigration and praised the contribution migrants have made in building the country.

By that time, five Asian tour groups – including a 160-person party from Singapore – had already canceled their plans because of 'political considerations,' and industry leaders were justifiably nervous. At the time of the uproar, tourism was already Australia's most lucrative foreign-exchange industry, bringing in almost $12 billion annually, and 60 percent of the tourists in Australia were coming from Asia. The number of Asian tourists in Australia has doubled since then, from 2 million a year to 4 million. This is a productive goose that the Howard government should make every effort not to kill.[208]

In addition to the massive tourism industry and the steady migratory stream, there is also an ever-growing number of Asian students at Australian universities. At Melbourne's huge Monash University, many of the 52,000 students are of Chinese origin. All of this points to one conclusion: Australia is at home in Asia. As an *Asiaweek* editorial pointed out during the immigration debate, 'Australia needs Asia. It needs the money and brains of Asian immigrants. The nation has an annual current account deficit of some $16 billion. The deficit is being funded by the sale of national assets, mainly property, hotels, shares and bonds. Asians are responsible for 80 percent of the purchases.'[209]

It is clear, then, that whatever overtures the Prime Minister might make toward the US, Australia's economic alignment with Asia will only grow stronger. Today, following David Ricardo, the nation is focusing upon a few key industries – with the huge Asian market clearly in its sights. We have already mentioned tourism and higher education (also a multibillion-dollar enterprise.) Not only are Asian students flocking to Australian universities; Australian universities are also opening 'branch campuses' in Malaysia, Indonesia, and Thailand. With only enough universities in China, for example, to accommodate the top 10 percent of students, Australia rightly sees this as a growth industry in Asia. Plus, since English is the accepted language of higher education, Australia has a key advantage over competitors like Japan.

Australia is also positioning itself to become the world's largest wine producer. The French are already buying Australian grapes, and Foster, Australia's beer giant, recently purchased Beringer, one of Napa Valley's major wineries. China, now the world's largest beer consuming country, may prove to have a palate for Australian wine.

Yet another special sector is heavy industry. The growth potential here is demonstrated by the A$25 billion deal between Australia and China signed in 2002. Australia's North West Shelf consortium beat out competition from the US and Europe to win the contract to supply Guangdong province with liquefied natural gas for the next 25 years.

In assessing Australia's current economic prospects, Tom Holland of the *Far Eastern Economic Review* comes to the right conclusion: 'Economists agree that both the government and business now need to concentrate on generating growth from abroad to counter likely cooling at home. Whatever can be gained from America, that growth will have to come from Asia.'[210]

Taiwan

Missiles in one hand, money in the other: this paradox seems to characterize the current relationship between Taiwan and its oversized sibling one hundred miles away.

With Taiwan president Chen Shui-bian's re-election in March 2004, we can expect political tensions between Taiwan and Mainland China to heat up. Chen represents the pro-independence Democratic Progressive Party, which has vehemently opposed the reunification of Taiwan with the mainland. Running behind in the polls, Chen hardened his stance against Beijing as a way to rally voters to the cause. For example, in September 2003, Chen's government – for the first time – issued passports with the word 'Taiwan' printed on them, rather than the official 'Republic of China.'

Meanwhile, the Pentagon reports that China now has 450 missiles pointed at Taiwan and is adding 75 a year. Alexander Huang, vice-chairman of Taiwan's Mainland Affairs Council, complains that the increasing threat doesn't leave the Taiwanese much room to maneuver. 'Chinese fighter jets take eight to 10 minutes to cross the Taiwan Strait. Missiles need five to seven minutes.' Many others share his concern; some want to acquire missiles capable of hitting Shanghai, while others want at least an upgraded anti-missile program. 'They threaten me, I need the ability to threaten them,' says Li Wen-chong, a member of Chen's DPP government.[211]

Will Taiwan's need for military hardware give the US a chance to strengthen its ties to the island – and at the same time an opportunity to retaliate against Mainland China's intransigence on current trade and currency issues?

Probably not. In fact, current arms sales negotiations between the US and Taiwan suggest America's waning influence in the bloc. The Pentagon has had an arms package – including the latest generation Patriot anti-missile system, as well as other advanced hardware – on the table for more than two years, and Taiwan has yet to close the deal. There are several reasons for Taiwan's reluctance to buy. First: the stuff is expensive, at a time when Taiwan is trying to reduce its defense budget. Second: China won't like it. Third, and perhaps most important: the Pentagon is trying to force the deal down Taiwan's throat. Deputy Assistant Secretary of Defense Richard Lawless exemplifies America's high-handed attitude when he says, 'We believe it is imperative that Taiwan... acquire an integrated air and missile defense capability.' Not surprisingly, some Taiwanese take offense at the US inclination to dictate what is good for the island. 'It's like they are giving us orders,' says a long-time member of the legislature's defense committee.[212]

Maybe the arms deal will go through after all. Ultimately, it doesn't matter. The fact is that the relationship between Taiwan and Mainland China will prove, once again, that money is more powerful than missiles. While the arms deal between the US and Taiwan is in limbo, the economic deal between Taiwan and China is already done.

Much like Singapore when Lee Kuan Yew became prime minister, Taiwan's first urgent goal, when Chiang Kai-shek established his Nationalist Party there in 1949, was survival. And like in Singapore, the economic success story that unfolded in Taiwan over the next 50 years is quite remarkable. In both cases, success was built on a strong antipathy toward bureaucratic corruption, the creation of an environment where entrepreneurs could flourish, and the building of an export-based economy.

US aid was critical during the 1950s and 1960s, when American factories allowed Taiwan to develop its low-cost, manufacturing-for-export sector. At the same time, increased demand for Taiwanese products elevated the island from an aid client to a trading partner. But with America's formal recognition of the People's Republic at the United Nations in 1971, Taiwan saw that it would have to make its own way into the world economy. The government offered help to export-oriented industries with low-cost loans and lower tariffs on imports that went into making exports. At the same time, Taipei also wooed foreign investment in order to speed technology transfer and improve quality. As a result, exports rose from $123 million in 1963 to $3 billion ten years later, and Taiwan was on its way.

Taiwan's success is measured by the fact that its per capita income has risen from $100 (in 1950) to $14,000, and that for several years its central bank held the largest foreign reserves of any country in the world. Today the country produces 30 percent of the world's notebook computers and half of the world's computer keyboards, monitors, scanners, and motherboards.

Of course, this over-reliance on tech exports has a downside as the world supply of consumer electronics has outstripped demand. Consequently, Taiwan finds itself in the same squeeze as other Asian countries of the first generation of high-growth – but no longer low-wage – economies. That is, Taiwan is pressed on one side by low-wage, newly industrializing countries (including Mainland China) and on the other by high-tech products from the established industrial countries.[213]

The solution is to follow Japan's example in evolving from a low-wage producer of basic manufactures to a high-wage producer of high-quality goods – not just manufactures but also services, research, and design. What happens to the manufacturing base that previously stoked the economy? Much of it has already moved to China.

Moreover China, despite the saber-rattling, warmly welcomes Taiwanese investment. Beijing needs capital, especially to develop the impoverished interior, and it has offered incentives, cut red tape, and relaxed regulations to lure Taiwanese business. More than 50,000 Taiwanese companies now manufacture on the mainland. Food-maker UniPresident Enterprises leads the way with a US$541 million investment, followed by such low-tech heavyweights as Nan Ya Plastic, Taiwan Glass Industrial, Cheng Shin Rubber Industry, and sneaker maker Feng Tay Enterprise.

As Taiwan moves up the value ladder toward services and research, its outsourced industries also move up. Televisions, DVDs, cables, modems, and laptops are now being made in China for Taiwan corporations. In fact, Taiwan-managed companies now account for nearly two-thirds of China's IT exports. And how's this for an example of economic ties that bind: Winston Wong, the son of the head of Taiwan's giant Formosa Plastics conglomerate, and Jiang Mianheng, the son of Chinese past president Jiang Zemin, have started a $1.6 billion chip-making venture in Shanghai.[214]

But this merely suggests China's importance to Taiwan as a low-wage manufacturing center. As Taiwan moves away from being a supplier for companies like Dell and Hewlett-Packard (HP), and toward being a distributor of its own brands, China's real value – as a huge market and trading partner – begins to emerge. For example, Taiwan runs a trade surplus of $27 billion with the mainland, just enough to offset the $22 billion deficit it runs with Japan. And Taiwanese electronics companies like BenQ, a spin-off of giant Acer, and MiTAC, which have been largely thwarted in North America, are developing their own brands with China's market in mind. With the world's largest cellular phone market right across the Taiwan Strait, MiTAC has begun producing its own Mio brand smart phone. Besides, explains a company spokesman, 'Dell's not in the phone business, and HP's not in the phone business.'[215]

Squabbling may continue as the political relationship between Taiwan and the mainland works itself out. For example, the 50-year-old ban on direct flights and shipping traffic between the two entities remains in effect, and Chen seems in no hurry to negotiate its removal. Beijing doesn't want to negotiate either, except under its mandated 'one-China' pre-condition, which is anathema to Chen and his DPP.

The economic ties between Taiwan and the mainland are already indissoluble. Even while it repudiates Chen and his ruling party, Beijing has been reaching out enthusiastically to everyone else in Taiwan. China has hosted Taiwanese opposition party delegations, overseen an exchange of visits between the vice mayors of Shanghai and Taipei, and celebrated Taipei's Kuomintang (opposition) Party mayor in Hong Kong. At the same time, some 320,000 Taiwanese businessmen and their families have relocated to the mainland.[216]

Will political reunification follow in the wake of mutual economic well-being? Most likely. As K. Y. Lee, Chairman of BenQ, observes, 'Taiwan has to think about how to live with this big tiger. We can participate in the prosperity of Chinese development.'[217]

Hong Kong

It might be said that Hong Kong's economic history opened a new chapter in 1842, when the Treaty of Nanking ceded it to the British at the end of the first opium war. If so, another chapter began in 1949 with Mao Zedung's victory over the Chinese Nationalists, when thousands of Chinese fled to Hong Kong from Shanghai and took their business assets with them. Yet another began in 1980, when Deng Xiaopeng located the first of his Special Economic Zones, Shenzhen, in Guangdong province right across from Hong Kong, giving Hong Kong entrepreneurs sudden access to the hinterland's vast pool of labor and resources. The current chapter began in 1997, with the expiration of Britain's 99-year lease and the return of the territory to Beijing.

Blessed with a deepwater harbor (and virtually no other natural resources), Hong Kong evolved to be an Asian trade hub. Under the influence of Britain's *laissez faire* philosophy, its economy was perhaps the freest in the world: no import duties (except on selected luxury items), no trade or exchange restrictions, a stock exchange but no central bank, little labor regulation, and low taxes. Furthermore, under the provisions of the Basic Law (which went into effect with China's resumption of sovereignty in 1997), the 'one country, two systems' concept guarantees the preservation of Hong Kong's capitalist economy for another 50 years. By 2047, we can safely predict, the 'two systems' will have become one, and it will look a lot more like Hong Kong's open market than China's traditional state control.

Like Taiwan and the other Asian tigers, Hong Kong grew as a low-cost supplier of manufactured goods, moving up the value chain from apparel and light manufactures to consumer electronics. The next step up, to service industries, was made possible by outsourcing the manufacturing sector to the Shenzhen SEZ right across the Pearl River in the 1980s. Now Hong Kong's services sector makes up four-fifths of its gross domestic product.

One of those service industries – the financial sector – deserves comment. The prevailing climate of freewheeling capitalism, along with the long-established trading houses known as *hongs*, formed the basis for Hong Kong's rise to preeminence as a financial capital with a world-class stock market. Economic integration with China deepened when the liberalized policies of the SEZs allowed mainland businessmen to raise capital through offerings on the Hong Kong exchange. Moreover, after the return of the territory in 1997, even state-owned enterprises began to feel Hong Kong's attraction. Quicker regulatory approval motivated Bank of China to float its initial stock offering in Hong Kong rather than New York, and the Industrial and Commercial Bank of China has set up a merchant-banking arm in the city.[218] The mainland is developing its own stock exchange in Shanghai but, in the meantime, Hong Kong's is serving well.

Deng's decision to locate his first SEZ in Guangdong province next to Hong Kong proved to be a wise one. Today 80 percent of the province's exports are shipped through Hong Kong, and most of its foreign investment comes from there. Hong Kong companies employ an estimated 12 million workers in Guangdong, almost twice the population of Hong Kong itself. A tangible symbol of the growing partnership between Hong Kong and the mainland is the so-called Delta Bridge project – a $2 billion bridge and tunnel complex linking Hong Kong with Zhubai and Macau on the western edge of the Pearl River Delta. The 29-kilometer bridge, targeted for completion as early as 2007, should bring to the relatively underdeveloped western side of the Delta the same kind of spectacular growth and prosperity that the eastern side has already enjoyed.[219]

Like in Taiwan, the only obstacles to economic integration grow out of political wrangling. In the case of Hong Kong, the wrench in the machinery is the controversial anti-subversion bill – Article 23 – handed down by Beijing in the summer of 2003. The bill had the support of Hong Kong's chief executive (and Beijing appointee) Tung Chee-hwa, but his enthusiasm cooled when a half-million Hong Kongers took to the streets in protest. Analysts say that Tung was not so much interested in the outcry of the citizens – who feared the bill would be used to undercut their civil liberties – as he was in the upcoming 2004 elections. In 2000, 24 of Hong Kong's 60 legislative seats were democratically elected; in 2004 that number will rise to 30. Tung's surprise at the outpouring of protest, combined with Beijing's alarm at the prospect of losing control of the Legislative Council, led to the scrapping of the controversial measure.

That's not all. In a classic case of economics coming to the rescue of politics, Beijing decided to rally support in the Hong Kong elections by offering a basket-full of incentives to jump-start Hong Kong's lagging economy. (Hong Kong's lingering effects from the 1997-1998 Asian crisis – collapsed real estate values and high unemployment – have been compounded by the SARS outbreak.) Among the new reforms is a policy change to allow mainlanders to travel to Hong Kong on their own rather than with government-sponsored tour groups. They can also take more money to spend there – an increase from US$2,000 to US$5,000. Thanks to the new policy, Mainland Chinese visitors to Hong Kong will soon number close to 10 million a year, according to a Hong Kong tourism official who welcomes this 'boon for our retailers.' Another carrot from Beijing was its offer to buy up 25,000 vacant public housing units, valued at HK$20 billion, in an effort to shore up the city's struggling real estate market.

The most significant gesture, though, was the newly signed free-trade agreement between Hong Kong and the mainland, part of their wide-ranging Closer Economic Partnership Agreement. Beginning in 2004, according to the agreement, Hong Kong will be able to set up wholly owned trading companies in China, an arrangement, which will allow tariff-free import of up to 4,000 new goods and services from Hong Kong into the mainland. Moreover, the 2004 start date gives Hong Kong firms a one-year advantage over their foreign rivals.[220]

Of course, a short-term fix for Hong Kong's ailing economy is not the long-term goal. For China, full integration – of both Hong Kong and Taiwan – under Beijing's banner is the goal. It is currently in progress, as a *Business Week* editorial points out: 'While America is preoccupied with the Middle East, directing an occasional nod to an expanding NATO and Europe, an economic supernova is rising in Asia – Greater China. The integration of Taiwan and Hong Kong into the fast-growing Chinese economy is creating a boom that is attracting huge amounts of technology, capital, and skilled immigrant labor from all over the world. We are witnessing a macro-event of immense geopolitical and historic significance... the rise of Greater China and the shifting fulcrum of international wealth and power.'[221]

India

'Why do we need 19 brands of toothpaste?' Jawaharlal Nehru wittily expressed his distaste for the excesses of capitalistic competition with this question. Unfortunately, his preference for a state-controlled economy consigned India to almost 50 years of stagnation.

Nehru came to power as the first Prime Minister of independent India in 1947. Mahatma Gandhi, whose radically anti-industrial economic program – symbolized by 'a spinning wheel in every hut' – was a source of contention between the two leaders, was assassinated a few months later. Thus, Nehru's vision was left unchallenged. He and his Congress Party set about building 'a proud new nation based on democracy, socialism, and secularism.' As we noted in an earlier chapter, in the first years after World War II, this didn't seem like a bad program. Unfettered capitalism had engendered the crash of 1929 and the agony of the Great Depression, while the Soviet Union's planned economy, with its emphasis on the development of the industrial sector, seemed to provide steady growth and high employment. Moreover, Nehru's central ambition – to alleviate his nation's massive poverty – was certainly worthy.

Unfortunately his program didn't work. Instead of lifting India out of poverty, Nehru's state-controlled economy degenerated into a bureaucratic morass of red tape, regulation, and corruption that became widely derided as the 'license raj.' By reserving seventeen 'strategic' industries for the public sector – including iron and steel, mining, electrical plants – and by a licensing system that squeezed the life out of private initiative, Nehru's system stifled growth and smothered entrepreneurship.

Nehru's daughter, Indira Gandhi, came to power in 1967, and – with her father's plan still in place – the economy continued to deteriorate. What's more, the national mood hit rock-bottom when, after being accused of election fraud, she declared an 'Emergency' and suspended civil liberties and imposed censorship for almost two years. After Mrs. Gandhi's assassination in 1984, her son, Rajiv Gandhi, ascended to the leadership of the Congress Party and the prime ministership. By now, state owned enterprises were bleeding profusely and government debt was rising to alarming levels. Rajiv spoke of reform but failed to achieve any, and by the time he was voted out of office in 1989, a crisis was looming.

'There were at least five flaws with our socialism,' writes Gurcharan Das in *India Unbound*. 'We adopted an inward-looking, import-substituting path rather than an outward-looking, export-promoting route, and thus we did not participate in world trade and the prosperity that trade engendered in the postwar era. We set up a massive, inefficient, and monopolistic public sector to which we denied autonomy of working. We over-regulated private enterprise with the worst (case-by-case) controls in the world, and this diminished competition in the home market. We discouraged foreign capital and denied ourselves the benefits of technology and world-class competition. We pampered organized labor and that led to extremely low productivity.'[222]

Meanwhile, on the geopolitical level, the price Gandhi and Nehru paid for independence was the partition of their country into Hindu-dominated India and Muslim Pakistan. Another border dispute arose in the 1950s, when despite Nehru's proposal for Sino-Indian 'brotherhood,' India and China clashed over sovereignty in Tibet. Animosity between the two nations was heightened when India offered asylum to the Dalai Lama in 1959, and even further during their brief border war in 1962.

Nehru preached India's 'non-alignment' but, not surprisingly, given his socialist proclivities and his admiration for the Soviet system, the Soviet Union increasingly became India's economic ally and trading partner. This Cold War-era alliance had the effect of pushing both China and the US into Pakistan's camp during the Pakistan-Indian conflict of the mid-1960s. Lal Bahadur Shastri, who won his country's loud acclaim by repelling Pakistan's advances over the Indian border, had by then succeeded Nehru.

The Soviet-sponsored Tashkent Agreement of 1966 restored normal relations between India and Pakistan, but the day after the signing, Shastri died of a heart attack.

The Soviet-Indian partnership was cemented in 1971 with the Treaty of Peace, Friendship, and Cooperation, and armed with Soviet military support, Indira Gandhi led India to its decisive victory over Pakistan in 1972 (in the war that saw the creation of Bangladesh, formerly East Pakistan). When the US, in a belated effort to support East Pakistan, dispatched a nuclear-armed carrier into the Bay of Bengal, India responded with the development of its own nuclear program. Now the lines were drawn. India and the Soviet Union on one side; on the other, Pakistan supported by both China and the US. As Das observes, the relationship between the US and India plunged to its lowest depth 'with Nixon and Kissinger's notorious 'tilt' toward Pakistan, which further pushed India into the chilling embrace of the Soviet Union.'[223]

Forty years of economic misrule were at the root of the crisis India faced in 1991, when Rajiv Gandhi was assassinated during a campaign he hoped would bring him back to power. His government (1985–89) had not helped; excessive short-term commercial borrowing to curb the nation's deficit had compounded the problem. The flashpoint occurred with Iraq's invasion of Kuwait in 1990. Iraq had been supplying cheap oil to India (thanks to the USSR's support of both countries), but suddenly, with Iraq facing off against the US, oil prices skyrocketed, and India had no money to pay for it. As Indian citizens lined up at the gas pumps, their government stared at a treasury depleted of foreign reserves. Nonresident Indians pulled their investments out of the country, and the hundreds of thousands of Indians who had been employed in Kuwait were suddenly no longer sending their wages back home. (They did get out with their lives, however. Forewarned by the Iraqis of the impending attack, some 600,000 Indians were removed from Kuwait in a massive airlift that went on 24 hours a day.)

It was 70-year-old Narasimha Rao, elected Prime Minister in 1991, who faced the stark fact that India was bankrupt. Only a loan from the IMF could save the country, but an IMF bailout would be contingent upon reform. In fact Rao, with Finance Minister Manmohan Singh and Commerce Minister P. Chidambaram, pushed reform much further than the IMF would have demanded – and in the process redirected India's economy toward the global market. They devalued the rupee by 20 percent, reduced the deficit by abolishing export subsidies, replaced import licenses with market incentives, spurred domestic growth by removing licenses from most industries, and allowed foreign investors to own majority shares of their Indian subsidiaries – thus welcoming additional foreign investment.

In just the first two years, the reforms brought vast improvement. The deficit came down from 8.4 percent of GDP to 5.7 percent. Foreign exchange reserves shot up from $1 billion to $20 billion. Inflation dropped from 13 percent to 6 percent. Large industry was now free from the control of the notorious Monopolies and Restrictive Trade Practices (MRTP) Act, which had virtually outlawed expansion and investment. Banking, airlines, electric power, petroleum, cellular phones, and other industries were gradually shifted from the public to the private sector (though many remain public sector dominated). Thanks to the Foreign Investment Promotion Board, foreign investment doubled year after year – rising to $3 billion by 1997. Customs duties gradually came down from a peak of 200 percent in 1991 to an average duty of 25 percent in the mid-1990s. Tax rates came down from 56 percent in 1991 to the 30 percent proposed by Chidambaram's 1997 budget.

'It seems astonishing,' writes Gurcharan Das, 'that a minority government led by a lackluster 70-year-old intellectual who was about to retire from active politics suddenly turned his party's 40-year socialist legacy on its head.'[224]

If India fell behind while Japan and the Asian tigers were exploding in the 1970s and 1980s, its great aptitude for the 'knowledge' industries will help it catch up quickly. There are now 325 software companies in Bangalore – India's Silicon Valley – including homegrown giants like TCS, Wipro and Infosys, as well as major internationals like IBM, Texas Instruments, and Motorola. What the foreign firms find in India is a vast talent pool, proficient in English, and with salary requirements roughly one-fifth of a comparable US worker. Thus India is poised to become the world's leading 'remote services' provider. Any work that can be done on the computer and transmitted through cyberspace – accounting, law, banking, customer service, back office, payroll – can be done cheaply and efficiently in India.

So India's economic future lies in software, the Internet, and IT-enabled industries – but that's not all. India has also become a global player in generic pharmaceuticals and entertainment (especially film). It is also a major manufacturer and exporter of two-wheelers, small tractors and auto parts. Moreover, it has a global competitive advantage in a dozen agricultural commodities, including tea, cotton, wheat, rice, horticulture, and diary products. With further reform in the agricultural sector, this should become a powerful performer in the Indian economy.

'In the globalized open economy governed by the WTO,' says Das in a familiar echo of David Ricardo, 'we will make only what we are good at – where we have a comparative and competitive advantage – and we will import the rest.... It is also worth remembering that the new economy is largely a service economy and creates many more jobs. The old economy is increasingly cutting jobs, downsizing, mechanizing, and becoming even more capital-intensive. India, with its vast intellectual capital – two million low-cost English-speaking graduates a year, including 75,000 in information technology – is in an excellent position to provide 'knowledge workers' to the global economy and benefit from the knowledge revolution. With competitive advantages in agriculture and the new knowledge economy, it may in the end be all right to skip the industrial revolution.'[225]

After the collapse of the Soviet Union, where would India look for the trading partners that would provide the vital link to the world economy? The nation first looked east toward ASEAN, but Lee Kuan Yew in Singapore rebuffed it. Lee preferred to push ASEAN toward a trade alliance with China, and he was well aware of the tensions that still simmered between India and China.

Well, given the current tension between Pakistan and its uneasy friend, the US, over the terrorism issue, perhaps the time has come for the world's two largest democracies to forge closer ties. In fact, this alignment is quickly falling into place.

As we have seen so often, the link was created first on the economic level, especially in the software and IT sectors. As *Global Information Network* points out, 'India's emergence as a supplier of software services and manpower to the US roughly coincides with the demise of its former ally, the Soviet Union, and the defeat of another close friend, Iraq, in the high-technology first Gulf War of 1991.' Software exports, now at more than $15 billion annually, have led India's entry into the world economy and represented the pride of the conservative Bharatiya Janata Party (BJP). Politics follows suit. The BJP, seeking a strategic alliance with Washington, refused to allow a resolution in Parliament criticizing the US war in Iraq. Moreover, contrary to its policy in the first Gulf War, India's Foreign Minister Yashwant Sinha indicated that, if asked, India would allow US military aircraft access to refueling stations.

The sea-change in attitude is represented by Rakesh Gulati, a recent IT graduate waiting for his H1B visa to come through: 'You won't catch me going anywhere near those Commie rallies in front of the US Embassy.'[226]

When India and Pakistan tested nuclear devices in 1998, the US imposed economic sanctions on both countries, temporarily cooling the US-India courtship. Soon, the alignment was back on track, however, visibly signaled by increasing US arms sales to its huge new partner. India continues to be the third-biggest arms consumer in the world (after China and South Korea), with an ever-increasing percentage of its purchases coming from the US. Or, with Washington's approval, from Israel, as in the case of the recently approved sale to India of the Arrow anti-missile system, jointly developed by Israel and the US.

The military component of the relationship between India and the US makes sense, and not only because of their alliance in the war on terror. Perhaps more important, Washington sees India playing a crucial role as a counter-balance against China in Asia. According to Lloyd Richardson of the Hudson Institute, 'India is the most overlooked of our potential allies in a strategy to contain

China.' To further that aim, the US has also been working closely with India's navy, as in the Malabar IV joint exercises involving thousands of sailors and pilots from both countries.[227]

Moreover, we are likely to soon see cooperation between NASA and India's aerospace industry, led by Hindustan Aeronautics Ltd (HAL). Complementing its software industry, Bangalore is fast becoming India's aerospace capital, and the technology is there for a productive US-India partnership. India recently announced its first moon shot, and NASA is investigating the feasibility of rocket launches from the sub-continent.

The only friction in the relationship now comes from US labor interests, who decry the loss of US jobs both to Indian immigrants and to outsourcing to India. The issue has become contentious. In the summer of 2003, the US Congress began considering bills to close a loophole in immigration law allowing foreign workers to service clients in the US on guest worker visas. At the same time the legislatures in several states were crafting laws to ban outsourcing of government tech-services contracts to low-wage countries.

The protests would seem unlikely to carry the day. In the first place, as India's software association, the National Association of Software and Service Companies (NASSCOM) has pointed out, while India sells $6.75 billion in software services to the US, it contributes twice that to the American economy in hardware and software purchases, customer savings, and US taxes paid by Indian workers. The industry also claims that it is creating jobs, rather than taking them, by hiring more US-based marketing and consulting executives than ever before – including 1,600 in New Jersey, one of the states considering anti-outsourcing legislation. Economics, not protectionism, will rule here, since the simple fact is that Indian software services deliver cost savings of roughly 60 percent over US companies. C. Srinivasan, of Electronic Data Systems, is probably correct when he predicts that 'in the next three to five years, the India solution will be a critical part of every portfolio.'[228]

Gurcharan Das offers a wise word to those who would stifle the natural expansion of the global economy: 'Statesmen in the

West need to reassure their citizens that in the long run, free trade is good for everyone, even though it causes pain to some in the short run. It is part of the rules of the capitalist game. The same fears were expressed in America some years ago when NAFTA was being debated. Bill Clinton had to reassure American workers incessantly that although some American jobs would be exported to Mexico and Canada more higher-paying jobs would in the end be created in America. And he was right.'[229]

In Conclusion

It is quite fascinating to watch these last pieces of the global economic jigsaw puzzle fall into place. Africa and the Middle East (including Israel) will strengthen their historic ties to Europe. China will clasp Taiwan and Hong Kong to its bosom, enhancing the power of an Asian super-bloc that will include Japan, Korea, ASEAN, and Australia.

As this scenario unfolds, America's sphere of influence would seem contained exclusively to the Western Hemisphere – except, that is, for India. Viewed in that context, America's ties to the world's most populous democracy become a matter of some urgency.

Chapter 7

Competition Between the Blocs

The forces driving the world towards the tripolar structure we describe in this book are powerful, and will not be denied. In the final analysis, we are confident that they will result in a world that is considerably more prosperous and peaceful in the 21st century than it was in the 20th century. However, many challenges remain for each of the three blocs in making the transition to this new structure. Overcoming these will require individual countries to make difficult choices and navigate sometimes-dangerous political currents. Instead of worrying about what may be politically or economically expedient in the short run, country leaders will have to stay focused on the larger goals of bloc economic integration: greater prosperity, security and opportunity for all the people in the bloc. To achieve this, they will have to convince their citizenry that it is wise for them to subsume a measure of their national identity into a shared bloc identity.

To remain prosperous and peaceful, each bloc will have to ensure that it is competitive with the rest of the world. In order to be globally competitive, each bloc will need to achieve very strong economic integration. Each bloc will also have to benchmark itself against the other blocs on a host of economic, social and political factors. If the differences across blocs become too great, there will be great pressure for change.

This chapter and the subsequent four chapters are about what each bloc must do to be globally competitive. We will make the case that doing so will require governments to take an activist approach in steering the economy at the national and trade bloc levels.

In this chapter, we start by describing the six flows that have to take place for true economic integration to occur. We then discuss the role of governments in shaping the evolution of the world in this direction. Market forces alone will not lead to this outcome; governments will have to engage in strategic planning to bring this vision of the future to fruition. We suggest that this will give rise to the notion of countries being managed as 'nation-corporations,' which in turn will be woven into the fabric of a bloc economy, similar to the way in which companies collaborate with each other within an economic ecosystem. Next, we will briefly describe the four major kinds of restructuring that will be necessary. These are the four policy main areas that governments need to address to enable a successful transition from national to trade bloc economies. Subsequent chapters will describe in detail what national and regional governments will need to do in each of the four areas. For each type of restructuring, we will provide an assessment of how well the three economic blocs are positioned to meet the challenges, and what needs to be done by each bloc to be successful in the future.

The Six Flows of Economic Integration

In perhaps the most stirring speech of his presidency, Ronald Reagan spoke these memorable words at the Brandenburg Gate in West Berlin on June 12, 1987:

> *General Secretary Gorbachev, if you seek peace, if you seek prosperity for the Soviet Union and Eastern Europe, if you seek liberalization: Come here to this gate! Mr. Gorbachev, open this gate! Mr. Gorbachev, tear down this wall!*[230]

On November 9, 1989, the wall was indeed torn down, signaling the beginning of the end of communism in Europe, and triggering a wave of national and even global euphoria as millions of East Germans poured into West Germany. Each 'tourist' was given a gift of DM100 by the West German government. A massive transformation of Europe was underway; the crush of people was so intense that there were 40-mile long traffic jams in certain places.

Rapid economic growth and development cannot occur without the free flow of products (including services), people, money, information, education and arts/culture. However, there are usually many obstacles to the flow of these elements, certainly across national boundaries and often within nations as well. Visionary bloc leaders of the future must work assiduously and on multiple fronts to remove all the walls that inhibit the free movement of any of the six elements within their bloc. The more they allow such free flows, the stronger their bloc will become. The role of the government is to remove all the barriers that arise because of religious, social or economic factors. By doing so, governments can remove the impediments that can prevent natural market forces from working their economic magic.

Unfortunately, the opposite can often happen in democracies; politicians may make emotional appeals to the masses based on creating and exploiting barriers. This was certainly the case in the run up to the last US presidential election, when the off-shoring of certain white collar work became a politically charged issue.

As shown in Figure 7.1, with true economic integration, no barriers would exist to inhibit the bloc flow of:

- *Products*: Products should be produced and shipped anywhere within the trade bloc without restriction. No tariff or non-tariff barriers exist to the flow of goods or services.
- *People*: People should be free to visit, live and work in any location in the trade bloc without restriction. This is perhaps the biggest weakness in the efforts of economic integration to date. Countries such as Australia, Ireland, New Zealand and Canada, which have opened up immigration in recent years, have reaped significant economic and social benefits, as we detail in chapter eleven.

- *Money*: There should be no restrictions on the flow of investment capital or the resulting profits to any part of the trade bloc.
- *Information*: It should be allowed to flow freely within the trade bloc, without censorship. This is where a country like China is vulnerable, since it still places significant restrictions on open access to information. In China, for example, it is impossible for anyone to view images of the citizen uprising and subsequent army action at Tiananmen Square in June 1989.
- *Education*: There should be no restrictions on the establishment of educational institutions within the trade bloc, or on the freedom of people to avail themselves of any educational institutions in the bloc. Educational standards should become more harmonized over time, and disparities within the bloc should become fewer.
- *Arts and culture*: Over time, there should be a greater internal flow and commonality of entertainment and cultural influence within the trade bloc.

To better appreciate this, consider what would happen if, instead of functioning as a single country, the US were to operate as fifty separate countries. Each 'country' would have its own culture, tax code, economic regulations and currency, and with significant restrictions on the movement of people, goods and information across borders. It is easy to imagine how economically and culturally grid-locked such an entity would be. Companies within each state would be largely restricted to serving their own small markets, and could only expand into other states with great difficulty. There would be enormous duplication of investments across states, resulting in the highly unproductive use of capital. Consumers would be forced to pay high prices for most products, without receiving high quality or getting access to a wide selection in return.

Without belaboring this unpleasant vision, it is abundantly clear that the US benefits tremendously from the open borders between its states. Each company within the country has ready

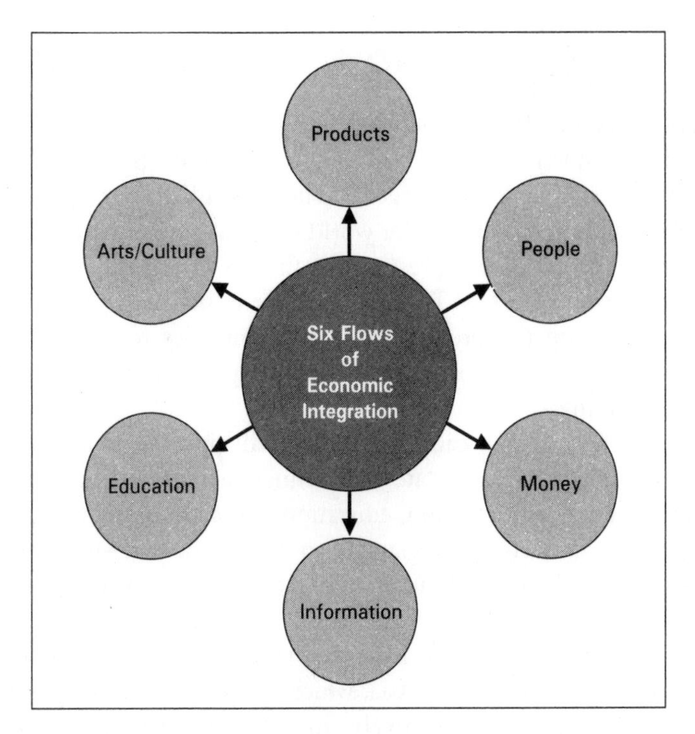

Figure 7.1: Six Flows of Economic Integration

access to a huge 'home' market, and consumers everywhere in the country benefit as a result. People can and do readily move to any part of the country, to suit their lifestyle choices or professional aspirations. A company in California can raise money in New York, while one headquartered in Delaware can manufacture in Georgia. Educational institutions can draw on a pool of students from across the country, while individual students can choose from thousands of educational alternatives available to them. While some regional differences remain, there is strongly shared national interest in books, music, television programs, movies and sporting events.

Europe has long envied these advantages, and is moving aggressively to emulate them by adopting a common currency and opening up the borders between its member states to facilitate the free movement of people and products. With ten additional countries (Czech Republic, Estonia, Cyprus, Latvia, Lithuania, Hungary, Malta, Poland, Slovenia and Slovakia) joining the fifteen existing members of the EU on May 1, 2004, the US already finds itself at a relative disadvantage.[231] The 'new' EU has a population of 450 million, making it the world's largest single market. This will result in additional pressure for the US to expand its 'home' market beyond the NAFTA region sooner rather than later. It will also ratchet up the pressure on Asian countries to move more quickly towards the formalization and expansion of their trade bloc economy.

Going forward, each trade bloc will operate as a kind of 'super-country' or 'trade-state,' permitting the free flow of products, people, money, information, education and arts/culture across all internal borders. Any bloc that does not do so, or that significantly lags the other blocs, will put at risk its own future economic well-being.

In essence, the world is headed towards the formation of a 'US of Europe' and a 'US of Asia,' which will join a greatly expanded 'US of America' to collectively dominate the world economy around the year 2020. While these broad entities will never quite take the form of today's nation-states, they will come close.

Rivalry Between Trade Blocs

In most industries, three large firms control the lion's share of the market and they compete, coexist and occasionally cooperate with each other. Likewise, the three huge trade economies that we see emerging will also compete as well as coexist and cooperate with each other. Just like companies in an industry, each trade economy will have its own 'core competencies,' vulnerabilities, and distinct formula for success within the global economy.

By no means do we envision a world in which the three trade blocs are shut off from one another, with little flow of people, information or products between blocs. There always will be sizeable flows of all kinds between the blocs; however, these will increasingly be dwarfed by the flows that take place within each bloc. The net impact will be two-fold. First, there will be rationalization of many ad hoc and haphazard relationships that currently exist for historical and geopolitical reasons that have become obsolete. For example, trading relationships established in the shadow of the looming threat of communism (e.g. between the US and Taiwan) will be replaced by new relationships that make a lot more economic, cultural and political sense (e.g. the burgeoning relationship between Taiwan and China). Second, there will be a significant net expansion of total trade flows, as countries enter into multifaceted, long-term strategic and mutually beneficial relationships with other countries within their bloc. Countries will be more willing to 'give up' certain sectors for greater positions in others. As more countries hone and leverage their comparative advantages in this way, it will result in the proverbial 'rising tide that lifts all boats.'

While each trade economy will undoubtedly put up barriers between itself and the other blocs (*a la* the notion of 'Fortress Europe'), those barriers will not be absolute. Since the boundaries will be permeable, each bloc will have to ensure that it is generally competitive with the other blocs in key industries.

In *Triad Power*, Kenichi Ohmae showed that 75 percent of world trade in the 1970s took place between the 15 nations of North America, Western Europe and Japan. These countries also accounted for 70 percent of the world's GDP. We expect that to change; approximately 75 percent of the trade will be *within* the blocs (earlier it was across blocs) by 2020. In a sense, what used to be known as 'Most Favored Nation' status (and is now known more accurately as 'Normal Trade Relations') will in the future only be conferred on countries within the same trade economy. For example, after joining the EU in May 2004, Poland has found that its imports from China have become more expensive, as a result of common EU tariffs. Un-connecting is difficult, because exit barriers are high; many companies have long-established physical presence (such as factories) in 'other' blocs. For example, some Japanese companies have reduced their investments in the US and invested in the ASEAN block and China instead.

Companies that are already heavily globalized, such as Coca Cola, IBM, HP and Siemens, will maintain a presence in all three trade blocs. The best way for them to do so would be to first ensure that they maintain dominance in their trade bloc, where they have a friendly political climate. In other blocs, they are likely to have joint ventures with powerfully entrenched local companies. They must localize and become part of the domestic economy. This is the old model, followed successfully by companies such as Xerox, which established Rank Xerox in Europe and Fuji Xerox in Japan.

Companies that do decide to pull out are likely to engage in the swapping of assets with other companies headed in the opposite direction – a sort of 'you take my China factory, I will take your India factory' approach. What is often done by product categories will be done by trade bloc. For example, General Electric (GE) and Thomson (a French electronics company) made a deal in 1987 in which GE traded its television manufacturing business worldwide (including the RCA brand name) – even though it was No. 1 in the US market. In exchange, it received Thomson's medical imaging business. Thomson walked away from that business because of Siemens' great strengths in that area. The move allowed GE to become a viable competitor to Siemens, in Europe, with 15 percent market share in medical equipment.[232]

In general, firms *outside* a trade economy will have to contend with a 15 – 20 percent cost disadvantage compared to those inside the bloc, representing tariffs and transportation costs. If a bloc does not do a good job of maintaining a reasonable level of global competitiveness internally, these firms will be able to exert pressure from the outside. If a trade economy can ensure that it has a high level of internal competitiveness, offshore companies – unable to compete in any significant way – will be relegated to serving only niche markets (if that) there.

We believe that non-tariff barriers will increase (such as quantitative restrictions and regulations on health, safety, and sanitation). Already, Europeans are starting to restrict imports from countries that have a different value system than their own. For example, the EU is asserting the right to restrict imports from countries that don't follow the 'right' environmental policies. The EU views the US as the worst offender, since it has refused to ratify global environmental treaties such as the Kyoto Protocol. As the rivalry between Europe and the US heats up even further (as we predict it definitely will), Europe will look for every possible way in which it can weaken the US or gain an advantage over it.[233]

Converging Bloc Approaches

While all the major economies in the world today are capitalistic, there are still strong bloc differences. Broadly speaking, there are three distinct types of capitalism being practiced in the world today:

- *Laissez faire capitalism*: Market forces operate with minimal government intervention.
- *Managed capitalism*: The government plays an active role in steering companies and industries to evolve in particular directions.
- *Social capitalism*: The government heavily taxes businesses and high-income individuals in order to provide extensive social security, healthcare and other services.

Currently, the US operates with relatively unfettered '*laissez-faire* capitalism,' while we see more 'managed capitalism' in Asia and 'social capitalism' in Europe. These varying approaches reflect very real philosophical differences across countries and regions, and are likely to continue to a degree. However, we expect to see convergence taking place over time, as countries in all three trade blocs move toward a more similar vision: strong faith in the virtues of free markets coupled with a degree of hands-on management of the economy by the government and a stronger focus on social issues than has traditionally been the case, for example, in the US Each bloc will seek to align societal, corporate and governmental interests in a synergistic way. We expect that Asians will temper their 'visible hand' approach to economic management and strengthen their social safety net (which is non-existent in many

Asian countries). Europeans will further deregulate their economies to subject them to greater free market forces, and dilute the more extreme aspects of the 'welfare state' that are counter-productive. Americans will be more willing to temper free market forces with a greater degree of control, and are already in the process of moving towards strengthening the social safety net. For instance, we believe that the US will have to join the rest of the developed world in providing its citizens universal healthcare in the next two decades. Otherwise, the widening gap between the US and the rest of the developed world – in per capita healthcare costs and as a percentage of GDP – will increasingly sap the competitiveness of the US economy and hence of the American trade economy. US companies are increasingly burdened – and rendered uncompetitive in some sectors – by the need to provide their employees with ever-more expensive health and pension benefits.

In addition to philosophical differences that will gradually be reduced through convergence, there are also major procedural differences across the blocs. The EU operates in a very formal way, especially now that it has created a regional government structure in Brussels. The American bloc is less formal in terms of process; for example, the US has a strong executive branch that is able to move ahead rapidly if needed (via Executive Order). In Asia, on the other hand, things happen silently and largely behind the scenes. Here, politics has always been driven by economics, and large industrial houses have had strong influence on the political process. Over time, we expect that both the American and Asian blocs will develop their own versions of Brussels, and adopt a greater degree of formalization in their operation. The competition between cities to become the home base for the Americas trade bloc is well underway, with contenders including Miami, Atlanta, Panama City, Port of Spain and Puerto Rico. For the Asian bloc, Singapore or Hong Kong may be the best-suited location.

All the blocs will have to come up with new approaches to address fundamental problems. The rapidly rising costs of healthcare and education, for example, are not sustainable in the way they have traditionally been supported by each region. Pan-regional approaches will be needed, including the outsourcing of more elements within each trade economy e.g. India is becoming a regional center for affordable, high quality healthcare, and is attracting a growing number of 'medical tourists' who come to the country for surgeries and other treatments from the US.

A Converging Process

Just as economic growth in the early 20th century was hurt by excessive ownership and control of economic assets by governments (as detailed in *Commanding Heights*), economic prosperity in the current century will be threatened if countries espouse blind adherence to *laissez faire* capitalism. As with many broad currents in history, there is cyclicality here. As *Commanding Heights* describes, many governments after World War I and II were heavily involved not just in guiding the economies of their countries but actually owning and running many key industries. This approach proved unsuccessful in the long run, so many countries moved towards pure *laissez faire*, especially in the West. That approach too has run into trouble. What is emerging now is a hybrid approach – a Third Way.

The 19th century was witness to a level of economic growth never before seen in the world. A combination of the Industrial Revolution and the adoption of *laissez faire* economic liberalism and free trade gave rise to rapid and sustained economic growth, particularly in the US and UK. In this era, politics and economics were viewed as separate and distinct. Companies were minimally regulated, and many grew to enormous size and power. In most industries, a handful of companies dominated the market. Around the turn of the century, trade unions and labor-oriented political parties emerged to challenge the power of corporations. They considered capitalists as the enemies of working people, a view that Karl Marx and Friedrich Engels popularized, and which became the basis for socialism and communism in many countries.[234]

In other countries, the approach was to curtail the power of companies by breaking them up and restricting them from adopting practices that were monopolistic or collusive. Governments enacted new laws and established new regulatory agencies to implement these policies. In many countries, governments even took ownership of certain industries away from the private sector by nationalizing them. This worked for a while, but eventually led to stagnation and economic pessimism. The move back towards freer markets based predominantly on private ownership began in Chile in the 1970s, emulated subsequently by Margaret Thatcher in the UK and Ronald Reagan in the US. Free markets came to be seen, almost without exception, as the engines of economic prosperity.[235]

The philosopher Georg Wilhelm Friedrich Hegel described this process as 'Thesis – Antithesis – Synthesis,' '…the inevitable transition of thought, by contradiction and reconciliation, from an initial conviction to its opposite and then to a new, higher conception that involves but transcends both of them.'[236] In a similar vein, we have moved from a philosophy of governments owning and controlling the 'commanding heights' of the economy to free market dogma and now to a form of managed competition and active steering of the economy.

Look at Russia, which represented the epitome of government controlling the commanding heights. After the Soviet Union collapsed, Russia became completely and suddenly market-oriented and almost destroyed itself in the process. Organized crime became a huge factor in the economy. Now, Vladimir Putin has moved toward a managed approach to doing things. Russia still will adhere to market processes, but the government will guide the economy in a more active way, thus emulating China, which has skillfully managed to gain the advantages of market forces while retaining a strong measure of control over how the economy evolves.

How can countries manage their economies in a way that blends the best of both worlds – the creativity and vigor of free markets and the steadiness and sustainability of managed market evolution? For an answer, we turn to an unlikely source – Sigmund Freud.

A Freudian Analog

For the most part, the economic and policy establishment in the US is deeply and instinctively hostile to any notion of managed competition. The US view is that the free market must be the foundation – there is no substitute for it, and tampering with it is tantamount to killing the goose that lays the golden eggs. But the free market is a wild force; it represents the rawest form of economic energy. Left to itself, it can result in many positive outcomes as well as some negative ones. For example, there are markets for all manner of vices. Most countries do not want to allow markets to emerge for socially undesirable or exploitative products, even though willing sellers and buyers no doubt exist.

The ways in which societies must harness and manage the market is analogous to the way that mature and well-adjusted adults manage their own behavior. According to Sigmund Freud, personality has three aspects - Id, the Ego and the Superego - that work together to determine our behavior. For a person to have good psychological energy and mental health, all three must be well-balanced.[237]

Table 7.1 describes the parallels between Freud's conception of the three aspects of personality and our economic analogs of those forces. Entrepreneurship is the way to harness the wild force of the market towards societally useful ends; but it can be a destructive force as well as a constructive one – just as a person's ego can become a slave to the Id. In that case, the pursuit of self-interest becomes so strong that it can become excessive and harmful to society. Entrepreneurs may exploit the environment, cheat consumers or defraud investors. When the native energy – Id – is allowed to drive the Ego, it can become wild and out of control. What is needed is the counterbalancing force of the Superego, which molds the Ego in a way that enables the person to survive and live in society. The economic analog to the Superego is the role of the government. Governmental policies can channel the energy of entrepreneurs in a way that it becomes less self-destructive and more useful to society. Of course, the effects of

Aspect	*Freud's Definitions*	*Economic Analog*	*Explanation*
Id	Functions in the irrational/emotional part of the mind; the seat of impulses Source of energy Ruled by 'pleasure principle;' demands instant gratification Equates to 'child' If too strong: Focused on self-gratification, uncaring to others	**Market Forces**	The fundamental energy – the drive to fulfill one's own material needs If too strong: Focused on satisfying material needs regardless of societal consequences
Ego	Functions in the rational part of the mind Ego's job is to get the Id's pleasures while being reasonable and mindful of long-term consequences; denies both instant gratification and indefinite delaying of gratification Uses some of Id's energy to plan and control Operates via 'reality principle' Ego recognizes the need for compromise and negotiates between the Id and the Superego Equates to 'adult' With no superego, or an extremely weak one, ego becomes all about satisfying the wants of the id – regardless of consequences to others	**Entrepreneurship**	Filling own needs by meeting the needs of others Can become wild and out of control in the absence of reasonable restraints, rules and regulations Can lead to exploitation of all stakeholders – customers, employees, suppliers, investors, community

	If too strong: Extremely rational and efficient, but cold, boring and distant		Is ultimately self-destructive if unchecked
Superego	The last part of the mind to develop Functions in the moral part of the mind; keeps people on the straight and narrow Embodies parental and societal values; it stores and enforces rules Enforces rules through ability to create anxiety Constantly strives for perfection Equates to 'parent' Two subsystems: • Ego Ideal: Rules for good behavior and standards of excellence (what parent would approve of or value) • Conscience: Rules about what constitutes bad behavior (what parent would disapprove of or punish) If too strong: The person feels guilty all the time and may have an insufferably saintly personality	**Government**	Policies that channel the energy of entrepreneurs in a way that is not self-destructive and is useful to society Self-interest is served in conjunction with the interests of society – the two are not opposed to one another The absence of an active and enlightened governmental role can lead to numerous marketplace abuses as well as tremendous waste of time and resources

too much dominance by the Superego are strongly negative as well. It is vital that the Ego be allowed to come out. It is the interaction between the two that can be the most positive.

Freud believed that early childhood socialization was key and that it is the responsibility of the parents to guide their child's native energy towards a self-identity. Likewise, governments have to play the role of a parent in society and in the economy. While this message may be anathema to many free market acolytes, we see it as an inescapable reality. The only difference is that good governments do it well and achieve great results for their citizens, while bad governments manage to destroy a great deal of potential value.

The policy debate between the pursuit of self-interest and the achievement of public interest is an old one. Adam Smith, the father of free market ideology, leaned heavily towards the promotion of self-interest because the monarchy was completely in charge of all economic assets at the time. Had that not been the case, the downsides of unfettered free markets would have been more evident to Smith. When the government plays a thoughtful and nuanced role in the management of the economy, it enables self-interest to be served in conjunction with the interests of society – the two are by no means inherently opposed to one another.

The Rise of the Nation-Corporation

Many companies today are so large and complex that managing them is akin to running a country (e.g. GE, Toyota and Siemens). The reverse is also becoming increasingly true: countries are increasingly amenable to being managed in ways that are similar to the ways in which companies are managed. Some of the key elements of corporate management that have implications for how countries and blocs are managed are: controlling their own destinies and managing externalities; engaging in formal succession planning to ensure continuity of vision and avoid major disruptions; engaging in strategic planning driven by market forces;

and having processes in place to integrate functional areas (just as countries need to coordinate their bureaucracies).

This approach is already engrained in the governmental mindsets of many up-and-coming countries. Pick up any business newspaper in India, for instance, and you will find references to the country's 'USP' (unique selling proposition), its 'core competencies' and its 'brand equity.' The publication of Michael Porter's landmark *The Competitive Advantage of Nations* in 1990 both explained as well as lent further momentum to this trend of countries seeking to define and refine their sources of competitive and comparative advantage.[238]

Strategic planning (based on understanding and leveraging market processes and forces) is now the hottest thing with governments. This is radically different from the 'planning commission approach' taken by the governments of centrally-controlled economies such as China, India and the Soviet Union in the past. Their 'five-year plans' were based on public ownership and control of resources and the setting of production targets for hundreds of sectors.

We refer to this trend as the 'rise of the nation-corporation.' A classic case in point is Singapore, a country with no natural resources and a tiny domestic market that was able to leverage its one key advantage – a central location – into sustained, long-term prosperity by becoming a highly efficient 'value-added switching hub' for air and sea shipments. Singapore also made itself an attractive manufacturing base for multinationals by investing in a highly sophisticated infrastructure for production. It subsequently took the lead in creating a highly automated, fully-networked society – a vision described as 'the intelligent island' initiative.[239]

A somewhat similar example from another part of the world is Dubai. Dubai is a city-state that has achieved success rivaling that of Singapore, and has become another testament to the power of visionary leadership for achieving radical transformation. In the 19th century, Dubai was known primarily for its role in entrepot trade or as a hub for the transshipment of goods; it also became known as a rich source of pearls. Dubai's importance was magnified because it was on the trade route between the UK and India. After the British left India in 1947, Dubai became a backwater known only for its role as the smuggling capital of the Arabian Gulf, primarily for gold smuggled into India. In recent decades, the ruling family has transformed Dubai into a regional hub for trade and tourism through judicious and farsighted investments. The discovery of oil in 1966 provided the initial resources for developing Dubai as a major port. Today, oil accounts for only 6 percent of Dubai's annual economic output. The country established a tax-free zone to attract foreign businesses, and today 2,600 companies use Dubai as a hub for shipments to and from China. Dubai has invested in a world-class airport (which is served by 100 airlines and whose capacity is being tripled to 60 million passengers a year) and has created a world-class airline (Emirates).[240]

Just as corporations have to anticipate the future and position themselves for long-term success by prudently investing in certain sectors while reducing their investments in others, countries too must increasingly adopt an activist stance in shaping their economic futures. 'Creative destruction' is not just a market process; it is also the deliberate result of corporate decision-making. For example, Kodak is consciously destroying its own chemicals-based film business, even as it invests heavily in digital imaging. GE, HP and IBM have also gone through major transformations. Heads of government need to play a role similar to that of a visionary CEO of a company, steering the national economy toward certain directions and away from others that may have been successful in the past. If they don't do this, the impact of outside forces will be much more dramatic and disruptive when it does come – as it inevitably must.

A Network of Nations

Companies exist in loose networks of suppliers, distributors, outsourcing firms, makers of related products, technology providers and other organizations. All the businesses impact, and are impacted by, each other. They are in co-destiny relationships;

each member shares the fate of the network as a whole. The complex interdependencies make the networks more productive and innovative than they would be as collections of stand-alone companies each pursuing their own profit maximizing agendas.[241]

Gomes-Casseres defines an alliance network as one in which groups of companies link together for a common purpose. Not all companies within a network have to link with one another. The linkages can be formal or informal, ranging from equity joint ventures to loose collaborations. Networks are often created to maximize joint volume and value to increase economies of scale, such as in airline industry networks.[242]

There are several characteristics of networks, each of which has a clear parallel in the case of trade economies:

1. Networks have advantages in battles over technical standards, trade economies likewise will enjoy similar advantages in attempting to set technological standards.
2. Networks enable companies to exploit global scale; trade economies will have a similar benefit for the countries and companies within them.
3. The composition of a network matters as much as its size. The network must cover all the technologies and markets that are crucial to success. Likewise, the composition of each of the trade economies is important; each must contain the 'right' mix of countries with complementary strengths and weaknesses.
4. Networks do have some degree of internal competition. The degree of competition is a matter of network design, usually determined by the leader. Similarly, each trade economy will have a healthy level of internal competition.
5. Networks must have effective collective governance mechanisms. The same is true for each trade economy.
6. Overall, networks that are well-conceived and well-managed will be highly synergistic – their whole is greater that the sum of their parts. This is the fundamental rationale for trade economies as well.[243]

In recent years, many American companies have embraced the alliance network model. For example, Chrysler's turnaround in the early 1990s was largely predicated on the company adopting the Toyota and Honda model of close and long-term relationships with a smaller number of suppliers. This resulted in lower costs, better product quality, faster product development, and higher profits per car – while the company's suppliers were highly profitable as well.[244]

The 'extended enterprise' model enables companies to achieve a 'virtual integration' that has the benefits of vertical integration without some of its drawbacks – such as inflexibility, mutual myopia and the exclusion of other customers or suppliers.

The three trade economies we are describing in this book are analogous to the alliance networks of the business world. Each represents a network or ecosystem of mutually dependent, long-term partner nations that come together to create greater value for each other than they could do by continuing to engage in arms-length trading relationships. The virtual integration of nations achieves most of the benefits of creating a single state without many of its drawbacks.

Restructuring for Competitiveness

In order to maintain its competitiveness with other trade blocs, each trade economy will have to undertake cross-national, intra-bloc restructuring in four areas (Figure 7.2): the realignment of industrial policy, renewal of bloc infrastructure, realignment of international trade and the rationalization of domestic industry. The blocs that are better able to make these changes are likely to be more successful.

Realignment of Industrial Policy

Each bloc (and the countries within it) will have to adopt formal and coordinated industrial policy to ensure that economic development proceeds in a planned and systematic manner. Rather

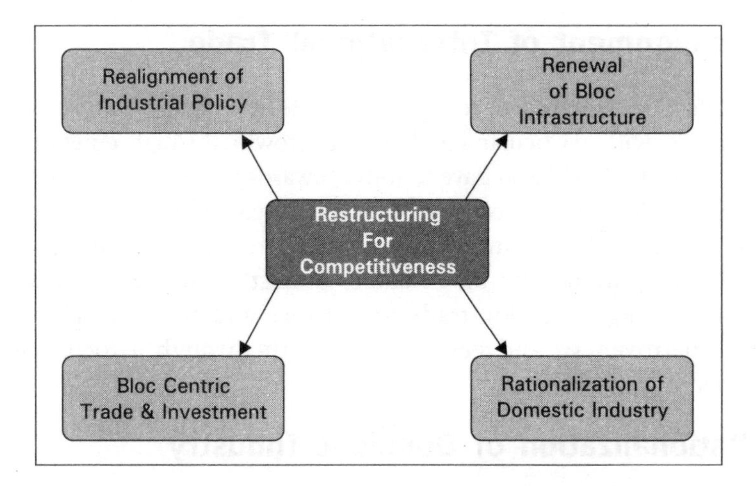

Figure 7.2: Restructuring for Competitiveness

than deploying their energies and resources at cross-purposes, bloc economies can ensure greater prosperity and limited economic dislocation by engaging in such planning. In particular, countries will have to focus on maintaining an ideology free policy; the privatization of public enterprises; providing incentives for quality, innovation and productivity; stimulating economic growth; and ensuring a high degree of environmental compliance.

Renewal of Bloc Infrastructure

Countries and trade blocs must invest to modernize and harmonize various types of their infrastructures. These include a transportation infrastructure to facilitate the movement of people and products; an information infrastructure to enable instantaneous 'any time, any place' sharing information of any kind; an energy infrastructure to reliably deliver any type of energy wherever it is needed; and a financial infrastructure to collect, manage and invest financial resources. There are also other infrastructures that are important and essential – infrastructures for water, waste and education, for instance.

Realignment of International Trade

Trade blocs will have to realign their trade flows within and across regions, with particular emphasis on growth through emerging markets. Each will also have to move towards a common currency. This chapter will discuss how blocs will have to address areas such as encouraging more intra-company trade; realigning of currency; promoting more intra-bloc trade to protect the domestic sector; encouraging inter-bloc trade to enhance and maintain global competitiveness; and generating growth through a focus on emerging markets.

Rationalization of Domestic Industry

Countries in each bloc will have to rationalize their domestic industries. This will include taking steps to facilitate sector specialization and focus, removal of governmental subsidies, permitting industry consolidation when appropriate, regionalizing domestic and global markets, and promoting bloc level standards and resource mobility.

In the next four chapters, we discuss each of these in detail.

Chapter 8

Realignment of Industrial Policy

How Ireland Became the Celtic Tiger

In the late 1980s, Ireland was widely regarded as a laggard in economic and social development. By the late 1990s, Ireland was growing faster than any other economy in the world. What happened to change its fortunes so abruptly?

This was not just the free market at work. Rather, it was the result of some very conscious policy initiatives by the Irish government, aided by heavy inflows of development funding from the European Union.

For centuries, Ireland had been known as a rural backwater with hardly any industrial base. Centuries of bloody conflict created a country known widely for its poverty, fueling the widespread emigration of many of its citizens to the US and other countries in the early 20th century. After gaining independence from Britain in the 1940s, the country had little on which to build a base of prosperity. The government sought to encourage foreign direct investment; however, the domestic market was tiny, and Ireland lacked access to export markets.

Despite its economic woes, the government in the 1950s took three steps that have paid off in the long-run: investing in higher education, lowering the corporate tax rate for exporting companies (Irish or foreign) to 10 percent (compared to 50 percent for other firms), and most importantly, joining the EU in 1973. The combination, over time, made Ireland a very attractive base for US companies, with low taxes, a highly trained English-speaking workforce, and ready access to the European market.[245]

By 1987, the economy was on the verge of bankruptcy, with a huge national debt and one of the highest unemployment rates in the developed world. By 1990, though, an unmistakable turnaround was in progress. The government maintained a consistent macroeconomic policy and continued to invest in infrastructure and education (aided by funds from the EU). It also created a 'social partnership' across the public, private and non-governmental sectors. Ireland's Industrial Development Authority (IDA) aggressively and carefully harnessed these advantages to attract companies in three or four key industries: ICT (information and communication technologies), pharmaceuticals and health-care, financial services and what is called the international service industry – software, customer service and support and shared service activities. The IDA's strategy was to target some of the world's most successful companies in these sectors, and it worked spectacularly well.[246]

There is no question that Ireland's membership in the EU was a critical factor in its economic rebirth. In addition to market access, the EU provided Ireland with billions of dollars of development assistance (so called 'structural and cohesion funds') starting in the 1990s, which allowed the government to continue spending on infrastructure and education while it tried to curtail its budget deficit. The EU also imposed a planning discipline that had previously been lacking in Ireland; structural funds had to be deployed under a six-year plan, necessitating a long-term approach to development.

Over 1,000 foreign companies now have a presence in Ireland. The country has embarked on an ambitious set of initiatives designed to foster an 'innovation culture' in the country. The National Development plan for 2002–2006 calls for investing 52 billion euros in infrastructure (in a country of just four million people), including 2.5 billion euros on research, technology and innovation. The initiative appears to be paying off; according to the annual Global Entrepreneurship Monitor, Ireland has the highest rate of entrepreneurial activity in Europe.[247]

An Active Role for Governments

We ended the last chapter with a Freudian analogy to show how governments need to play a role in harnessing 'wild' market forces. Natural forces of any kind must be properly harnessed in order to become socially useful. For example, many rivers are wild, and can be very destructive if allowed to remain the way they were created by nature. By thoughtfully and systematically channeling the potential of such forces of nature, societies can generate many social goods, from improved irrigation for agriculture to the generation of electricity. Of course, this must be done right – if not, it can result in terrible long-term ecological damage and social displacement.

In the economic arena, this calls for the adoption by governments of thoughtful, well-considered industrial policy. In contrast with Europe and particularly Asia (e.g. Singapore and Japan), the US has traditionally been reluctant to adopt a formal industrial policy, preferring to allow market forces alone to determine the direction that industries take. Given the broad economic success that the US has enjoyed so far, it would seem to be difficult to argue against such an approach. However, the world in the future will be quite a different place than it has been in the past half-century or so, and the US (and Americas trade bloc in general) will have to adopt a more explicit industrial policy than it has done before. Otherwise, it will find itself increasingly disadvantaged by rival blocs that use active industrial policy to target more industries where the US currently enjoys certain natural advantages.

It could be argued that the *absence* of a more active, interventionist industrial policy by the US government has contributed to the diminishment of US competitiveness and global presence in industries such as consumer electronics and, more recently, wireless communications. In the case of the latter, the proliferation of incompatible standards has placed US manufacturers of cellular equipment and handsets at a distinct disadvantage to their European and Asian counterparts, where governments played a more active role in setting standards. Likewise, the government's hands-off approach has kept the penetration of broadband Internet connectivity at a level far lower (22 percent of homes) than that in many other countries. South Korea, for example, has opened up an impressive advantage in both the penetration (69 percent) as well as average speed of broadband networks.[248]

Governments need to provide well thought out incentives to encourage industry to evolve in particular ways. Incentives usually are of two types. 'Push' incentives are provided on the supply side, in order to overcome initial barriers to production and to create new markets. This is clearly needed in social and environmental areas (e.g. funding for a vaccine for AIDS/HIV or R&D for alternative sources of energy such as cell fuels). Generally, new markets are created through new technology. Therefore, push incentives should be directed at encouraging upstream activities, such as R&D, the development of a shared infrastructure or refining manufacturing capabilities. For example, Germany has always been a strong exporter, far more so than its size would warrant. One reason is that the German government years ago instituted a policy that once an exporter's product was out of the factory, the exporter had to take no risk whatsoever; the government insured the transaction. That is why Germans were able to respond to export orders very quickly; there was no risk of collection.

Pull incentives are given on the consumption side to induce customers to buy. Often, the key problem for consumers is affordability, and financing is therefore a key issue to the consumption sector. This is what the US government did for real estate purchases when it helped create an entire industry of savings and loan institutions and provided tax benefits for home ownership.

The targeting of industries for global dominance, as Japan has done, is going to become more popular for several reasons. First, as the world moves towards bigger markets, countries will have to focus their resources on particular industries that are better suited to become bloc or globally dominant. The second reason goes back to classical trade theory: countries should do more of what they are good at. Once its strengths are identified, it makes sense for a country to move rapidly to focus its efforts in those areas. The third reason is that governments are able to galvanize the nation towards a common vision through targeting. India has been successfully doing this in recent years, targeting the software and pharmaceutical industries for an expanded role in world markets.

The onus falls on governments to play an active role in this because the market process can be pretty inefficient at targeting. Market processes are strictly evolutionary; they take much too long, they basically operate on trial and error, and live by maxims such as 'the survival of the fittest.' Targeting, by definition, calls for some sort of an intervention, and thus much more of an active role for the government. For example, most basic manufacturing has left the US, which has become an economy dominated by services and high-end non-labor intensive manufacturing. The same end-result could have been recognized upfront, and expedited on a more proactive basis once it was clear that it was going to happen down the road anyway. The death of an industry is a tremendous human tragedy; communities are destroyed, people are displaced, the tax base is decimated. Instead of watching an industry that is clearly doomed go through this painful process, it is better for governments to facilitate a smooth transition to a new business model.

Any kind of fundamentalism – whether market based, heritage or culture based, or religion based – is inherently wrong. We believe that the time has come to discard dogmas concerning market processes versus public policy. Of course, free markets are very desirable and generally highly effective, but they have to be tempered with sound public policy initiatives. The 'visible' hand of public policy is an important element in bringing about the goal of sustainable, positive-sum growth throughout the world. This debate came up frequently in the early 1990s, but then the tide shifted against it, especially as Japan's dominance declined. However, Japan's collapse had far more to do with needed financial reforms than with shortcomings in its industrial policy.

A purist free market economist would argue that the 'visible hand' approach could never be better than the 'invisible hand' of the market. We disagree. The US essentially lost the global cellular telephony industry by relying only on market processes at a time when the Europeans were taking an activist approach in the sector. Plus, it is important to emphasize that the visible hand should never try to move in the opposite direction of what the invisible hand would do; it should simply guide and channel market forces in a 'natural' direction.

Countries in each of the three trade blocs will have to realign their industrial policies, paying particular attention to the following:

- Ideology free policy
- Privatization of public enterprises
- Incentives for quality, innovation and productivity
- Stimulating economic growth
- Environmental compliance

Ideology Free Policy

Governmental policy within each bloc must become less dogmatic and ideology-driven and more pragmatic and market-driven. By ideology, we mean any strongly held perspective. If any trade bloc over-emphasizes ideology (such as religious or social ideology, or excessive nationalism), it is likely to fail. Trade blocs that demonstrate greater pragmatism will be more successful.

The key to this is that one shared ideology – a market-orientation – replaces all divisive ones. Gradually, free market forces are injected into virtually all areas of society. US President Bill Clinton did this remarkably well in the 1990s. For example, he converted the US welfare system to a 'workfare' system without any political hiccups, getting Congress to enact landmark welfare-to-work legislation in 1996. He was able to achieve this because he had a strong economic growth engine going. In 1993, there were over 14 million individuals on welfare in the US, representing 5.5 percent of the population – the highest percentage ever. By 2000, the number had been reduced to 5.8 million, representing just 2.1 percent of the population – the lowest percentage since 1963. As of June 2003, there were only 4.95 million individuals on welfare, or less than 2 percent of the population.[249]

So how are the three trade blocs likely to fare on this score? This dimension is likely to be a significant source of comparative advantage or differentiation across the blocs. Our conclusion is quite straightforward: the most ideology free trade bloc will be Asia Pacific. The region has a minimal religious base; the dominant religions of the world that have had huge influence elsewhere and have been the source of much religious strife (Christianity and Islam) are practiced by relatively few people in Asia. There is also no longer a strong belief system based on social policy after the collapse of Communism. So there is nothing in Asia's history that will come in the way of moving towards a market-oriented economy. The Asian trade bloc is highly pragmatic; countries there have been able to move beyond the dictates of their history much more quickly than in any other region. For example, Thailand today welcomes Japanese tourists in a big way, despite the memory of atrocities committed by Japanese soldiers during World War II.

After their disastrous experiment with Communism (which continues in name only), the Chinese have become the ultimate pragmatists. Consider China and Taiwan. Despite their history and all their differences, they are doing a great deal of business together. Though direct trade between China and Taiwan was cut off in 1949 when the countries split after a civil war, trade between the two is now growing at over 25 percent annually, and already exceeds $50 billion a year. Most of the cross-strait trade takes place indirectly, through Hong Kong.

Japan and China first fought a war in 1894–95, for control of Korea. They fought the second Sino-Japanese War from 1937 to 1945. Japanese forces occupied virtually the whole coast of

China, and committed severe war atrocities, especially in the capital, Nanking. Today, there is a huge flow of economic activity between the two countries; Japan is now China's number one trade partner, while for Japan, China ranks second after the US. Two-way trade between the countries totaled a record $132.4 billion in 2003, and Japanese direct investment in China rose 50 percent to $7.96 billion.[250]

South Korea and Japan have been able to overcome the bitter legacy of 35 years of colonial rule to become close economic allies. The two countries now enjoy over $45 billion a year in two-way trade and are discussing a bilateral free trade agreement.

Europe will have the hardest time on this dimension. Religion may become an issue, especially in Southern Europe. Once Islamic countries from the Middle East join the trade bloc (adding to already sizable Islamic populations in Germany and France), religious diversity will rise, and religious strife could follow unless it is managed properly. Another potential area of concern is social ideology, especially in relation to health care and education. The Nordic states, even today, believe strongly in a firm social safety net. Germany still has a very generous welfare system. Europe also has a strong presence of unions; they have not been able to curtail the power of unions to nearly the degree that the US has. In general, Europe is bound by many more traditions than the other blocs, which becomes a liability in the move towards economic pragmatism.

Privatization of Public Enterprises

All three trade blocs still have a strong presence of public sector enterprises. These 'assets' are in many cases a huge burden on the taxpayers and on the governments. In order to be competitive, countries and trade blocs will have to privatize most state-owned commercial enterprises, reducing the direct role of the state in the economy to a bare minimum.

Inspired by the success of the 'Chicago boys' (mostly Milton Friedman's former students, who became key financial decision makers) in reviving the moribund Chilean economy in the 1970s, British Prime Minister Margaret Thatcher initiated a massive program of privatization in 1979. The benefits of shifting assets from public to private ownership were seen as two-fold: the discipline of private ownership and capital markets would greatly increase economic efficiency, and substantial amounts of money would be raised for state coffers.[251]

The impact of this sea change in governmental participation and control of the economy has been huge. The share of the GDP controlled by state-owned entities in Britain dropped from 12 percent in 1979 to a mere 2 percent in 1997, when Tony Blair became prime minister. Other countries in Europe have followed suit, though none have been able to go as far as the British. Even the Socialist Jospin government in France raised a total of $18.1 billion through two offerings of France Telecom in 1997 and 1998. Germany has sold shares in Deutsche Telekom. Spain and Portugal have embraced privatization: Spain sold Iberia, the national flag carrier, in 2001. All told, between 1990 and 2002, European governments raised a total of $675 billion through privatization.

Privatization has become a worldwide phenomenon, accounting for 30 of the 35 largest ever share offerings. It rapidly spread from Europe back to Latin America (where it had actually originated). Now India, after decades of being burdened with a highly inefficient but dominant state-owned sector, is moving aggressively to privatize. Two extreme examples of the inefficiency of state-owned enterprises: an airport hotel in New Delhi with a 3 percent occupancy rate and inoperable toilets, and a fertilizer company in West Bengal that had produced nothing in 14 years.

India is now in the midst of a three-year campaign to divest the 250 companies controlled by the central government. So far, stakes in 34 companies have been sold, including India's long-distance telephone company and its largest automaker, as well as companies producing aluminum, petrochemicals and zinc. India plans to sell off oil companies, shipping concerns, and hotels, and is expected to largely privatize its banking sector, which was nationalized in the early 1970s. It is also likely to privatize its two state-owned airlines and many airports. Some of the sales have been spectacularly successful. For example, the offering of shares in Maruti, the carmaker, was oversubscribed ten times and triggered a bull market on the Bombay Stock Exchange that stalled only when a new government was elected in May 2004 and signaled that it would be more cautious in continuing the policy.

Achieving this was not easy, as the previous Indian government faced entrenched opposition from trade unions. However, it demonstrated a newfound sense of resolve in the matter. For example, in March 2001, strikers opposing the sale of Bharat Aluminum went on a hunger strike, threatening to fast until they died. The minister in charge of privatization was unmoved, and the strike ended in three weeks.[252]

To appreciate the potential impact of privatization, countries have to consider their 'balance sheets,' not just their 'income statements.' The governments of many countries have acquired assets that have huge economic value. Just as in selling a house, they must spruce up the assets before making a sale. China is doing an excellent job in this area, as has Mexico with Telmex and Japan with NTT. Venezuela's Petromas is a world-class oil company. The key point is that in regards to state enterprises, only the largest are capable of becoming global enterprises. For example, Duetsche Telecom is now expanding all over Europe, and NTT will become a global player. These are all giant enterprises waiting for their value to be unlocked through privatization and the removal of previous restraints on what they are permitted to do.

Starting in mid-1990s, the Chinese government kicked its privatization program into high gear, with a policy of 'keeping the large and releasing the small' and 'strategic realignment of the state-owned economy.' After initially privatizing only small and midsize firms, the government has proceeded to privatize large state-owned enterprises that compete with the private sector.[253] Provincial governments have been given the authority to dispose of state-owned enterprises in their domains and retain the resulting income. This has become a significant incentive for them to promote privatization even more aggressively. As a result of these efforts, there was a 40 percent decline in the number of state-owned enterprises between 1996 and 2001.

A key factor keeping the status quo going is that public sector enterprises were always used for political patronage. However, this must be overcome if countries are to make progress.

We are not advocating that governments get out of everything. But they do need to learn how to improve the efficiency of what they do through downsizing, outsourcing and privatization. A strong incentive for governments is to raise money, which can be used to reduce debt, pay for needed social programs, etc.

In assessing how the three emerging trade blocs stack up on this, it is immediately evident that the US has a big advantage because it has always had a minimal amount of public sector enterprise. The rest of the Americas trade bloc does have a challenge on its hands, though the process of privatization has been underway in the region for nearly two decades already, especially in sectors such as telecommunications.

We believe that this challenge will be met in Asia as well. This is China's biggest opportunity to change, since it still has massive public sector enterprises in numerous industries. Many are being prepared for privatization, and are likely to be major forces in their industries virtually from day one.

Europe is likely to have the most difficult time achieving a high level of privatization, though as we wrote above, the region has made considerable progress on this dimension already.

Incentives for Quality, Innovation and Productivity

Each trade bloc will have to provide incentives for quality, innovation and productivity, as these are the platforms for global competition. Governments should give incentives to the private sector to encourage all three, as well as invest in them directly. For example, to generate innovation, the US has invested huge amounts of public money to fund R&D for defense, agriculture and health care.

The Quality Movement's Impact on Japan

The origins of 'Total Quality Management' (TQM) can be traced to the development of Statistical Quality Control (SQC) in the

1930s, specifically the invention of the control chart by W.A. Shewart of Bell Labs. The impact of SQC was so great that many believed it helped the Allies win World War II. Indeed, American quality control techniques were treated as military secrets until after the war.[254]

In 1946, the US Occupation Force in Japan was charged with reviving Japan's communications equipment industry, so that General Douglas MacArthur could undertake to educate the Japanese public about what the US intended to do there. Homer Sarasohn, an engineer from MIT, headed the Civil Communication Section (CCS), and was put in charge of restarting the industry, including repairing and installing equipment, establishing an equipment test laboratory (ETL) and setting quality standards. Since wartime managers could not be employed in positions of responsibility, new recruits were brought in to run the factories but they proved to be highly inept. The CCS started to train Japanese engineers and managers in management techniques, including SQC. The Union of Japanese Scientists and Engineers (JUSE) wanted more training, and asked the CCS to bring in an expert. Since Shewart was not available, Sarasohn recommended W. Edwards Deming, a Columbia University professor.

For two months in 1950, Deming trained hundreds of engineers and managers in SQC. So great was his influence that the Deming Prize was established soon thereafter and was first awarded in 1952 to Koji Kabayashi, whom Sarasohn had appointed president of NEC. In 1954, JUSE invited Joseph M. Juran to come to Japan and teach managers how to promote quality efforts. This marked a shift from dealing primarily with technology and manufacturing to overall total quality management, spanning company-wide education in quality control, the use of QC circles and audits, and the promotion of quality management principles.[255]

By 1960, JUSE had trained 20,000 engineers in SQC methods, and Deming was declared a 'living treasure' by Japan's emperor. The Prime Minister awarded him the Second Order of the Sacred Treasure to recognize the role he had played in reviving Japanese manufacturing.

Over time, the Japanese advanced quality management techniques beyond what they had learned from Deming and Juran. In 1965, Bridgestone Tires released a report summarizing the quality management practices of companies that had been awarded the Deming Prize. The techniques came to be known as Hoshin Kanri, and were soon widely accepted and practiced throughout Japan. In the 1980s, some Japanese divisions or subsidiaries of US companies, including Hewlett-Packard's YHP unit, Fuji-Xerox and a Japanese manufacturing facility of Texas Instruments, were awarded the Deming Prize. This resulted in the adoption of Hoshin practices in the US by their parent companies.[256] In 1987, going full circle, the US Congress established the Malcolm Baldrige award to recognize US companies for achievement in quality and overall business excellence. Thus, the Japanese inspired the US to renew its commitment to the principles of TQM, after having learned the same from US companies and experts more than 40 years earlier!

At the trade bloc level, we could say that Europe is No. 1. This is because most of the markets there are mature. The Americas are second; while the US has generally high quality standards, its emerging trading partners, namely Brazil and India, bring down the overall rating. In the US, quality is purely driven by the market; in Asia and Europe, it is more regulated or mandated by the government.

Asia (other than Japan) is still lagging today, but is rapidly gaining ground. In recent years, quality levels for Taiwanese and South Korean products have risen rapidly; for example, in the 2004 J.D. Power and Associates Initial Quality Study, South Korean brands outpaced both European and US brands, having cut initial quality problems by 57 percent in six years.[257] Asian companies and governments clearly realize that they cannot compete without attention to quality.

China is now investing in quality in a big way. Starting in 2003, China requires a new certification mark for products marketed and distributed within the country. The new mark, CCC (China Compulsory Certification), replaces China's two 'old' marks – CCIB (safety approval) and CCEE (Great Wall approval). The new system requires manufacturers of 132 product categories to obtain the CCC mark before exporting those products to China or selling them in the Chinese market. Products not meeting CCC requirements can be held at the border and are subject to other penalties. Attaining the CCC mark is difficult and expensive for organizations seeking to enter the Chinese marketplace, especially since it usually requires in-country testing. Not all information is available in English, making it essential for foreign companies to seek assistance from Chinese experts.[258]

Innovation and Intellectual Property Rights

As the world moves ever faster towards knowledge-centered economies, intellectual property rights (IPRs), which include patents, copyrights, and trademarks, have become a prominent issue in economic policymaking at the national, regional and global levels. We expect that each trade bloc will eventually have its own patent system.

During the 1990s, many countries moved unilaterally to beef up their laws to protect IPR. The World Trade Organization successfully completed an Agreement on Trade-Related Aspects of Intellectual Property Rights (TRIPs), through which member countries committed to protecting IPRs.

The benefits of stronger IPR enforcement are clear. Foremost among these is the increase in incentives for innovation and the returns on international technology transfers. On the downside, it increases the costs of acquiring new technology and gives technology producers an edge over technology consumers with respect to global terms of trade.[259]

The conventional view on IPR has been that these are almost exclusively to the benefit of mature, developed economies. While this may have been largely true in the past, it is not the case any more. China and India, in particular, have potentially a great more to gain than lose by better enforcement of IPR. Both countries have huge pools of trained scientific manpower, and are beginning to generate technological breakthroughs on their own as well as through domestic research labs run by multinationals. In industries such as software, consumer electronics, biotechnology and pharmaceuticals, India and China are likely to generate substantial new knowledge and intellectual property in years to come. China is already No. 6 in patent filings, and we predict that it will become No. 2. Though it hasn't adequately done so yet, India needs to emphasize the same thing.

Currently, the Americas trade bloc is the most aggressive in protecting the IP rights of its citizens and companies. Asia is last, almost by default, given the rampant piracy (movies, music, software, fake branded products) that prevails there. The Europeans are in the middle.

The Government's Role in Raising Productivity

Improving productivity at the national and bloc level is vital to raising living standards. A major driver of productivity is the quality of the overall infrastructure, which we will discuss in the next chapter. Beyond that, the government can play an important role in raising productivity by investing in and facilitating automation and integration. Uniquely among societal institutions, governments are in a position to mandate or at least greatly accelerate the adoption of technology in general and information technology in particular. For example, the US government is steadily moving towards the automation of tax filings and patent applications. Many state governments in the US have also automated many common services they provide to residents, including processes related to the Department of Motor Vehicles. Governments throughout the world have used the Internet to great advantage to provide more convenience to citizens at lower cost.

The government can also provide incentives for the market to move in the direction of greater efficiency and productivity. For example, the US government is now proposing the automation of all record keeping for healthcare. Such automation will displace labor, which becomes a political issue. The government can provide training for displaced workers to make career transitions. This is something the US does not do very well; it relies on the market to address the need.

Stimulating Economic Growth

Politicians who are unable to create jobs soon lose their own. There is, of course, no magic wand that a politician can wave to create jobs. Jobs come from economic growth: pure and simple. A stagnant economy with little or no growth cannot create new jobs. So the first job of political leadership is to generate economic growth, even in economies that are otherwise mature.

As we have stressed in this book, and as economists have pointed out since the age of Ricardo, no country can grow its economy in a vacuum, and any country that seeks to create growth at the expense of another will not succeed for long. The only way to create sustainable economic growth, and the job growth that comes with it, is through mutually beneficial trade partnerships with complementary economies.

With such approaches, there is immediate job creation in developing countries through the outsourcing of manufacturing and now service sector jobs. The greater challenge is to generate growth in the mature economy from which such jobs are being displaced. Part of the answer comes from rising demand for the output of the mature economy in the developing country, as a result of its rising purchasing power. Another part of the answer is that governments in the mature economies have to invest in transitioning industries and in retraining programs. For example, there is a shortage of 250,000 nurses in the US currently. The government should have stepped in earlier to encourage the creation of more nursing programs. The state of North Carolina has done a good job of phasing tobacco farmers out and creating more high tech jobs. Virginia has done the same thing. On the other hand, Wisconsin and Oregon have not done much to reduce their dependence on the agriculture sector.

Comparing the three trade blocs on their ability to provide employment, Asia is in the best position currently, as it is seeing an influx of jobs (through the outsourcing of services from developed countries and export-oriented manufacturing) as well as creating its own through growth in domestic demand (though unemployment or underemployment is still a major problem in many countries). The Americas bloc, especially if India is included, comes next. The US has a relatively low unemployment rate compared to most developed economies. This is even more impressive considering that the US has a far higher proportion of its population in the workforce than any other industrialized nation, including young teenagers, most women and many elderly. Most unemployment in the US is of just a few months' duration, compared with endemic long-term unemployment in many other countries. The US has a high availability of good jobs for educated people, with virtually no unemployment for college graduates. Notably, the workforce in the US has seen a tremendous influx of women in the last three decades, as the proportion of women working full-time has risen rapidly. The economy has been able to absorb all of these new workers with little strain – a remarkable accomplishment. The US is also the only country that has a broad continuing-education system. As a result, people can retool to move from one type of work to another. This is not as easy to do in Europe or Japan.[260]

Job growth is a key short-term vulnerability for Europe. Since most of the countries within the bloc are already mature economies, there is little potential for job growth unless Europe is able to tap into some emerging nations. However, the largest emerging nations – China, India, Brazil and Mexico – are going to be part of other blocs. This makes it even more urgent that Europe look to integrate countries with sizable populations and strong growth potential – such as Russia, Turkey, Iran, Egypt, South Africa and even Iraq – sooner rather than later.

European unemployment rates have been stubbornly high for a long time, with some exceptions. Jobless rates in German, France and Italy have been around 9 percent, while the overall unemployment in the 'Euro area' stood at 8.9 percent in 2004. Contrast this with a rate of 5 percent in the US in 2005. Economists have suggested that high tax burdens, high welfare benefits and lack of flexibility in hiring and firing workers all contribute to Europe's high rate of unemployment. Britain has managed to bring its rate down to 4.8 percent through greater labor flexibility, though its welfare state is proportionately larger than that of the US. As a consequence, the wage differential in Britain is now greater than in other parts of Europe. On the other hand, the Netherlands has lowered its unemployment rate by shrinking its welfare state while preserving job security. Finally, Ireland has lowered its unemployment rate to 4.8 percent through a combination of labor market flexibility and aggressive promotion of export-oriented development.[261]

Environmental Compliance

Economic growth that is accompanied by environmental devastation is a Faustian bargain indeed. Few issues today are more self-evidently important than the need for *sustainable* economic development, which results in greater prosperity with no degradation of the environment.

The US environment has been improving over the past few decades, due to less heavy manufacturing, stricter regulations and the innovative injection of market forces (e.g. the granting and trading of pollution rights, known as the 'cap and trade' program). Overall, air quality in the US improved 42 percent between 1980 and 1997, based on the air-quality index. Likewise, water quality improved 27 percent since 1980. The number and amount of oil spills also declined over the past 20 years.[262]

Data from 2002 indicate that:

- Since 1970, emissions of six principal air pollutants have been cut 48 percent.
- Sulfur dioxide emissions from power plants were 41 percent lower than 1980.
- Nitrogen oxides emissions from power plants showed a 33 percent decline from 1990.

This impressive environmental progress comes even as the country has experienced a 164 percent increase in gross domestic product, a 42 percent increase in energy consumption and a 155 percent increase in vehicle miles traveled.[263]

Clearly, the US has made great strides in arresting and even reversing its environmental decline. However, the rest of the Americas are in poor shape (e.g. Mexico City, Santiago, Sao Paulo). Overall, we assess Europe as the leader, followed by the Americas and then Asia. Though many parts of Eastern Europe were in disastrous shape environmentally at the end of the Communist phase (such as many areas of East Germany), many of the countries are making progress in cleaning up the environment.

Going forward, the anticipated economic development could lead to very adverse environmental impact. The explosive growth in energy consumption by China and India, unless properly dealt with and managed, could have devastating environmental implications.

Summary Assessment of Trade Blocs

Our summary assessment is that the Americas trade bloc is best placed on the realignment of industrial policy, while Europe has significant challenges. The challenges for Europe are primarily in three areas: shedding ideologies when formulating economic policy, speeding up true privatization (i.e. relinquishing governmental control as well as ownership fully) and generating greater employment by stimulating growth. For Asia, the challenges are to rapidly improve quality and productivity, and to foster a better climate for innovation by affording stronger protection for intellectual property rights. Several of Asia's fast growing economies, such as China, Indonesia and Thailand, face potentially devastating environmental degradation in years to come unless they move quickly to reverse the slide.

Chapter 9

Renewal of Bloc Infrastructure

Singapore, a small island and city-state located at the southern tip of the Malay peninsula, has been the site of astonishing economic and technological achievements. Singapore's story demonstrates the capacity of a country with almost no natural resources to create economic advantages with influence far beyond its region. It represents one scenario for what can happen when a government assumes an instrumental role in shaping and managing the economic environment. Singapore's success is reflected in its ranking as the world's second most competitive economy in 2004 (after the US), and years of consistently ranking high prior to that.[264]

Reduced to its essentials, Singapore's economic strategy has been straightforward: it has leveraged its single natural advantage of strategic location by establishing world class transportation and materials handling facilities; extended such 'hubbing' into the financial and other service domains by establishing a sophisticated communications and information technology infrastructure and continually upgraded the skills of its workforce to keep up with the ever more challenging demands placed on it.

Singapore's strategy reflects an emphasis on the 'four flows' that are essential for economic vitality: people, products, money and information.

- ***People***: Singapore's Changi Airport is a well-oiled operation widely acclaimed for its aesthetics and efficiency. Though it has had extraordinary success worldwide, a conscious decision was made to disconnect Singapore Airlines (SA) from the airport. The company realized that it could make more money by serving other airlines under the 'open skies' approach. SA excels in baggage handling, kitchen services, reservations, etc., and has been able to handle those services for the many other airlines that have made Changi a key base for their regional operations. Changi has become a hub for most north-south traffic in the region, such as from Australia to China. The Singapore subway, likewise a model of cleanliness and efficiency, was completed in the 1980s, two years ahead of schedule and under budget. Its development reflects the government's pragmatic approach to infrastructure development. By reclaiming several large parcels of land from the sea and using the profits from selling leases on the land to pay for the subway, the government simultaneously developed an important infrastructure element, expanded prime real estate and attracted more overseas investors.
- ***Products***: Singapore's port, one of the largest in the world, handles cargo more efficiently and at rates lower than any other port in the world. Hundreds of information technology applications have been implemented to streamline every aspect of its operations. Given the symbiotic relationship between Singapore's airport and seaport, it can complete sea-to-air shipments in a matter of hours, faster than anywhere else.
- ***Money***: Singapore has a stable currency, an extensive international banking system, no restrictions on the flow of foreign exchange, and many private investment companies.
- ***Information***: Singapore has one of the most advanced information infrastructures in the world, encompassing high-speed Internet access and ubiquitous wireless communications (well over 80 percent penetration and now moving to third generation technology).[265] The government

early on set a policy that Singtel (the state-owned phone company) would always have the most modern technology possible. It also set a policy that every outbound international call would be cheaper than a corresponding inbound call. This caused a great deal of telephone traffic – especially between Japan and the US – to be switched in Singapore.

The Importance of Infrastructure

Arthur C. Clarke, the well-known author and futurist, has observed that if it weren't for the telegraph and the railroads (which provided the communications and distribution infrastructures for the industrial age), the United States probably would not exist. It is widely recognized today that a nation's competitive advantage derives in large measure from the quality of its infrastructure. The same will be true at the trade bloc level as well.

As Robert Reich has observed, fluid movements of raw materials, finished goods, capital and technological know-how characterize the global economy; the only elements that cannot flow freely across borders are people and infrastructure. These elements are crucial drivers of a nation or trade bloc's competitive advantage.[266]

In this chapter, we focus on four major types of infrastructure – all essential for the well-being of a country or trade bloc. First, transportation infrastructure to facilitate the movement of people and products; second, information infrastructure to enable instantaneous 'any time, any place' sharing of any amounts of information of any kind; third, energy infrastructure to reliably deliver any kind of energy wherever it is needed; and fourth, financial infrastructure to collect, manage and invest financial resources.

Other important infrastructures include those for education, public health, human services, and water and waste. A sound legal system is also a crucial infrastructure element; it is said, 'A foreign investor is more interested in the answer to the question – whether his property rights are protected under the law – than in the availability and accessibility of electricity lines.'[267]

A good infrastructure must be sharable, ubiquitous, easy to use and cost effective.[268] Any infrastructure that does not meet all these criteria will fail to serve its basic purpose: to facilitate and expand its own usage. The more intensively an infrastructure is utilized, the more it contributes to economic wealth creation. Conversely, an idle infrastructure with huge amounts of excess capacity is an enormous drain on the economy.

Any economic system is constrained by its weakest links; fixing those weak links can thus have a dramatic impact on productivity and prosperity. Each trade bloc must ensure that all its infrastructures are built, operated and maintained at a high level of efficiency and effectiveness.

The development of infrastructure may appear to be a somewhat mundane and boring matter; it is anything but that in today's world. Indeed, it is too critical an issue to be left to purely market processes. Governments must set priorities and provide incentives to ensure steady yet stable infrastructure development.

Governments often, but by no means always, make infrastructure investments. In the US, the road transport network has largely been publicly financed; however, most other infrastructures are predominantly in private hands. Even the rail network, almost exclusively developed by governments in the rest of the world, was developed by the private sector in the US.

Infrastructure costs cannot be loaded onto transaction costs without significantly depressing demand. The costs of creating infrastructure are enormous, and usually cannot be absorbed by any one company on the basis of its own requirements. Nor can a single company afford to maintain and upgrade an infrastructure once it is built. Bringing about a comprehensive infrastructure is therefore impossible without coordinated and visionary public policy. In the case of the US information infrastructure, for instance, cable, telephony and satellite companies have been working at cross-purposes to develop competing broadband infrastructures. Capital is being wastefully deployed to create overlapping, substitutable assets. This dilemma can only be resolved through the catalytic effects of public policy. Rather than merely adjudicating between rival industries seeking to define and dominate the future infrastructure, the government must play a more visionary role: determining national and trade bloc interests, facilitating a speedy and coordinated movement in that direction, and ensuring that the resulting infrastructure is inclusive and not exclusive.

Infrastructure and Economic Development

Public investment in infrastructure results in rising productivity and thus faster economic development. Of course, not all investments in infrastructure are equally effective.

In the US, annual public investment in infrastructure was about 2.5 percent of GDP in the 1950s and 1960s. By the 1990s, it had dropped to about 1 percent of GDP; the reduction was due to the completion of the national highway system in the 1970s, and a gradual shifting of governmental spending priorities towards social programs starting in the 1960s (President Johnson's Great Society initiative). As US productivity growth slowed significantly in the 1980s, there was renewed interest in infrastructure investments.

Generally, economists have had little influence in determining what kinds of public investments should be made. Many have underestimated the value of infrastructure, as they tend to take a micro rather than macro view of such investments. Many major infrastructure projects have thus been undertaken on faith. For example, the interstate highway system was built because there was a perceived need to tie the country together for defense reasons.[269] Similarly, the Internet infrastructure was originally built and used for defense purposes (ARPANET).

There is now a large body of research that has established that public investments can generate very large returns to society – in many cases far exceeding the returns generated by private capital. In the 1950s and 1960s, rates of return on public investments in infrastructure exceeded 30 percent, well above returns on private investments in the same time period. By the 1990s, the returns had fallen to 10 to 15 percent.[270]

Research has also shown that the benefits of investment in infrastructure tend to be far greater for developing countries than for developed countries. The reasons for this are quite evident, but it does illustrate the essential dilemma for developing countries: most cannot afford infrastructure investments because they are poorly developed industrially, but their industrial development cannot pick up without such investments. The World Bank can help to some degree, but in the future, investing in the infrastructures of developing countries will be one of the biggest growth opportunities for governments and corporations from developed countries, especially those in the same trade bloc economy.[271]

It is important to emphasize that not all the benefits of good infrastructure can be captured in purely economic terms. In addition to the primary benefit of enhancing the standard of living by raising productivity (ready availability of electricity and running water, for example), a superior infrastructure can also enhance the quality of life. For example, the impact of cell phones and cable television in rural areas can be huge. This can be just as important, or more important, than raising the standard of living.[272]

The education system is a key element of infrastructure. As an economy develops, a poor education system can become a critical bottleneck; the more advanced the economy, the greater the need for skilled, educated workers. Education is important at all levels – primary, secondary and post-secondary. Cross-country studies have found positive, statistically significant correlations between schooling levels and GDP growth on a per capita basis. The data show an average of 0.3 percent faster annual growth in per-capita GDP over a 30-year period for each additional year of schooling.[273]

Research has shown that the highest returns tend to be when the public invests in large infrastructure systems that transcend any single locality. For example, research has found returns on national spending on infrastructure to be as high as 60 to 146 percent per year, while the corresponding rate at the state or regional level was small or negligible.[274] In recent years, however, the trend has been the opposite – to decentralize infrastructure investments. While this may be appropriate in some cases, it can often be counter-productive. In the US, public works spending is often referred to by the pejorative 'pork barrel' spending, as it is heavily influenced by the power of politicians to steer resources to their constituencies. Instead, the federal government should be looking for opportunities to make national investments rather than funding a myriad of local initiatives.

Taking this logic a step further, investments that cut across blocs have the potential to deliver an even greater pay-off. As nations blend together into trade economies, infrastructure-related thinking will have to further transcend national boundaries and become bloc-wide in nature. National governments intent on raising the domestic quality of life never prioritized such investments in the past.

As our understanding of the social and economic multiplier effects of infrastructure grow, new market-oriented approaches to financing infrastructure are emerging. For example, rather than requiring that the tolls on a new highway pay completely for the cost of its construction, many localities are coming to realize that the spillover benefits of such new projects can be so high that a much lower threshold can be applied to the question of whether to approve a new project. The objective is to invest in projects that have synergistic benefits for the private sector as well as for society at large.[275]

Transport Infrastructure

This includes roads, highways, railroads, public transport, airports, seaports and river freight. The benefits of a good transportation system are evident: for example, companies can deliver their products to customers faster, they can lower their inventories, centralize workers to gain economies of scale, and hire people from a wider geographical area.

The economic multiplier effect of a sound transportation infrastructure can be seen by examining the impact of the interstate highway system in the US, which transformed the business landscape, dramatically reduced regional economic disparities and altered numerous aspects of everyday life for all Americans. According to former US Secretary of Transportation, Rodney Slater, the Interstate Highway System 'changed the way we live and the way we work. It is an engine that fuels our economy, creates jobs and serves as a gateway to opportunity. It is truly the tie that binds, a system that connects all of us to this wonderful land.'[276]

The federal government began to spend money on roads in 1916, but its role was limited. In the mid-1930s, a widespread impetus developed for the creation of limited-access highways without stoplights or crossings, similar to Germany's autobahns. Franklin Roosevelt was an enthusiastic backer, but it was difficult to find the money for the development of a national superhighway in the midst of World War II. In the meantime, the wealthier states of the Northeast and the Midwest began to develop their own highways. The first was the Pennsylvania Turnpike in 1940, followed by the New York State Thruway and the New Jersey Turnpike. California also began to develop its network of freeways in the 1940s.

It was in 1956 that President Eisenhower signed highway legislation that earmarked new higher fuel taxes for a Highway Trust Fund, which would pay for 90 percent of the Interstate Highway System, with the balance to come from states. By the 1970s, when the bulk of the work was completed, this proved to be an enormous boon for the economy as a whole, but especially for the less developed South. With a better transportation network, the South finally was able to attract heavy manufacturing and retailing companies, and the economic gap between the South and the rest of the country started to shrink dramatically. The same effects are likely to occur at the bloc level once the overall regional infrastructure is upgraded.

The shipping container was also invented in 1956, and coupled with the rapidly growing network of superhighways this allowed foreign and domestic producers much faster, broader and more efficient access to the entire US market.[277]

The Interstate Commerce Commission (ICC)

As the boundaries of the US grew in the 1800s, and as the notion of 'national markets' became more feasible due to improved communication and transport networks, it was increasingly evident that federal legislation was necessary to deal with changing and inconsistent state regulations related to commerce. For example, railroads were often frustrated by conflicting requirements placed on them by individual states. The public was also indignant over the 'malpractices and abuses' of the railroads. In 1886, the Supreme Court ruled that states could not regulate interstate railroads. This led to the formation of the Interstate Commerce Commission in 1887, which was tasked promoting commerce by assuring fair dealings between carriers and the public, and the oversight of interstate and foreign commerce within the US. Starting with railroads, the ICC gradually acquired jurisdiction over all surface common carriers, including buses and trucks (1935), barges (1940) and freight forwarders (1942). In 1910, the ICC began regulating telephone, telegraph and cable communications; this lasted until 1934, when the Federal Communications Commission (FCC) was formed. The creation of the Department of Transportation in 1966 removed the safety oversight of railroads and trucks from ICC's jurisdiction. In 1980, the ICC's powers over rates and routes in railroads and trucking were further curtailed. ICC's powers over trucking were ended in 1994, and the agency itself was terminated in 1995, with the newly formed National Surface Transport Board taking over its remaining functions.[278]

The European Transport Infrastructure

The European transportation sector accounts for approximately $1.2 trillion in annual economic impact, representing about 10 percent of the EU's GDP. It employs over 10 million people.

Recognizing the crucial role of transportation in the EU's competitiveness and for commercial, economic and cultural exchanges, the European Commission issued a Transport Policy report in 2001, outlining approximately sixty proposed policy steps to be taken until the year 2010.

The document outlines a 'Common Transport Policy' designed to harmonize transportation systems throughout the EU. Some of the objectives of this policy are to reduce the imbalance between modes of transport, facilitating ready intermodality between types of transport systems, reducing congestion and improving overall safety and reliability. For example, the policy recognizes that transportation congestion is becoming an ever-bigger problem for the EU, which, if left unchecked, could consume 1 percent of the EU's GDP by 2010 and would prevent the outermost regions from being well connected to the central markets. The policy also aims to outline principles for fair pricing that would encourage the use of less polluting and less congested types of transportation systems, as well as to better facilitate infrastructure financing.

The challenges of moving to a standardized pan-European transportation system are by no means trivial. Consider the obstacles facing the railroad system. The share of goods transported by rail fell from 21.1 percent to 8.4 percent between 1970 and 1998, in a time of huge overall growth in volume. During the same time period, the share of rail transport of goods in the US rose to 40 percent. What was happening here was that as EU integration proceeded, more companies were selling products across Europe. As more goods crossed internal EU boundaries than stayed within those boundaries, the inherent inefficiency of dealing with disparate rail systems became more obvious. For example, it was not until 2000 that a limited number of locomotives capable of running on both the French and Italian rail systems were put in operation on the Lyon–Turin line. This has reduced waiting time at the border to 15 minutes, from an average of 90 minutes earlier. However, major challenges remain:

- The Italian side requires two drivers, while the French side requires only one
- Drivers from France are not permitted to operate on the Italian network, and vice versa

- ❑ Since the passing tracks are of different lengths, trains must sometimes be split in two
- ❑ The Italian locomotives can only operate at half power in France, since the voltage there is only half the 3,000 volts used in the Italian system

Imagine if the same challenges faced rail transport managers attempting to get steel from Pennsylvania into Michigan or automobiles in the reverse direction! Understandably, many customers might opt for road transportation instead.

In 2001, rail infrastructure managers from nine European countries formed an association aimed at promoting the development of the European rail network. Their vision is to create a 'borderless, international railway network... in a transparent, neutral and effective way alongside the national and regional networks that are funded by the Member States.' In 2002, the RailNet Europe (RNE) organization was created, which now includes European railway infrastructure managers from 21 different countries. These include private as well as public companies.

In Europe, the rail infrastructure has traditionally been managed as a national matter, often through state-owned companies (European taxpayers contribute about $36 billion every year to the railway sector). Companies wishing to ship goods across national borders had to coordinate individually with each national rail company, and trains would have to stop at each border for technical, operational and legal procedures.

To address these obvious problems, in 2001, the EC passed a directive that requires railway infrastructure managers to cooperate in order to achieve better quality in cross-border traffic and to offer customers a single point of contact for coordinating the shipment.

The RNE organization has gone beyond the EC mandate by starting earlier, offering a broader slate of services and including non-EU countries such as Hungary, Norway, Slovakia and Switzerland.[279] Harmonization and coordination are needed for decisions on matters such as international capacity allocation, track access agreements, safety matters, technical standards and norms, processes for approval for rolling stock and certification of personnel, traffic control rules and train control systems.

So how do the three trade blocs compare on transport infrastructure? There is no question that Europe is definitely No. 1; the high quality roads, railroads, seaports and airports of Europe represent a major advantage for the bloc. With the recent sprouting of low-cost air carriers such as easyJet and RyanAir, Europeans now have access to cheap airfares for intra-Europe travel, something that was a distinct disadvantage earlier. In our view, the Americas rank second (given the wide disparity between the US and other countries in the bloc), and Asia third. India and especially China are investing heavily to create and upgrade their transportation infrastructures, primarily to build better national highways. Both countries have good railway systems. Though India's rail system is only the fifth largest in the world in terms of length of track (63,518 kilometers), it is the most heavily utilized system, with well over 400 billion passenger-km per year. Indian Railways employs around 1.6 million people and carries around 13 million passengers and over 1.4 million tons of freight every day.

Japan has a decent highway system, but all the highways are toll roads. The tolls are outrageously high (the money is used to pay down a $358 billion debt from wasteful public-works projects). A two-hour trip typically runs up tolls of $47, and crossing a bridge can cost as much as $50. Driving from one end of the country to the other (similar to driving the length of California) costs $330. The Japanese highway system fails to meet a fundamental requirement for good infrastructure: that it be affordable and heavily used. While some highways around Tokyo are heavily used, most of the rest are very lightly used.[280]

Information Infrastructure

Even as countries and trade blocs move to repair and upgrade their crumbling physical infrastructures, they must also focus on the urgent need to formulate public policy that will result in the creation of an advanced information infrastructure. The development of an advanced information infrastructure is an increasingly critical element to ensure the competitiveness of an economy. Such an infrastructure can improve economic performance across all industries, leading to increased international competitiveness. While business will certainly become more productive, we are also likely to see significant improvement in the quality and productivity of sectors such as education and healthcare – two enormous segments of the economy whose costs are rising rapidly. The implications of widespread working at home, shopping at home, videoconferencing and reduced demand on physical transportation systems will be felt throughout society.

Governments clearly must play a significant role in this. The government aided all the previous infrastructure deployments (such as railroads, electrification and civil aviation). Many countries now have three very large and successful network providers: wireless networks, wire-line phone networks and cable networks. In order to achieve the objective of universal affordable access to a broadband information infrastructure 'anytime and anyplace,' the government cannot simply seek compromises between the positions advocated by rival industry groups. Instead, it must fashion a clear vision of what is needed and then create incentives and craft regulatory policy to ensure that it is realized within the desired time frame. The government must also ensure that some important aspects of the public interest be served. Primarily, it must address three issues: individual and organizational privacy, information security and assuring universal access (to prevent the creation of information 'haves and have-nots'). The government can use its regulatory authority to shape the information infrastructure in desirable ways. It can play a lead role in getting industry to establish technological standards, and it can spur the development of key component technologies through targeted incentives.[281]

To compare the trade blocs in this area: Europe ranks first, followed by Asia and then the Americas. Europe consists largely of mature economies with sound information infrastructure.

Though the US does have a good information infrastructure, it is moving very slowly to upgrade to next generation technology. The US infrastructure is the oldest, and because of massive budget deficits, it will be difficult to make the public investment necessary for expansion and modernization. The regulatory system has been foundering since the Telecommunications Act of 1996, and arguably even before that. The quality of the information infrastructure in the rest of the Americas is quite poor, especially outside the metro areas.

As with its transport infrastructure, Asia is investing heavily to create and upgrade its information infrastructure. Many countries are building brand new, state-of-the-art infrastructure, leapfrogging generations of technology. Already, South Korea has the highest penetration of broadband Internet connections anywhere. Japan has taken the lead in integrating wireless technology into the fabric of society, and China already has the two largest cellular operators in the world. China is growing fast in terms of landlines as well, adding 15–20 million each year.

The UK has made a commitment to put in place the most widely available and competitive broadband infrastructure by 2005 among the G7 nations. As of 2003, 80 percent of UK households had access to broadband (either through cable or ADSL), and the government is making a concerted push to get that to 100 percent by 2005. According to E-commerce Minister Stephen Timms, 'The challenges of globalization and new technology are driving businesses to be more efficient, innovative, productive and competitive; information technology and broadband in particular have a critical role to play.'[282]

Energy Infrastructure

Abundant, affordable and ecologically safe energy is the lifeblood of commerce and of society. As the demand for energy grows, each trade bloc will come under severe pressure to develop new and improved sources, and to provide reliable delivery. The quality of the energy infrastructure depends on the supply as well as reliability. For electricity, the focus is not just on the quantity of generation but also on reliability of the grid.

As the world's population grows from approximately the current 6 billion to 7.5 billion by 2020, the demand for energy will grow at an even faster rate. Thus, while the population grows by 25 percent, energy demand is expected to grow by 57 percent. The fastest growing component of this is electricity, which is expected to see an increase in demand of 85 percent by 2020 (shockingly, some two billion people around the world still have no access to electricity).

Coupled with growing concerns about the environmental impact of dependence on fossil fuel energy sources, there is a great sense of urgency to increase the proportion of electricity generated cleanly. One of the solutions will have to be nuclear power, which currently provides over 16 percent of the world's electricity (with coal providing 40 percent, oil 10 percent, natural gas 15 percent and hydro and other 19 percent). Nuclear power accounts for almost 24 percent of electricity in OECD countries, and 35 percent in the EU. Interest in nuclear power is growing again, because it remains the most environmentally friendly way of producing electricity on a large scale.[283]

The use of nuclear power is growing rapidly in Asia, which is the only trade bloc where overall electricity generating capacity is expanding significantly. There are currently about 100 nuclear power reactors in operation in East and South Asia, twenty under construction and plans to build forty more. There are also about 56 research reactors in fourteen countries in the region. The greatest growth will be in China, Japan, South Korea and India.[284]

An interesting win-win development in recent years has been the use of nuclear fuel derived from warheads. In the US-Russian 'Megatons to Megawatts' program, nuclear material from Russian warheads is recycled into reactor fuel and sold to US electric utilities. Almost every one of the 103 nuclear power stations in the US has used this fuel. The program has resulted in the elimination of nuclear material from over 7,500 warheads. By 2013, when the program is scheduled to end, this will reach 20,000 nuclear warheads. A similar initiative has been launched to recycle highly enriched uranium from US warheads. Thus, growth in nuclear power has twin benefits, helping the environment while also aiding nonproliferation efforts worldwide.[285]

Other sources of energy will also have to be tapped further, and new ones developed. The projections for how long humankind will be able to rely on fossil fuels for energy have recently been called into questions. In his recent book, *Out of Gas,* Professor David Goodstein of the California Institute of Technology, suggests that we may have already consumed more than half the oil known to exist, and that what is left will not last long because of the increased rate of consumption.[286]

In China, which recently surpassed Japan as the world's second largest consumer of oil, demand is growing at 30 percent per year.[287] What this means is that oil prices are unlikely to decrease to any substantial degree, and we may be looking at a scenario where countries make increasingly desperate attempts to secure reliable sources of supply. Some geologists have predicted that oil supplies could start to run out ten years from now, although many geologists don't agree. Even so, oil is likely to become much more expensive than it is now, making it unaffordable for most of the world.

There will be two primary alternatives to expensive or limited oil supply. The first is increased use of coal: this, however, will accentuate the greenhouse effect and accelerate its climatic impact. The second will be increase in the use of natural gas. Neither of these is a long-term option. To that end, the world must increase its use of solar and nuclear power, and hope that new technologies such as fuel cells and nuclear fusion become viable. One thing is clear: sometime during this century, and probably during the first third of it, humankind will have to close the short but eventful chapter of its heavy reliance on fossil fuels that began when 'Colonel' Edwin Drake struck oil in the valleys of Western Pennsylvania in August 1859.[288]

Which bloc is well-positioned with respect to energy? In terms of access to oil, the European trade bloc will have a distinct edge, with the Middle East and Russia together controlling a huge supply of petroleum. China has some oil reserves, but is relying heavily on Indonesia and Brunei. How vulnerable does this make the Americas? Venezuela and Mexico do have significant resources. The largest suppliers to the US used to be Saudi Arabia, Iran and Iraq; but Iran ceased to be a supplier after the Khomeini revolution, as did Iraq after the first Gulf War. Now Canada and Venezuela are the largest sources for US oil, followed by Saudi Arabia and Mexico. The US is getting nearly half its imported oil from within the Americas, and only a quarter from the Middle East. Given that the Americas will have fewer fossil fuel resources than Europe, it is more likely to move faster towards alternate sources of energy: renewable sources such as ethanol, as well as nuclear power and fuel cells. India is pushing fuel cell R&D in a big way as a key to its future energy needs.

With regard to electricity, the generation is less of an issue than the distribution in the Americas. Europe is much better in distribution. As with railroads, Europe has already linked together its national electrical grids.

The ASEAN+3 Energy Partnership

The energy ministers of the Association of the Southeast Asian Nations (ASEAN), the People's Republic of China, Japan and the Republic of Korea met in Manila, the Philippines on June 9, 2004, and agreed to work together to strengthen their energy partnership. The ASEAN bloc consists of ten countries – the 'original' six namely Brunei, Indonesia, Malaysia, the Philippines, Singapore and Thailand, and the newest members namely Vietnam, Laos, Myanmar and Cambodia – with a combined population of 500 million. The ASEAN+3 represents a population of approximately two billion, and will soon be the largest energy-consuming region in the world.

The countries have established a common energy goal of 'greater energy security and sustainability.' The general principles of the partnership include:

- A determination to diversify primary energy supply sources to reduce the region's dependency on imported oil;

- A commitment to enhancing energy exploration and wider utilization of indigenous energy resources;
- A preference for primary energy options such as natural gas, coal and renewable energy;
- An extension of oil stockpiling programs in the region, building on existing programs in Japan and Korea, and a commitment to concerted emergency response measures;
- A recognition of the value of natural gas as a cleaner energy source, a commitment to promote investment in the exploration and production of natural gas, and developing a gas transport infrastructure;
- Close cooperation in promoting and commercializing renewable energy for energy security and environmental sustainability;
- Recognizing that coal is an abundant, effective and economical energy resource in the region, a commitment to disseminate clean coal technology and the environmentally friendly use of coal; and
- Emphasizing joint action to enhance energy efficiency and conservation.[289]

This example of 'regional thinking' bodes well for the Asian trade bloc, and shows how – despite an initial reluctance to embrace the vision of a world comprising three major trade economies – may in fact be further along the path to making it happen than the other two blocs.

Financial Infrastructure

The financial infrastructure of a country or a bloc comprises three components: capital markets, financial institutions and taxation. Capital markets (public equity, private equity and debt) are driven by the monetary policy of a country. At the bloc level, there will therefore need to be a common monetary policy and a common currency. The debt market especially depends on the interest rate, which is set by monetary policy. Trade facilitation also requires currency harmonization. The ideal situation is to have a common currency, which the European region already has, along with a common monetary policy. The Europeans therefore enjoy a distinct advantage in terms of capital markets.

The five key types of financial institutions are commercial banks, investment banks, industrial development banks, brokerages and insurance companies. All three blocs are quite well developed in this regard; the main disadvantage for financial institutions in the US is that they are still relatively fragmented compared to European institutions. US banks, in particular, were restrained until 1999 from growing in both scale (i.e. national banking) and scope (i.e. adding other financial services) by the provisions of the Glass-Steagall Act of 1933. Now, 'universal banking' (in which there is no separation between commercial banking and investment banking), which has long been prevalent elsewhere, will also gradually become the norm in the US.

An important category of financial institutions is development banks, which primarily provide long-term, low-interest financing for infrastructure projects. The big change we predict here is that, gradually, the World Bank will become marginalized (just as the UN will be for political and security matters), and will only be used in places where none of the blocs can or will do it on their own. For developmental needs within each bloc, each trade bloc will have its own development bank. In fact, these banks already exist: the Asian Development Bank (based in Manila and started in 1966 by 31 countries), the Inter-American Development Bank (based in Washington DC and started in 1959) and the newest one, the European Bank for Reconstruction and Development (based in London and started in 1991; proposed by President François Mitterrand of France in 1989, primarily to aid formerly Communist countries).

The third area is taxation. It is important that countries within a trade bloc harmonize their tax codes, otherwise there would be significant shifting of economic activity based on tax treatment alone. This includes individual income tax rates, corporate taxation as well as sales and VAT (value added tax, also referred to as GST or general sales tax). Europe is trying to harmonize VAT within the region; right now, there is still broad variation across countries, ranging from a low of 15 percent in Luxembourg to a high of 25 percent in Denmark and Sweden. Right now, Germany has perhaps the most complicated tax code in the world. The code is so complex that more academic research articles are published on German taxation than on any other subject. In the US, individuals pay more than 90 percent of all taxes, and corporations less than 10 percent. This suggests that companies are able to take advantage of the complexity of the tax code and pay less tax than they otherwise might.

Trade blocs that have high taxation rates and complex tax systems will be at a competitive disadvantage. The objectives of all the regions should be to simplify as well as lower taxes, on business as well as individuals. This would reduce the unproductive administrative burden on both sides – for taxpayers as well as tax agencies. It would also have the effect of paring down social welfare programs to a more sustainable and economically sensible level.

Another important aspect of financial infrastructure, especially from the demand-side perspective, is easy and efficient access to consumer credit. In most developed countries, this is exemplified most clearly by the extensive penetration of credit cards into virtually every segment of society. The widespread availability of credit cards acts as a definite spur to consumption, which in turn adds to economic growth. In much of the developing world, credit cards are still relatively rare, suggesting that a great opportunity exists for growth in this key infrastructure element.

The concept of credit is an ancient one, dating back at least 3,000 years to Assyria, Babylon and Egypt. However, credit cards, which made the granting and accepting of credit simple and widespread, are a relatively recent phenomenon. It was in 1951 that Diners Club issued the first credit card to 200 customers, who could only use them at 27 restaurants in New York City. American Express followed in 1958. Later the same year, Bank of America issued the BankAmericard (now Visa), which was the first bank-based credit card. In the 1970s, Bank of America entered into licensing arrangements with other banks so they could issue

BankAmericards. This led to the formation of a bankcard association and the adoption of the Visa name in 1977. Banks that decided not to join the association later formed their own group and launched MasterCard International. Until 1978, banks had to choose which of the cards they would offer. In 1978, MasterCard and Visa entered into an agreement that allowed banks to issue and honor both cards.[290]

The early cards required payment in full in a relatively short time (usually ninety days). Soon, bankers realized they could create a highly profitable business by extending the repayment time and charging interest. The use of credit cards received a major boost in 1970, when the establishment of a standard for magnetic stripes led to their popularization.[291] Credit cards became so popular by the mid-1970s that Congress had to regulate the industry, banning practices such as the mass mailing of active cards to people who had not applied for them.[292] Today, there are over one billion Visa cards alone, issued by 21,000 financial institutions and accepted at 20 million locations in 300 countries and territories.

Looking at the overall quality of the financial infrastructure across the trade blocs, we conclude that the Americas lead here, followed by Europe and then Asia. While Europe has an edge in capital markets due to its shared currency, it has huge disparities in taxation within the region. All trade blocs need to move towards simpler tax codes with relatively low rates that are more or less consistent within the region. This is a thorny issue, because of philosophical differences across countries within a bloc with regard to the provision of government-sponsored benefits such as retirement and healthcare.

Summary Assessment of Trade Blocs

It is clear that Asia has a major weakness in terms of infrastructure, relative to the other two blocs. At the same time, it is worth noting again that Asia is also investing most aggressively in upgrading its infrastructures, especially with respect to transportation and information. This will lead to a paradoxical situation: it is quite likely that Asia will have pockets of state-of-the-art infrastructure along with larger areas of highly backward infrastructure. Instead of concentrating their resources in this way, countries in the bloc would be better advised to invest in developing a strong infrastructure across the board.

Chapter 10

Bloc Centric Trade and Investment

The Japan–China Economic Axis

Japan's economy and its stock market have been in the doldrums seemingly forever. As one of the fastest aging countries in the world (with the longest life span and one of the lowest birthrates), Japan has seen domestic demand wither away in category after category. The collapse of the 'bubble economy' in the early 1990s ushered in a historically long period of deflation and general economic malaise. Real estate prices crashed, as did the stock market. The recovery always seemed to be around the corner, but never quite came.

Now, suddenly, the Japanese economy is growing faster than the US economy, and the stock market rose 45 percent in 2005. The biggest reason for this turnaround can be encapsulated in one word: China. Two-way trade between Japan and China has been growing explosively. In 2004, two-way trade rose 28 percent to $167 billion, eclipsing US–Japan trade. China has overtaken the US to become the largest single source of imports into Japan, and is growing rapidly as a destination for exports, having doubled its share in the past few years. In a few years, this will be one of the largest trading relationships in the world. At the same time that Japan's trade with China has been exploding, its trade with the US and the EU has been flat. Within East Asia in general, the trend towards greater regionalization of trade is quite evident; exports and imports have been growing much faster within the region than between the region and the rest of the world.[293]

Demand in China has been particularly strong in industries that are Japan's strengths: household electronics, mobile phones, televisions, digital cameras, automobiles and construction equipment. Moreover, growth potential in most of these categories remains huge; for example, only about 2 percent of Chinese in the middle class own cars.[294] Another factor that has contributed to the growth in two-way trade has been China's accession to the WTO in December 2001, which resulted in significantly lower tariffs, removal of some non-tariff barriers and freer entry by foreign firms.

What is underway here is a fundamental re-division of labor between Japan and China in a way that is beneficial to both countries. The Japanese have long excelled at this most important aspect of mutually beneficial global trade: the ability and willingness to gradually vacate certain industries in which they have long held a strong global position (e.g. textiles) and invest in other sectors, such as chemicals, pharmaceuticals, sophisticated information technology, retailing and financial services. In recent years, Japan has moved much of its automobile and consumer electronics industries overseas. We anticipate that the steel industry will gradually migrate from Japan to China. In shipbuilding, the Japanese consciously moved into more sophisticated products, leaving basic cargo ships to the Koreans. Now, the Koreans are moving upmarket, and Japan may eventually exit the business altogether. Japan dominated the global shipbuilding business for 40 years, starting in 1956. Today, the Koreans dominate, with over three times the market share of the Japanese. The three biggest shipbuilding companies in the world are now Korean: Hyundai Heavy Industries, Samsung Heavy Industries, and Daewoo Shipbuilding and Marine Engineering.[295]

Rationalizing and Stimulating Trade and Investment

As we move towards a tri-polar world of integrated trade economies, current trade and investment flows will get redirected as well as enhanced. We expect to see significant declines in bilateral trade and investment between entities that are in different trade economies (such as the US and Germany), which will be more than offset by rapid gains in bilateral trade and investment between countries that are part of the same trade economy (as has happened between the US and Mexico after NAFTA, and as we expect to see happen in a major way between Australia and China in the future). Certain bilateral trading relationships will gradually replace others. For instance, we expect that trade and investment in US–India will rise, as trade and investment in US–China declines.

In order for this transition to occur smoothly and with maximum benefits for countries in each of the three blocs, certain structural barriers will have to be removed (e.g. the lack of a common currency). At the same time, countries and blocs should accelerate certain trends (such as increasing intra-company trade) that are likely to enhance the benefits of trade blocs.

The Growing Alignment Between Russia, Germany and France

Germany is Russia's largest trade partner as well as its biggest investor. Two-way trade between the two nations exceeds $30 billion annually, and Germany has cumulatively invested over $20 billion in Russia. Recent events have seemingly brought the countries closer; in St. Petersburg, after the start of the Iraq War, German Chancellor Gerhard Schroeder[296] declared, 'German-Russian relations are the strongest they have been in 100 years.' While that may not be saying much (given the history of the last century), it is still significant.

The economic linkages between the two countries would have become considerably stronger had a plan to swap Russian debt for German equity been implemented. The plan, negotiated over six months, would have given German banks equity stakes in Russian firms in exchange for billions of dollars in debts owed by the Russian firms. On December 20, 2000, Stratfor, an Internet news service, carried an article stating, 'Such a development would significantly weaken US influence in Europe while dramatically strengthening Germany and Russia and helping them to advance to the front stage of world geopolitics.' The deal would 'help Russia's revival and Germany could emerge as the leader of a united Europe with Russia on its side.'[297] The deal was cancelled after the Bush administration objected to the growing 'intimacy' between Berlin and Moscow.[298] Notwithstanding that setback, it is almost inevitable that Germany and Russia will get closer, economically, politically and – eventually – militarily. The relationship between the two will shape the future of Europe, as it has shaped its past.

While trade between France and Russia is much less than that between Germany and Russia, they too have been coming closer together. In January 2004, French Foreign Minister Dominique de Villepin met with his Russian counterpart, Igor Ivanov. They agreed to coordinate their policy on the Middle East and Iraq, and to cooperate against the 'hegemony' of the US. Ivanov commented: 'The approaches of Russia and France to these problems coincide in many respects. Such closeness is not accidental. It is explained by the adherence of the two countries to the multipolar model of the world order, where the central role, as the main guarantor and instrument of maintaining international security and stability, belongs to the United Nations and its Security Council.'[299]

While Russia is not yet part of the EU, and has not yet gained entry to the WTO, we believe these steps are inevitable and just a matter of time. In the short term, Russia is being squeezed further by the entry of ten new states (including three former Soviet republics and five former members of the Warsaw Pact) into the EU in May 2004. Russia fears that it is losing some of its traditional markets in those countries. It also questions the fate of the various bilateral agreements it had in place with some of those countries.

Russia objects that its food exports to those countries would now have to adhere to strict EU hygiene standards, and its steel exports to them would be subject to the overall EU quota for steel imports from Russia.[300]

These skirmishes will ultimately be seen as minor distractions on the path to the full integration of Russia into the EU in years to come.

In this chapter, we discuss how countries and trade blocs need to realign their trade policies in the following areas:

- Encouraging more intra-company trade
- Encouraging more intra-bloc trade and investment
- Inter-bloc trade to enhance and maintain global competitiveness
- Realignment of currency
- Generating growth through a focus on emerging markets

Intra-Company Trade

Most trade now occurs between industries that are tightly integrated across borders. Intra-company trade – also known as foreign affiliate sales – accounts for a growing proportion of international trade – as high as 70 percent and growing, according to a study by the United Nations Conference on Trade and Development (UNCTAD).[301] When multinational companies have branches and subsidiaries in other countries, commodity flows between countries are largely intra-company flows. Intra-company trade used to be largely focused on natural resources; in recent decades, it has increasingly been based on intermediate products and services.[302]

This is particularly true of cross-border flows between the US and Canada and between the US and the EU, reflecting the high levels of integration and joint ownership between the markets. An estimated 54 percent of US–EU trade is intra-company trade, while approximately 70 percent of the exports by US-controlled firms in Canada are conducted on an intra-company basis. This also suggests that there is a clear link and that foreign direct investment (FDI) and trade compliment each other to a high degree. FDI has risen precipitously (e.g. from $25 billion to $315 billion between 1973 and 1995) in the past few decades. This has raised the issue of whether and how entities such as the World Trade Organization (WTO) should be involved with setting rules for such investment.[303]

The rise in intra-company trade reflects the growth of foreign direct investment by companies in locations other than their home base. One reason for this is the implementation of functional specialization by country. For example, when a US-based multinational such as Ford exports engines to its assembly plants in Ontario, Canada or Sonora, Mexico, it counts as an export from the US. Ford may then import the cars back into the US, which includes the originally exported parts. This phenomenon will grow as companies are encouraged by governments to become more regional in nature (i.e. to maximize efficiency by performing work in locations where it is most effective to do so).

Europe is by far the leader in this. The trade data is mind-boggling; there is over $3 trillion of trade within the bloc, most of which is intra-company. This is because most large European companies have a pan-European presence, created largely through merger and acquisition activity that started about five years before EC92, in anticipation of the change to a common market. Asia is second strongest on this. Aggressive moves by companies from Taiwan, South Korea and Japan are one reason for this. American companies currently do have extensive operations within Asia and Europe, but they are weak within the Americas. They are only now initiating the process of shifting factories from Asia to the Americas. For example, HP recently announced that it is going to shift some of its production from Taiwan to Mexico. Other American companies, such as Motorola, are shifting some activities from China to India.

In the past, the rise in intra-company trade has been viewed with suspicion. Intra-company trade poses a clear challenge to the jurisdiction of the nation-state, according to Wolfgang H. Reinicke, an economist at the World Bank.[304] In particular, it creates huge problems for tax authorities, as companies become highly adept at using transfer pricing between subsidiaries to move profits from high-tax jurisdictions to those with lower rates.[305] In our view, encouraging companies to set up subsidiaries within the same economic bloc, and harmonizing tax laws and rates across the bloc so that companies do not use artificial transfer pricing mechanisms between subsidiaries to minimize corporate tax can prevent such abuses. Once such measures are implemented, encouraging intra-company trade would lead to more efficient investment allocation decisions within the bloc, and more rapid economic development across the entire bloc.

Intra-Bloc Trade and Investment

The formation of mega-blocs is akin to creating three huge trade nations. Over time, a greater proportion of trade and investment flows will happen *within* each of the trade blocs, just as the vast majority of US commerce is domestic. This 'trade' happens with few if any barriers, and creates great efficiency within the economy. That thinking is now expanding outward. Countries and trade blocs will promote heavy intra-bloc investments and flows of goods and services. What used to be considered exports and imports across national borders will now become like the domestic flow of products and services.

Figure 10.1 shows the extent to which trade in each bloc is dominated by internal flows. As it indicates, Europe is heavily dominated by intra–EU trade and intra–Americas is the least dominated. Going forward, we expect that each of the blocs will have approximately 75 percent of its trade concentrated within the bloc.[306] Trade flows within Europe already account for approximately 75 percent of the total European trade. While internal percentages are lower for the other two blocs, the trends are clearly in that direction.

Increased volumes of trade between nations represent a form of shallow economic integration, while escalating amounts of foreign direct investment is suggestive of deep integration. It is interesting to note that the Americas continue to have strong

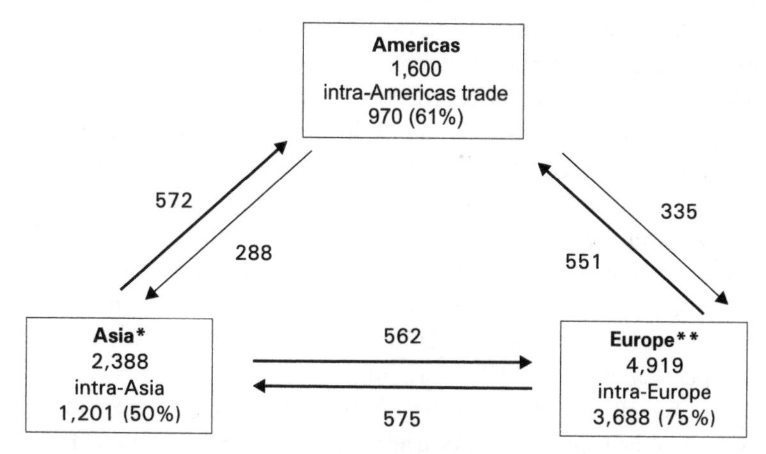

Figures are in $ billions. Total trade equals exports plus intra-bloc trade.
Source: World Bank, Intra- and inter-bloc merchandise trade, 2004
*Includes South Asia
**Includes Africa, Middle East and Commonwealth of Independent States

Figure 10.1: Trade between and within Blocs

bi-directional FDI with Europe, while its trade volumes are rising faster with Asia. Our assessment is that over time, both trade and FDI will be more concentrated within each trade economy. In other words, we expect sharp declines in FDI between the Americas and Europe as well as between the Americas and Asia (other than South Asia). We anticipate much higher levels of FDI between the US and South America, and between the US and South Asia. Likewise, we expect heavy FDI flows to occur within North and East Asia, as well as between Western and Eastern Europe (including Russia), and between Europe and the Middle East and Africa.

The Impact of NAFTA

NAFTA came into effect on January 1, 1994, though many of its provisions have only gradually been phased in. Nonetheless, enough time has elapsed that it is now possible to make a reasonable assessment of its impact on trade between the US and Mexico, and its incremental impact on each economy.

Most impediments to trade and investment between the US and Mexico have been removed. The overall average tariff on Mexican products entering the US is now only 0.2 percent, and 87 percent of imports have no tariff at all. The overall Mexican tariff rate in 2001 was 1.3 percent, down from 12 percent in 1993. It is interesting to note that Mexico's economic liberalization started long before NAFTA was enacted, though it was certainly given a major impetus with the prospect of NAFTA. Mexican tariffs fell from 27 percent in 1982, to 12 percent in 1993. Inflation was also brought under control, falling from 187.8 percent in 1987, to 6.4 percent when NAFTA was implemented.[307]

Overall, the growth in trade in the post-NAFTA period has been highly impressive. US trade with Mexico has grown faster than with any other country, including China. Two-way trade between the US and Mexico has grown dramatically, from about $80 billion in 1993 to $250 billion in 2000. Mexican exports to the US were growing at 10.1 percent annually in the five years leading up to NAFTA; they have grown at an average annual rate of 16.1 percent in the years since. Export growth has contributed to more than half of Mexico's real GDP growth since 1994 and more than half of the new jobs created. NAFTA also triggered an FDI boom; the average annual inflow over a seven-year period tripled after 1994.[308]

Assessing each bloc's success at promoting more intra-bloc trade and investment, Europe is the clear leader, Asia is No. 2 and the Americas is at No. 3. The Europeans have already rationalized manufacturing capacity and created a high degree of sector specialization within Europe. The US is still heavily weighted towards Europe and Asia in terms of exports as well as imports; while 37 percent of US exports go to Canada and Mexico, 30 percent go to Japan and the EU each. On the import side, Canada and Mexico account for 30 percent, while the EU, Japan and China account for almost 40 percent. These ratios will change significantly in years to come as the US aligns itself more closely within its own trade bloc. Consider that Argentina sends 45 percent of its exports to the US, Chile and Brazil, and 44 percent of its imports come from Brazil and the US. For Brazil, trade with the US and Argentina accounts for 36 percent of all exports and 41 percent of all imports. For Canada, the US represents 85 percent of exports and 73 percent of imports. For Mexico, the numbers are even more skewed; the US and Canada account for 91 percent of exports and 70 percent of imports.[309]

Inter-Bloc Trade and Investment

If a bloc is exceptionally strong in an industry, it can use its domestic market power and excess manufacturing capacity to try to dominate the world. The Asian bloc, for example, virtually owns the global consumer electronics industry. In order to continue to gain favorable access to the other two trade markets, companies may try to get some kind of backdoor entry into the trade bloc. For example, the Europeans have used Mexico as a beachhead into the Americas, because Mexico has signed a bilateral agreement with Europe. Michelin entered the North American tire market years ago through Canada, because French Canadians were favorably inclined towards French companies. These kinds of loopholes will continue for a while, but the Europeans must realize that the US and Canada will not allow them to do so indefinitely. Companies that have truly global aspirations will have to find other ways to enter markets outside their home trade blocs.

Some companies from each trade bloc will establish a significant presence within other blocs to make them more competitive globally. Industries that would fall into this category include consumer electronics (where the Asians dominate), technology industries (where the US is very strong), and automobiles (where the Japanese – especially Toyota and Honda – will continue to do very well globally).

There is interesting geopolitics at play here. China appears to be going out of its way to align with Europe, apparently to spite the US. It is deliberately inviting European manufacturers to come to China to marginalize US manufacturers. China appears to subscribe to the mindset that 'the enemy of my enemy is my friend.' It correctly sees Europe and the US becoming greater economic rivals rather than partners in the future. China also sees itself and the US becoming rivals, a further reason for it to get closer to Europe.

We believe the recent US moves toward a greater presence in India are really a reaction to Chinese policies. The Chinese are starting to demonstrate a stronger sense of nationalism, which worries the US; China is the only country in the world that will be in a position after a few years to rival the US as a military and economic superpower. China's inevitable ascension to great power status in the future is likely to be accompanied by a desire to dominate the East Asian region. This will become an ever-greater source of rivalry and contention between the US and China.

For two centuries, the US has been in the unique position of being the only global power with unchallenged hegemony in its region. With the Monroe Doctrine (promulgated in 1823), the US made it clear to France, Spain and other European powers that it would not accept any attempts to establish or maintain colonies in the Americas. By recognizing Argentina, Chile, Peru, Colombia and Mexico in 1822 (all of which had fought for independence from Spain), the US upped the ante. The Monroe Doctrine stated that the American continent could no longer be colonized by Old World powers, and that any efforts to do so would be viewed by the US as 'dangerous to our peace and safety.'[310] Since that time, the US has strenuously combated any attempts by other powers to attain hegemony in their own regions. Germany's attempts to do so were dealt with in both the World Wars. When Japan showed signs that it had similar ambitions in Asia, the US imposed a devastating embargo on it and then defeated it in the war. The US then placed hundreds of thousands of troops in Europe to prevent the USSR from attempting to gain European hegemony. In the future, if China were to attempt, on its own, to become a regional hegemon militarily, it is a sure bet that the US will do everything it can to counter that. Indeed, all evidence is that planning to that end has already begun.[311]

However, the future is more about geoeconomics than about geopolitics. While the two are certainly intertwined (and always have been), geoeconomics will be the driver going forward. Our position is that Germany (or a combination of Germany and France) and China (as part of the Asian trade bloc) will achieve economic hegemony over time within their own blocs, and that the US will be unable to stop it from happening.

Many US companies have moved into China but few have had any success there. It is believed that not a single large US company has made any significant money in China (except when they have used China as a sourcing mechanism for low cost manufacturing and assembly). None have succeeded in penetrating the domestic Chinese market. On the other hand, many European companies are making money there. For example, Volkswagen (VW) is doing well in China, with a 15 percent share of the passenger car market, which is growing at 30 percent a year. However, VW's share has fallen from nearly 50 percent, and the Japanese have captured nearly 30 percent of the market. The trend is clear – Japanese companies will far outspace others in China.

Overall, Asia has the edge over the others on this dimension, due to its superior manufacturing performance, the power of domestic market scale and the availability of skilled labor. Europe is number two and the Americas number three.

Realignment of Currency

Each trade bloc will eventually have a common currency. This has become imperative for the other two blocs now that Europe has successfully adopted a common currency (with the notable holdout of the British pound).

As trade and investment goes more within trade economies, currency alignment becomes key. Thus, the Russian ruble will link with the Euro, and the Indian rupee will link with the US dollar. China will have to allow its currency to float sooner rather than later, and coordinate its management with that of the Japanese yen and the Singapore dollar.

The journey towards monetary union in Europe began in 1972, when the Europeans implemented the 'currency snake' system, so called because the currencies would only be allowed to fluctuate within a narrow 2.25 percent band of one another, much like the undulations of a snake. The countries were Germany, Netherlands, Belgium, France, Italy and Luxembourg. They were worried their currencies would collapse after the US government pressured other countries to float their currencies against the dollar. So they anchored to the Deutsche Mark, which gave them a safe haven – Germany would bail them out by intervening in the market and buying and selling their currencies. In 1979, the European monetary system was launched, and two more countries were added to the snake group.

The history of currency unification in the US is fascinating. There was no common currency in the early years of the federation. The first central bank was created in 1791, to oversee banks that were run with permission from state governments. Another central bank was created in 1816, but only lasted until 1832; thereafter, states were in charge of bank supervision, a function they performed poorly. By 1860, over 10,000 different types of bank notes were in use! The currencies traded against one another and fluctuated frequently. There was widespread counterfeiting, and commerce across the country was hurt. Finally, a National Currency Act was passed during the Civil War in 1863, and national bank notes began to be circulated. The Federal Reserve Bank was created in 1914 to produce and regulate America's modern national currency.'[312]

Internationally, the dollar had little influence until after World War II. Instead, the British pound was the dominant global currency from the 18th to the early 20th century, due to the strength and scope of the British Empire. Most world trade was done in pounds sterling, which was viewed 'as good as gold' because of its gold backing. By 1925, however, Britain's economy was foundering, and it was forced to devalue the pound, ultimately taking it off the gold standard in 1931. After World War II, the US dollar became the dominant currency worldwide, reflecting the ascendance of the US as the dominant world economic power. The dollar was pegged to gold at the rate of $35 per ounce. Most other currencies were pegged to the dollar, with fixed exchange rates that were periodically adjusted. This stable international financial system came under severe pressure in the late 1960s from the huge deficits created by the Vietnam War and the Great Society programs implemented by Lyndon Johnson. As US inflation soared, the dollar was no longer viewed as 'good as gold.' In 1971, the Nixon administration took the dollar off the gold standard. Floating exchange rates became the norm and the dollar was sharply devalued.[313]

Europe is clearly the leader on this, since they have already done it. The new countries that are joining the EU will also adopt the Euro. The Americas are number two, because the US dollar is already a *de facto* common currency in Latin America and elsewhere. However, the Americas are far from being a dollar economy. Argentina did link its currency to the dollar, but the arrangement collapsed. While the dollar is being used in the informal market, there is no monetary and currency unification, whereby each country's central bank would subordinate to a single common central bank. This is precisely what the British don't want to do, and they have thus stayed out of the European Monetary Union. The dollar will be the currency of trade, even though countries may keep their own currencies. It will become a widely used second currency, just like in Canada, where you can use either US or Canadian dollars for virtually all purchases. Even in India, the rupee and the dollar will be freely interchangeable. The central banks of individual countries, even if they do not adopt the dollar, will use the dollar as a backup.

Because of its head start, we expect that the Euro will become the lead currency worldwide, not the US dollar. Asia is the weakest bloc in terms of currency alignment. The Japanese yen is not the currency of the future, because China will eventually dominate the Asian bloc. Eventually, the trade bloc currency has to be the Chinese yuan, but that is a long-term evolution. The yuan is currently pegged (at what many believe to be an artificially low rate) to the US dollar; it is likely to be switched to a peg with a basket of currencies before being allowed to float freely.

Growth Through Emerging Markets

The greatest potential for win-win outcomes in international trade comes from 'North-South' integration i.e. the tapping of emerging markets by firms from mature economies coupled with the opening of those mature markets to goods and services from developing countries.

As discussed in chapter one, all nations can be described in terms of two simple but critical dimensions: growth and prosperity (Figure 1.4). The ideal situation is when a country has both high prosperity and high growth. Advanced countries tend to have very high prosperity but low growth, whereas newly industrialized countries (NICs) have both high prosperity and rapid growth, and less developed countries (LDCs) have good growth but poor prosperity. Stagnant countries are those that are stuck in an economic morass in which they have neither growth nor prosperity.[314]

Growth can come from one of two sources: domestic demand or export markets. This depends upon access to markets and access to supply functions. If a country has a large domestic market and a well-developed infrastructure, it can grow by stimulating and serving its domestic demand. An example of this is the US in the late 1800s.

For most LDCs, however, the best initial growth model is export-based. The reason is that the domestic market infrastructure is not ready because consumers lack the ability to pay. What they need is income through employment; this is where China has excelled, especially over the past decade. Success with this strategy requires that a country be granted ready access to large lucrative markets. Taiwan and South Korea, for instance, got access after the 1950s to the large and attractive US market because of the alignment of their political ideology (anti-Communism) with the US. Japan was given access to the American market as part of the US effort to rebuild that nation after World War II.

For a small stagnant nation that has neither good prosperity nor good growth (for example: Nepal, Myanmar, the Pacific Island nations or other countries whose economies have been primarily based on tourism), the only viable approach is an export-based one. Exporting success can be achieved without having a good domestic infrastructure because all you really need is 'export' island within a nation – a sort of duty-free zone. It is very simple to put an infrastructure in a small territory. This is exactly what has happened with the Special Economic Zones in China, and more recently in India.

When countries reach the NIC level, their growth has to be balanced between domestic and export markets. They cannot sustain themselves on the export market forever because the aspirations of their people rise along with their incomes. They aspire to a better life than they had in the past. At this stage, these export-oriented economies must begin to invest in a big way to build the domestic infrastructure. So an NIC goes from being export-oriented with a production sector plan, towards emphasizing investments in domestic infrastructure with a consumption sector plan. Individuals as well as governments accumulate a lot of savings by this time. In recent years, Taiwan has spent over $70 billion of its reserves on its infrastructure. China is starting to do so in a big way, as is India on a smaller scale.

For LDCs, exports may account for 80 percent of the total economy. For NICs, the split may be 50–50. And for mature countries, exports may be only 20 percent and the domestic market may be 80 percent.

Some LDCs have a tough time cracking export markets, either because they don't belong to one of the trade blocs or because they simply don't have a competitive offering. For such countries, it is really difficult to get off the ground. The only way for them to bootstrap growth internally is for the government to have a very disciplined economic policy. In that case, they may be able to get an infusion of outside capital and know-how. But nobody would like to invest in the domestic market if it is a very small country, particularly if they cannot export their production. In the case of Singapore, the government provided a stable, highly disciplined environment with a trained and peaceful workforce.

Multinationals came in droves to manufacture and export from Singapore. Similar examples are Mauritius and Dubai.

India and China are different from South Korea, Taiwan and Singapore, in that they have huge domestic markets. Such countries can create growth by inviting multinationals to develop domestic markets for them, in which case the multinationals take the risk. The role of the government then is to mitigate that risk and invest in the domestic infrastructure. In the past, many LDCs have been reluctant to go down this road because of their past experience with colonial powers that exploited or conquered them.

The process of economic integration between advanced and less developed nations is very interesting. In uneven economies there is typically a redistribution of economic activities. For example, manufacturing usually goes south. This happened in the US in the aftermath of the Civil War when machinery and textile industries went from New England to North and South Carolina.

The first reason for this migration is that the south is typically less developed and has cheap labor. Second, there is usually pent up demand and therefore markets can be created through employment and infrastructure investments. Third, the natural resources (such as oil, minerals, or basic raw materials) needed for manufacturing are generally still available in such regions, since they are usually unexploited. The ideal nation to tie in with an advanced nation is one that has cheap labor, a large domestic market, and abundant natural resources. The advanced nation can then deploy capital and know-how to trigger rapid economic change. That is what the ASEAN, Mexican and Chinese miracles have been all about.

Since manufacturing does go south, it means that advanced countries will have to give up something in the process of achieving economic growth. This is the big difference between economic integration and colonialism. The traditional approach to integrating economies used to be a colonial model that involved taking over a country. That must shift to the integration of economies, or the linking of economic destinies for mutual benefit (Figure 10.2). Rather than being driven by a colonial mindset, it is driven by economic partnership and mutual interdependence,

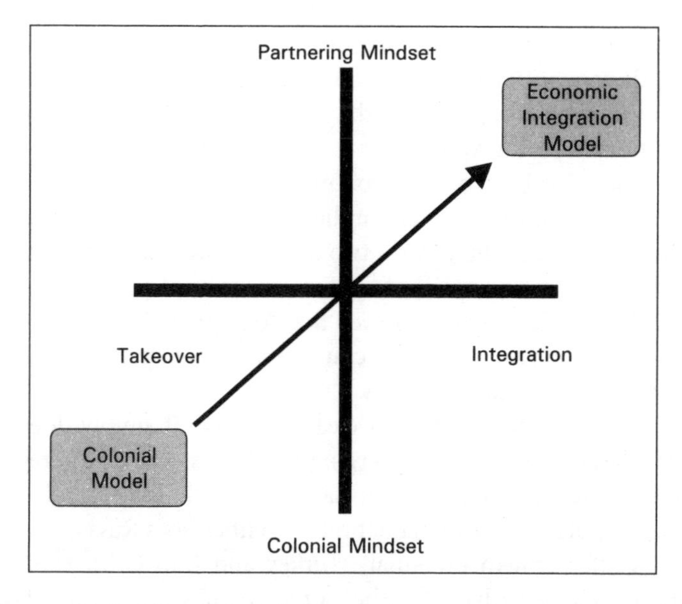

Figure 10.2: Non-Colonial Approach to Economic Integration

reflecting a newfound economic pragmatism. Advanced countries must, therefore, permanently give up some industries. Thus countries have to learn not only how to create industries, but also how to give up industries. This is a skill only a few countries in the world have. The country that best practices this is Japan. As it targets new industries for the future, Japan gives up old industries to its less developed partners. And this, of course, was Ricardo's theory in the 1800s for the rise of the British economy.

In the past, it has been common to speak of 'sunrise' and 'sunset' industries. However, sunset and sunrise industries are man-made rather than natural phenomena. A sunset industry for a mature economy can become a sunrise industry for a developing economy. Sunset industries are not the ones that are dying of old age or lack of global competitiveness; they are industries that mature nations consciously exit in their prime because they no longer generate domestic growth. The industries are then transplanted into places where they can generate growth once again; they become rejuvenated or 'dematured.' For example,

Matsushita took all of its manufacturing capacity for room air conditioners out of Japan and into Malaysia, which – coming out of nowhere – soon became the leading exporter of room air-conditioners in the world.

With North American economic integration, Mexico quickly became a major player in two industries for all of North America: cement and glass. The world's two largest glass manufacturers and third largest cement manufacturer are now Mexican. Colonial powers would have never allowed that to happen. In North–South economic alliances, advanced countries are giving up something in exchange for market access.

The weakest bloc here is clearly Europe; it simply does not have a large and growing emerging market as part of the region. None of the ten countries that have joined the EU recently have young populations or high birthrates. Neither does Russia (though it does offer growth potential). Turkey and Iran (with about 70 million people each) offer the potential of younger and faster growing markets. The African continent has about 800 million people, with the largest concentrations in Nigeria (134 million), Egypt (75 million), Ethiopia (64 million), the Congo (56 million) and South Africa (43 million).

The Americas will have Brazil, Mexico and India (and potentially Pakistan and Bangladesh as well). The Asian bloc will have China and Indonesia. The net result appears to be a slight edge for the Americas; the primary reason being that it will have more large, emerging and young countries.

Summary Assessment of Trade Blocs

Our summary assessment is that Europe has a significant head start in the realignment of trade, primarily because it has been the prime mover behind regionalization for several decades now. As a result, European companies are already pretty much there in terms of making the necessary changes. The Americas is vulnerable because the FTAA has not yet been signed, and US companies have barely begun the process of thinking 'Americas first.' As a result, US companies are still facing East and West, towards Europe and Asia, when they should be aligned North and South. If the Americas can successfully integrate South Asia into its bloc, it will enjoy a significant advantage over the Europeans in having access to a large and growing population base. As the world population peaks – sometime in the next few decades – and then starts to decline, this will be a big advantage.

CHAPTER 11

RATIONALIZATION OF DOMESTIC INDUSTRY

Change Begins at Home

Countries in each bloc will have to facilitate the rationalization of domestic industry so that the advantages of trade blocs can be achieved. This includes the following areas:

- Facilitating sector specialization and focus
- Removal of government subsidies
- Removing barriers to industry consolidation
- Bloc-centric markets
- Promoting bloc standards
- Permitting intra-bloc resource mobility

Facilitating Sector Specialization and Focus

The town of Akron, Ohio was founded in 1825 at the highest point on the Ohio & Erie Canal's route from the Cuyahoga River to the Ohio River. The town was created so travelers would have a place to stay while they waited to travel the canal, the route of which was so steeply downhill that 15 locks were needed to cover one mile. The first canal linked Akron and Cleveland in 1827, and was followed by a canal that linked Akron to Pittsburgh in 1840. By 1897, the railroad had arrived in Akron. The combination of a well-developed shipping infrastructure and an abundant water supply were the attractions that brought B.F. Goodrich, a New York physician-turned-realtor, and his business partners to Akron to set up Goodrich, Tew & Co. They initially produced rubber tires for bicycles and carriages and then, in 1896, started making pneumatic tires for a Cleveland automaker. This attracted other tire makers to town. In 1898, Frank A. and Charles W. Seiberling founded the Goodyear Tire and Rubber Co. (It was named after Charles Goodyear, who invented the rubber vulcanization process but had nothing to do with the company). Next came Harvey S. Firestone, who moved to Akron in 1900. He formed the Firestone Tire and Rubber Company, initially making rubber tires for horse-drawn vehicles, but switched to automobile tires in 1903. Harvey S. Firestone developed the first pneumatic tire, as well as the first tires that could be taken off the rim, enabling motorists to change a flat with a spare tire.[315]

By 1915, several other rubber companies were established in Akron, including General Tire & Rubber Co., Miller, Kelly-Springfield, Swinehart Tire & Rubber, Stein Double Cushion Tire and Union Rubber. Between 1910 and 1920, Akron's population tripled to over 200,000 people, and it became known as the 'rubber capital of the world.' By 1930, the city accounted for more than two-thirds of all tires sold in the US.[316]

The story of Akron is perhaps surprising, but is not unusual. In fact many industries end up gravitating, naturally, to a single location.

Traditionally, countries around the world have prided themselves on their self-sufficiency in what they consider to be key economic sectors. To that end, many have supported and often propped up companies in major industries such as airlines, telecommunications, steel and automobiles. To ensure the survival of these companies, governments have granted them subsidies, tax advantages and, in many cases, protection from more efficient foreign competitors.

This type of thinking has long become outmoded. It is important that countries within a bloc allow industries to migrate to locations within the bloc to make the whole industry more productive and globally competitive. This requires shedding the last vestiges of a parochial mindset that prizes the presence of 'national champion' companies.

When such migration is freely permitted, it usually leads to the concentration of an industry's major companies in a small geographic region, as we described above with Akron and the tire industry. Similarly, all the major US carmakers ended up in Detroit, the steel industry became concentrated around Pittsburgh, while the personal computer industry centered on Silicon Valley and the wine industry in Napa Valley.

Michael Porter refers to this phenomenon as 'clustering.' According to him, clusters impact competition in three ways: they increase the productivity of companies located within the cluster, they impact the direction and speed of innovation and they lead to the creation of new businesses within the cluster.[317]

Why do clusters form and what role do governments play in their formation? As Porter describes, clusters usually emerge and begin to grow naturally, usually due to the success of a particular company. As a company begins to establish itself, buyers, suppliers and related industries may locate nearby. Other firms soon arise nearby as well, to take advantage of the favorable infrastructure that is taking shape. Often, individuals leaving the pioneer firm may start these firms. Once a cluster starts to take shape, state and local governments can do a great deal to 'turbo-charge' the process. A good example of this is investment in university-based technical institutes and training centers, such as the 'Research Triangle' in North Carolina.

In some cases, governments seek to trigger the formation of new clusters by investing in Special Economic Zones, complete with specialized infrastructure and technical centers. These 'magnets' for clusters are sometimes successful, but can also have a high failure rate if poorly conceived and implemented.[318]

While the US has already gone through this process on a national level, it will now have to facilitate a second round of clustering at the bloc level. At present, Europe is leading the way. Through the EC92 architecture, the Europeans have had a number of years to determine how certain industries will migrate within Europe. One example is the negotiation between the Germans and French over the aerospace and automobile industries, both very large and key industries. In the future, Germany is likely to become the automotive capital of Europe, while France will become the aerospace capital. Countries in the bloc must surrender their positions in the industry in which the other country has a clear strategic edge. France will dominate the aerospace industry all over Europe, and will compete globally. This has major implications for aerospace companies all over Europe. A similar scenario is likely to emerge with Germany and the auto industry.

The emerging architecture is governed in part by the existing locations of major companies that are already globally competitive in a given industry. Thus, the European petroleum industry is likely to be anchored to the Netherlands, because of the presence of the giant Shell group there. Interestingly, the Europeans may prevent British Petroleum (BP), which has become an archrival competitor to other European petroleum companies, from making further inroads into Europe; consequently, BP is now focusing more on the Americas through its mergers with Amoco and Arco.

Consider the European airline industry. Switzerland is exiting the business because Lufthansa has bought Swissair. The Netherlands' KLM has been bought by Air France. Iberia and Alitalia are up for sale. British Airways, most likely, will align on the other side with a US carrier. We have seen this phenomenon in Europe across about a dozen industries.

The Europeans are very worried about the prospect of American companies dominating any industry in Europe. One consequence is that some previous mergers that have taken place between European (not British) companies and US companies may be disbanded via demergers. For example, we would expect that Cap Gemini would divest itself of Ernst and Young; it would be better served to acquire other smaller profitable computer services companies across Europe, or to partner with SAP of Germany. We also do not see a long-term future for the combination of

Daimler and Chrysler. Finally, when Citibank tried to buy Duetsche Bank, the latter's CEO, Joseph Ackerman, got in trouble as a result. The message is loud and clear – such mergers will not be encouraged.

Within a given country, there will be multiple players from a particular industry. In essence, a number of Detroits (automotive), Akrons (tires) and Pittsburghs (steel) will emerge. For most major industries, then, the Big Three in Europe are likely to come from a single country or a single sub-region within Europe. This is a major change from earlier historical reality: the European Big Three usually consisted of a German company, a French company and a third company that was either British, Italian, Spanish or Scandinavian.

The US has already gone through this kind of rationalization, which started after the Civil War and accelerated with the development of national rail and road networks. The challenge now is to take this to the next stage and re-rationalize at the bloc level. All labor-intensive manufacturing is likely to head south, as it always does; only now, instead of going to the Sun Belt within the US or to Asia, some of it will head to Latin America or India. Our forecast is that Brazil or India will become the steel capital for the Americas and the US will exit the steel industry except for specialty steel. For education and health care, the US will be the base and US universities and hospitals will establish satellite locations throughout Latin America and India. The cement industry has already been surrendered to Cemex of Mexico. The glass industry (bulk glass) has likewise been surrendered to Mexico. Agriculture has to go south or to India, which means the US will have to give up most of its heavily subsidized agriculture industry. In agriculture seeds, Mexico is already No. 1 in the world, and India is No. 2.

Comparing the three trade blocs, it is evident that Europe is far ahead on bloc clustering; European companies have been clustering at a bloc level since before 1992, while in the Americas, the process happened within the US long ago but has not yet happened across the region, except for NAFTA. Asia is further along than the US; industry mobility across countries has been quite high in the bloc. For example, electronics manufacturing and assembly has moved from Japan to Singapore, Taiwan, Malaysia, and now to China. The Japanese have been practicing this art of 'vacating markets' far more than most other countries. As soon as they realize they have a competitive disadvantage in a particular industry, they move to outsource it. Japan initially outsourced low-end automobile manufacturing and shipbuilding to South Korea; now they are concentrating on China.

There are two ways in which countries vacate markets. One is to set up manufacturing in the other locales, while maintaining ownership. This is what happened in automobiles. The other way is to simply get out of a sector altogether, and let companies from other countries take over. For the most part, the latter phenomenon is what we are seeing. For example, the Japanese government is likely to encourage the 'zaibatsu' (the large trading houses) to cap investment in certain industries. Instead, they can train companies in other countries to perform the tasks, but not directly invest in those companies. This is the old British model where the government gave signals to companies as to what it would or would not favor. Japan's MITI and Ministry of Finance did the same thing. Governments also give incentives or disincentives to steer companies in one direction or another or to remove existing incentives or subsidies. Even the US government does this, despite all its protestations that it relies solely on market forces. Companies get the signal; they disinvest out of certain areas and diversify into new areas.

So Asia is ahead of the Americas because of the pace with which non-competitive countries and companies have vacated markets. In the US, lobbying and election-year political pressures work against these movements. Changes take a long time to happen, as the adversarial system plays itself out.

Removal of Government Subsidies

One of the most significant barriers to economic integration and the achievement of a true win-win outcome for developed and developing countries alike is the presence of government subsidies. The impact of these subsidies is particularly dramatic in the agriculture sector, which continues to command a disproportionate amount of political power in the US, Europe and Japan. Removing such subsidies is an extremely important step that all countries have to undertake.

There is clear distinction between acceptable incentives and unacceptable subsidies. Acceptable incentives are those designed to move the market in a direction that it is already likely to go. Unacceptable subsidies, on the other hand, prop up an unproductive sector of the economy that clearly does not have a chance of existing under normal market conditions. They are usually the result of disproportionately high political strength enjoyed by a relatively small group.

The US government has long protected farmers through trade restrictions and enormous subsidies. The reality today is that the US agricultural sector simply cannot compete in an open market. It is a cherished myth in the US that American farmers are the most competitive in the world and can produce a bushel of wheat at a lower cost than farmers anywhere else. The reality is that without subsidies, most US farmers would not be able to compete. Many farmers get more money from the government for *not* farming than what they could make if they did farm. This is a corporate welfare system; it is not a market economy.

In 2003, the US spent approximately $16.3 billion subsidizing corn, peanuts, rice, and many other crops. The Bush administration recently approved spending $125 billion over the next ten years. Even worse, the EU spent an astounding $41 billion subsidizing its farmers in 2003, representing 60 percent of its budget. Likewise, Japan spends tens of billions of dollars a year on agriculture subsidies.

The impact of all this misplaced largesse on developing countries is devastating, even tragic. Some estimate that it leads, indirectly, to thousands of additional deaths every day, as it pushes the incomes of farmers in poor countries below subsistence levels.

US farmers just recently started to lose their political power, even though their numbers began to decline a hundred years ago.

Increasingly, Congress is shifting its attention towards the power base towards the industrial and commercial sectors. Many of the traditional agriculture states have taken steps to adjust to this new reality. For instance, the state of Kentucky is permanently transforming itself from 'tobacco country' to more of a 'knowledge economy.'

In a world free of heavy agriculture subsidies, corn production is likely to shift from the US to Argentina, which is already the largest corn producer in the world. Soybean would go to Brazil, wheat to Argentina. We forecast that in less than 20 years, there will be no more orange groves in Central Florida. Already, 50 percent of the orange juice sold in the US comes from Brazil; it is simply blended in the US. In the future, Minute Maid and Tropicana will put their factories directly in Brazil, and bring in value-added products rather than raw materials. So in 2020, what you will see in Florida instead of orange groves will be 'Disney County.' If you are skeptical, think about Orange County in California. Only 25 years ago, it used to be filed with orange groves. Now it has been transformed into a commercial and residential area. In fact, our forecast is that Napa Valley in California will be gone as a major wine producing area in fifty years. Today, the bulk of 'California white wine' comes from Chile; it is just blended in Napa Valley. So, why not move the entire operation there? Argentina is very good in red wine, because of its Italian heritage, and Chile is very good in white wine. So why make wine in Napa Valley? That land is highly valuable for other things; we expect that Napa Valley will become an extension of Silicon Valley, a sort of knowledge colony.

Comparing the three blocs, it is clear that Asia has the fewest subsidies (though Japan and Korea do prop up their agriculture sectors). Interestingly, ASEAN has signed an agreement with China that would lead to the creation of a common free trade area by 2010; the pact includes 'early harvest', a package to liberalize trade in agriculture products much earlier than that. The Europeans and Americans are relatively close; their farm subsidies are equally huge. Overall, we would put the Americas as No. 2 and Europeans as No. 3. The reason is that Europe still has a much more significant presence of public sector enterprises e.g. railroads, education and health-care, which are all subsidized.

Removing Barriers to Industry Consolidation

After the EC92 plan was announced in 1987, the number of mergers and acquisitions in the EU rose significantly. Between 1987–88 and 1992–93, the annual number of mergers and acquisitions involving EU firms rose from 3,021 to 4,831.[319] Approximately two-thirds of the mergers were between companies based in the same country.[320] In the manufacturing and construction sectors, mergers and acquisitions rose from 673 between 1984 and 1986 to 6,850 between 1990 and 1992, a more than tenfold increase. The proportion of cross-border deals rose from 32 percent in 1983–85 to 54 percent between 1990 and 1992.[321]

Governments must allow the 'natural' consolidation of markets through market processes. If they do not do so, industries remain fragmented and highly inefficient. We have examined this issue in detail in our book, *The Rule of Three*.[322] Basically, we have found that competitive markets tend to evolve in a way that best balances overall economic efficiency and consumer choice. Almost without exception, such markets end up with three major players, who we refer to as 'full line generalists,' controlling 60–80 percent of the market. The balance of the market is served by specialist companies – which can be product specialists, market specialists or product-market specialists.

The Rule of Three emerges after successive waves of industry shakeouts, during which weaker players are weeded out and stronger players either merge with one another or gradually move towards becoming specialists. This process is repeated as a market evolves from local to national to global.

The Rule of Three is most evident in the US market, but less so in Europe and Asia. While European merger and acquisition (M&A) activity has been growing rapidly, the Japanese government has been especially reluctant to allow mergers between competing firms. As a result, the Japanese market remains relatively fragmented and inefficient.

Governments can facilitate such consolidation by removing regulatory barriers and other impediments such as incompatible standards. In particular, they can encourage mergers within a trade bloc, while discouraging mergers across blocs. In the future, they must also eschew parochial nationalist thinking, and let mergers occur across national borders. The vestiges of such 'national champion' thinking in Europe are perhaps strongest in France, where two recent cases show how difficult it can be for governments to allow market forces to operate. First, the French government aggressively intervened to facilitate the merger between French pharmaceutical companies, Aventis and Sanofi-Synthelabo, by issuing a warning to Novartis, a Swiss company, not to challenge the merger. Then, the French government intervened to rescue industrial giant Alstom from bankruptcy and a sale of assets. Alstom makes power turbines and the famous TGV high-speed trains, and also owns the Chantiers de l'Atlantique shipyard. The move was strongly opposed by Siemens, which had hoped to buy some of Alstom's businesses in a breakup. The French government was determined not to let this 'national champion' perish. However, this approach runs counter to the consensus Franco-German industrial policy that seeks the creation of European champions that can compete globally with large American or Asian companies.[323]

The US is more liberal in allowing mergers and acquisitions than the other blocs. The Europeans apply a 'dominance' test, which seeks to determine whether the merged company will have an excessive market share. This was used to block General Electric Co.'s proposed 1991 acquisition of Honeywell International Inc. In the US, companies may be allowed to merge if they can show that consumers would benefit through lower prices or new products, even though competition may decline.[324]

India is now seeing significant M&A activity for the first time. In India, most major industries have been dominated by the large industrial houses, many of them family controlled. Until a few years ago, foreign companies faced stringent restrictions on their ability to participate in the Indian economy. Capacity rationalization was nearly impossible to achieve as a result of licensing and the inability to 'downsize' (reduce the labor force) when market conditions so dictated. Several factors are now triggering the Rule of Three across the Indian commercial landscape. These include the rise of public sector companies from many industries as consolidators, the removal of many governmental controls on growth, the rising ability to rationalize capacity and curtail the size of a company's labor force, the freer entry of multinationals into the Indian market, the explosive growth in national media (especially television), the growth of the organized retail sector, and the recognition by the large business houses that they must focus on their core competencies and exit marginal business lines.

As discussed above, Europe puts up more barriers to mergers than the US. Asia does not put up as many barriers, but there has not been much of a culture of mergers. The explanation for the lag in Asia has to do in part with the greater domination of family-owned businesses; the lack of separation of ownership and management makes it less likely that a company would agree to subsume its identity into that of another company's. Asia is also home to many highly diversified conglomerates. The degree of subsidization across businesses that is typical with conglomerates is not sustainable in the long run. As conglomeration declines, and companies focus more on their core businesses, consolidation will follow. In fact, the hotbed for mergers and acquisitions in the future is likely to be Asia. We expect that Australian, Korean and Japanese companies will buy out companies in the ASEAN bloc. The Asian bloc will bypass the domestic Rule of Three, and will go directly to a Rule of Three at the bloc level.

Bloc-centric Markets

Ultimately, large companies will have to learn to play the game at three levels: national, trade bloc and global. Of these, the importance of national and global strategies will decline, while that of bloc strategies will rise. This has two dimensions: domestically focused companies expanding their horizons to the bloc level, and already-global companies reorienting themselves to place greater focus on their home trade bloc.

Many companies will increasingly look to dominate *within* a given bloc rather than *across* multiple blocs. In other words, trade blocs will prevail, and the dominant share of both investment and trade will take place within blocs. If you look at the trade between France and Germany today compared to 10 years ago, you see the patterns clearly. The growth rate of trade with the US is declining while trade within Europe is growing rapidly. Similarly, trade between Japan and China is growing at a faster rate than their trade with the US.

As a result, most major industries will become more bloc-centric than global; instead of competing globally, most companies will seek bloc dominance. Indeed, most companies are not truly global at all, and have never been. A few exceptions (e.g. Toyota, Honda) will rise to a global architecture. However, Toyota is barely present in Europe, and American automakers are barely present in Asia. Companies that strive to be truly global players will follow Kenichi Ohmae's prescription of producing locally within each market (as many are already doing). Many of the 100 or so largest multinationals will fall into this category. For many of those companies, the overwhelming majority of their sales still come from one bloc. For example, Coke and IBM still depend heavily on North America. Just because companies are present all over the world does not mean that they are dominant all over the world.

It appears that the consumer electronics industry will be an Asian stronghold for the foreseeable future. US companies such as HP and Dell are becoming more prominent in the converging consumer electronics industry. Dell is emerging as a major consumer electronics company, while Apple is emerging as a key niche player. HP has recently moved some manufacturing from Taiwan to Mexico for computers and peripherals, and many American companies will follow suit. When companies in the US and Europe lost the volume advantage in the industry, they became niche players (e.g. Bang and Olufsen in Denmark). India is likely to become a major trading partner of the US, and should emerge as a global manufacturer in consumer electronics and textiles.

In the service sector especially, we expect to see a greater degree of bloc-centric markets. Trade in services tends to require more cultural homogeneity (or at least compatibility), as well as greater physical proximity. This is one explanation for why Indian software companies have made limited headway in the Japanese software outsourcing business: the cultural differences are too great. On the other hand, Chinese companies are able to do quite well with Japanese clients.

Bloc-centric thinking also means that countries within a bloc will have to remove any bilateral barriers that may exist. Consider India and Pakistan, two natural trade partners that in practice have been hostile neighbors. Even a modicum of economic integration between them could play huge dividends. The continual state of tension between the neighbors over ideological issues costs each side billions of dollars a year in excessive and economically devastating defense spending (Pakistan spends 30–40 percent of its government's budget and an estimated 5 percent of its GDP on defense, money it desperately needs for economic development) and thousands of lives lost annually (many soldiers succumb to the bitterly cold conditions on the border in the Himalayas). Currently, official trade between the two huge countries (with 1.3 billion people between them) is virtually non-existent (estimated at $1 million a year). A recent study by Ilmas Futehally of Pakistan and Semu Bhatt of India estimates that there could easily be $13 billion a year of trade between the two populous countries. The many complementarities and closely aligned heritage (including shared languages) make open trade between the two neighbors all the more desirable. An obvious area of mutual benefit is electricity, where India has a shortage and Pakistan a surplus. The two countries could also reap the benefits of a common pipeline that would deliver natural gas at a fraction of current costs.[325]

On this dimension, Europe is definitely ahead. There is already over $3 trillion of trade *within* the Europe trade bloc. Asia comes next, as many Asian companies are now focusing on the region. The Americas come in third, since most US companies have not yet turned their energies inwards to the bloc.

Promoting Bloc Standards

There will be battles between blocs over technical standards. Each bloc will create standards of its own and try to impose them on the rest of the world. Sometimes they will succeed, and sometimes they won't. Just as with electrical plugs, cars with left hand and right hand drive, electric voltage and so on, governments will use standards as a mechanism to protect or promote industries in their bloc.

China has such a huge domestic market that it will be able to win many such standards battles in the years ahead. For example, as the world's largest cellular market (with the two largest cellular service companies in the world), China is developing its own '3G' (third generation) standard for broadband wireless communications, called TD-SCDMA. Today, China pays royalties to Qualcomm (the originator of the CDMA standard). In the future it is likely to be the other way around. China has also unilaterally developed and commercialized a new standard for videodiscs called EVD (Enhanced Versatile Disc), which delivers five times the image quality of DVD movies and a higher computer data-storage capacity. This is only one among several projects initiated by the Chinese government in order to reduce licensing payments and 'shake off dependence on foreign technologies in production.'[326] In fact, China is trying to create its own standards for office software, operating systems, wireless computing, Internet protocols, video compression, RFID and several other technologies.[327]

In some industries, dominant standards from one trade bloc will emerge as *de facto* global standards, particularly if their licensing terms are liberal. However, in many other industries, we expect to see intra-bloc standards predominate.

Comparing the trade blocs on this dimension, we find that the Europeans are the most aggressive in using standards to dominate and protect a market. The US generally employs a hands-off policy on the setting of standards, preferring to let industries run the process. This is why the US has been losing some standards battles. The Asians occupy a middle ground. But China is becoming increasingly assertive in setting its own standards in several areas, and all of Asia may adopt Chinese standards. This may ultimately give Asia an advantage in this arena.

Permitting Intra-Bloc Resource Mobility

In the future, trade blocs must ensure that any company operating within the bloc is basically unconstrained in terms of its ability to use resources from anywhere in the bloc. Blocs must facilitate the mobility of labor, money, raw materials and other resources. Current business relationships and processes, which are generally domestic or in some cases global, will have to be reengineered to become bloc centric. In the US, no one thinks about whether a worker is from Florida or California. Likewise, Nokia hires people from all over Europe – it may have Italians working in Finland and Germans in Sweden.

Among industrialized nations, the US has some major advantages. It is the cheapest place to produce sophisticated products in advanced industries, although not because wages are low (they are not). The advantages come from the fact that employee benefits are cheaper, and employees are much more flexible; they can physically be moved from one location to another without much of a problem. This cannot be said of Germany, to pick one European example. Because of highly generous employee benefits, it is cheaper to keep an unemployed employee in one location rather than move him or her to another location. The same is true of much of Europe as well as Japan.[328] This will have to change.

At the bloc level, however, Europe is still definitely in the lead here, as EU passport holders are free to move and work anywhere. The Americas are second (there is high mobility between the US and Canada, but limited elsewhere in the bloc), while Asia remains very restrictive. Even though countries have been more willing to vacate markets, they are still not permitting the free flow of people, money, information and products.

Some trade blocs have huge disparities in terms of population density; they have tremendous density in some places (e.g. China, Japan, South Asia) but very low density in others (Argentina, Australia, Canada, Brazil). Ultimately, there will be pressures for large-scale migration. This is where Europe has an advantage, because it doesn't have huge disparities. On the other hand, there is greater opportunity for synergy when you have disparities, such as between Australia and China. Australia needs people, so it has radically changed its immigration policy. After resisting for decades, it is now opening up to immigration in a big way.

The much-feared global population explosion has now been revealed to be a non-issue. Although the population continues to rise, it is projected to peak and then to start declining in the next few decades. For most developed countries in the world today, the issue is not too many people, but too few, especially working age people. These countries face a demographic meltdown – too few workers supporting too many retirees and stagnant or declining demand for most products due to a net loss of households.

It is becoming increasingly evident that low population density countries must invite more people. With bloc integration, we believe very strongly that people should be encouraged to settle in new places. It is our observation that outsiders are always the ones who are able to revitalize a place, because insiders tend to become complacent. This happens within countries as well. For example, in India, the people of Rajasthan (*Marwaris*) have revitalized the economically backward states of Bengal and Bihar. People from the Indian state of Gujarat revitalized many east African economies during the colonial era.

The problem is that many of the countries with the most severe problems of population shrinkage are also the most culturally insular, to the point of xenophobia. Many nations in Western Europe and Japan have been concerned about having their culture overrun by 'alien' influences.

In addition to the economically stimulating effect that a growing population brings, immigration also has many other economic benefits for host countries, when it is done thoughtfully. The five countries most open to immigration in the world in recent years have been the US, Israel, Canada, New Zealand, and Australia. Of these, the latter four have strict requirements that potential immigrants must possess desired skills or substantial economic clout. Many other countries permit limited immigration to individuals marrying citizens, to fill specific job needs, for wealthy investors, for asylum seekers or as a condition of multilateral agreements, such as in the European Union or between Australia and New Zealand. The consensus view of analysts who have examined the economic impact of immigration on these and other countries has been that it is a strongly positive force.[329]

Indeed, many economists argue that the free movement of people would have a greater beneficial economic impact than the free trade of goods and services. Others disagree with this view, arguing that unrestricted immigration can depress wages, degrade the environment and lead to unsustainable population densities and growth. In our view, encouraging planned and steady immigration is a sound policy for countries to follow. The market for the best human capital is not as liquid as are other markets, but it is a reality that the best opportunities will attract the best talent. It is in the best interest of countries and blocs to permit this to occur, and to do everything they can to attract the best human capital themselves.

Summary Assessment of Trade Blocs

The pattern here is quite clear. Europe is in the lead because it had a considerable head start in this journey. Its advantages will become even stronger if it can remove heavy subsidies and allow more consolidation to take place. The Americas are lagging on this front; it is important for the governments in the bloc to start thinking more regionally, and encourage companies within the bloc to do the same. They must communicate to them the reality that, while their past has been inextricably linked with Europe and to a lesser extent with Asia, their future lies in the Americas. This will require simultaneous disinvestments and reinvestment on a massive scale.

CHAPTER 12

OBSTACLES TO THE REALIGNMENT OF MARKETS

The evolution we have described here has a certain historical logic and momentum, but questions remain and obstacles loom. As we conclude, let's look ahead at some of the difficulties that must be negotiated.

Who will Lead?

Nothing can happen without visionary leadership. The realignment we envision may yet founder unless far-sighted leaders of key countries take up the cause with passion and commitment.

We believe that the three trade economies will take optimum shape only if at least two countries in each bloc step forward as leaders to make it happen. In the EU, we have already seen the effectiveness of the leadership of France, Germany and in the future, Russia. In the other two blocs the situation is different in that most of the nations joining the alignment will represent emerging economies. Therefore, in both the Americas and in Asia, it will be critical for leadership to take the form of a close partnership between a dominant developed economy and a major emerging economy. This seems to be happening between Japan and China, and between the US and India. Such partnerships will best exemplify the 'win-win scenario' that must lie at the heart of this whole evolution. It must be convincingly demonstrated that increased trade among member states in each bloc constitutes a rising tide that will lift all boats: the most advanced economies will find new room for growth in the least advanced, while the least advanced are given opportunities to ascend the economic value chain.

We might note, also, that smaller countries are often less subject to historical inertia and can take the lead in suggesting the way forward. In the Americas, for example, Chile has long been at the forefront of efforts to achieve broader economic integration. In Southeast Asia, Malaysia (under former Prime Minister Mahathir) was the first country to formally propose that Asian countries start thinking about an Asian regional economy along the lines of the EU or NAFTA.

Furthermore, the success of ASEAN suggests that, as a practical step forward, smaller FTAs can be entered into which ultimately get woven into a broad trade union. As the US, Canada and Mexico joined to form NAFTA, which will be subsumed into FTAA, so Japan, China and Korea could enter into a North Asian FTA, which would eventually merge with the ASEAN FTA (AFTA) to form the East Asian Economic Union (EAEU).

Effective leadership will be all the more critical because the journey ahead will be difficult, beset by a variety of obstacles. Change always encounters resistance, especially from those whose interests are vested in the status quo. In the pages that follow, we look briefly at some of the challenges that will confront the evolving realignment.

1. An Entrenched Domestic Private Sector

Some of the most strategic victories lie in surrender. The creation of long-term value through trade blocs can only come when individual countries willingly 'vacate' certain industries in which they lack comparative advantage, while enhancing their efforts in industries where they do enjoy such an advantage. But it's easy to see that private companies devoted to such industries will not be happy about giving them up. The US textile industry, long a mainstay in the Southeast, offers a great example. It's no wonder that the captains of such industries fight to hold onto subsidies and other trade practices that, in the long run, make little economic sense for the country.

Perhaps surprisingly, the bloc managing this obstacle with the most success is Europe, despite its strong labor unions. Two factors explain this relative success. First, Europeans have already said, 'We are one market,' thus committing to the free movement of products. The French company that did business only in France because of market restrictions is now doing business in Germany as well. It begins to export products to Germany, for example, or even decides to buy out a Germany company. (Again, it has been easier for Europe to become 'one market' because of the relatively large number of similarly advanced economies within the EU.) The second advantage for Europe is that it already home to a large number of diversified conglomerate entities – companies that can engage in pan-European deal-making with one another. A company like Siemens, for example, may decide that, rather than having 30 businesses scattered across Europe, it would rather be in ten pan-regional industries and surrender the other 20 to firms from other nations. When companies can 'trade chips,' so to speak, everyone comes out a winner.

Asian nations like Japan, South Korea and Taiwan are showing how to overcome this obstacle by vacating industries and moving up the value chain. Korea's progress has been astounding here. Not long ago a low-end manufacturer and the butt of a thousand 'made in Korea' jokes, Korea is now a world leader in high-tech gadgetry, and Samsung is one of the world's most respected brands.

The bloc likely to have the hardest time overcoming this obstacle is the Americas under the FTAA architecture. We see every day how reluctant the US is to surrender its entrenched sectors, and trade negotiations with its hemispheric neighbors are contentious. The problem is much bigger than just farm subsidies, though that is its most visible aspect. Steel and textiles are among the other industries in which the US no longer enjoys any comparative advantage, but, needless to say, there is much opposition to letting such industries go. Too, the problem in the US is exacerbated by the incredible power of lobbyists, who seem able to run roughshod over legislators and other political officials who might otherwise see the wisdom of pursuing a free trade agenda.

Solutions

The trading bloc governing bodies must offer economic incentives for the private sector to get out of certain industries. Traditionally, companies have looked to governments for incentives for entry. Now they'll have to be given incentives for exit – job-retraining programs, tuition plans, retirement packages, anything to ease the pain of upheaval. In the US, North Carolina and Virginia have managed to transition their economies away from dependence on tobacco and towards high tech. The orange groves of central Florida have been transformed into the Mecca for tourists, Orlando.

2. Political Gridlock

In a system that depends on the mutual cooperation of dozens of nations, political gridlock is bound to seem an intractable problem. Difficulties already exist in each of the three blocs, and as the realignment we have foreseen moves toward its final shape, many more will be encountered.

In Europe, the problems associated with the drafting of the EU constitution seem to be insurmountable, with some member states refusing to adopt it altogether. At issue: where will the power lie – in Brussels, or within the governments of member states? It is an issue that almost sundered the US 150 years ago. More problems will arise with the inclusion of Eastern European states. Poland's support of the US in the war in Iraq was a slap in the face to France and Germany.

In Asia, long-festering political problems will prove an obstacle for bloc cooperation. To read the newspapers, you would think that China might blow Taiwan off the map at any minute. As for China itself, as it evolves into a world economic superpower, how will its one-party, Communist government, which still lays a heavy hand on industrial development, ever be truly reconciled with the mandates of a free market?

The Americas may be in the worst shape of all. Look at the situation between the US and Cuba, for example, where sheer hardheadedness seems to characterize both sides. Or consider US relations with Venezuela, or the US's questionable history in Central America. Many of the nations of the proposed FTAA perceive the US as a bully out to take advantage of them, and they may not want to play.

Solutions

Patience will certainly help. The benefits that will accrue to the three trading blocs – and ultimately to the world – will not be seen overnight. As small free-trade agreements blend and merge into larger ones, as the pluses begin to outweigh the minuses, economies will improve and, as China demonstrates so remarkably, people will rise out of poverty. Progress will trump political gridlock, eventually.

Wisdom will help also. Governments must be willing to recognize and acknowledge what is happening, even when it runs counter to an established political agenda. The long view will have to be embraced, and short-term special interests will have to be shunned.

Now, where will we find the requisite patience and wisdom? Of course, they will have to emerge in each bloc's leaders. Each bloc will have to be led by men and women with vision to see the future and courage to bring change – leaders like Margaret Thatcher, Lee Kuan Yew, Mahathir Mohamad of Malaysia, or Manmohan Singh in India; leaders who understand that 'economic pragmatism' is stronger than any ideology. Perhaps foremost in this company is Deng Xiaoping, patient enough to wait until he was 74 years old to become paramount ruler, and wise enough to understand that China's economy was in ruins and that it would have to be transformed by market forces.

3. Rising Expectations

Paradoxically, progress that doesn't march forward fast enough appears not to march at all. The US learned this lesson during the Civil Rights upheaval of the 1950s and 1960s. Thanks to advances in technology (the Internet, especially) and the democratization of information, the paradox is more apparent all the time. People want the future yesterday. And who can blame them? Free trade agreements promise a rising standard of living, uplift out of poverty, an end to starvation, jobs and wages, and people in the developing world want that promise fulfilled *now*. When it is not thus fulfilled, the trade agreements are blamed, and the slow progress that has been made is at risk. Thus, people's rising expectations become a formidable obstacle to the realignment underway.

Europe faces this problem as it tries to bring the less developed economies of Eastern Europe (and eventually Turkey) into the union. (The consequences of the sudden collision of mismatched economies were dramatically illustrated in the reunification of Germany, when Kohl allowed the one-to-one conversion of East German Ostmarks into Deutschmarks and virtually destroyed the East German economy.) The problem will be even worse in the Americas, where the vast gulf between American affluence and the impoverished regions of Central and South America will likely be a source of tension. Vicente Fox's inability to speedily deliver the full promise of NAFTA already imperils his regime and that of the reform-minded National Action Party (PAN). The huge differences between the developed and developing economies in Asia will cause problems in that bloc as well, though the incredible progress in China, where 300 million people were lifted out of poverty in just two decades, can be held up as an example of what is possible.

Solutions

As with political gridlock, there is no programmatic solution to the problem of rising expectations. People in need will continue to demand change faster than change can be delivered. Common sense and human nature tell us that much.

A partial solution might be found in relaxed emigration laws and policies. That is, to the extent possible, people should be allowed and encouraged to move to wherever they discern the greatest opportunity, thus precipitating a global 'leveling' of the economic playing field. One problem with this approach is seen in the bitter 'border wars' going on right now between the US and Mexico. Countries with open borders are going to be pressured to close them again by citizens who feel that their own jobs and opportunities are threatened. An even greater problem here lies in the fact that the vast majority of the world's impoverished people lack the means to travel. Economic development must come to them.

Good leadership is again the real key, but note the paradox. Leaders will be measured by how quickly they deliver economic progress. Those who understand that real progress comes slowly have a huge selling job on their hands, shouting a truth nobody wants to hear.

We believe that these three – an entrenched private sector, political gridlock, and rising expectations – are the chief obstacles to trade bloc realignment. Let us take a brief look at a few others.

- **Privatization of the public sector:** Here, the weakest bloc is Europe, where state governments continue to own or control a number of industries and enterprises, despite an announced policy of privatization. For example, the Chirac government has proven unable to privatize France Telecom, and Airbus Industrie continues to be subsidized by not one but four European governments. India's privatization efforts continue, haltingly, as reformers work to throw off years of communist influence. In China, the battle between state ownership and free enterprise continues to simmer. Eventually it will come to a boil.
- **Cultural and ideological diversity:** Oddly, the Americas, and specifically the US may face the biggest challenge here, because cultural diversity has transformed the melting pot

into a smorgasbord. There seems to be no national consensus on anything (gay marriage, abortion, immigration, the war in Iraq) and, consequently, no national identity. The US is widely viewed internally as being evenly split between 'red' (Republican-leaning) and 'blue' (Democrat-leaning) states. The proposed FTAA likewise splits the country, and typically, both sides are vilified: those who are for it are corporate/capitalist exploiters, and those opposed are dreamy-eyed socialist-environmentalist tree-huggers. Unlike the Americas, Europe and Asia appear to be further along in the process of building identity. Cultural differences persist, of course, but the very existence of the European Union and ASEAN testifies to the power of a common purpose and a unifying cause.

- **Corruption:** This is perhaps Asia's biggest problem. Japan's keiratsu and Korea's *chaebols* have left a lasting legacy of corruption, especially in the banking systems, and elsewhere in the bloc political instability continues to breed widespread corruption. Europe is not immune, of course; nor is Central or South America. The US, for all its current woes, insists on a level of transparency that others would do well to emulate.

In Conclusion

The dominance of the US is already over. What is emerging is a world economy of blocs represented by NAFTA, the European Union, ASEAN. There's no one center in this world economy.

Peter Drucker[330]

The pattern is very clear, and the Europeans, who want to create a 'more perfect union', are driving it – analogous to the 'US' of America that established itself as a world power once it emerged from the devastation of the Civil War. As the Europeans succeed in integrating their union – and creating a huge market in the process – the US will take the next logical step to create a hemispheric coalition of 'American states.' The US of America, in essence, will evolve into the United *Countries* of America. Meanwhile, Asia cannot ignore the process, and the combination of Japan's mature economy with China's immense emerging one, both in alliance with the ASEAN nations, will provide the countervailing third force.

In the Western Hemisphere, the FTAA-propelled economic integration throughout Central and South America will happen by the year 2020. In sectors such as finance, insurance, airlines and telecommunications, northern partners – the US and Canada – will command most of the business throughout the regional community. In the classic Ricardian scenario, the north will 'vacate' its agriculture sector and the traditional manufacturing industries – processed foods, automobiles, steel, textiles – and allow them to migrate southward, giving the necessary boost to the agricultural and manufacturing-driven economies of Latin America. While those economies diversify and grow healthy, the US and Canada will move further up the value chain to service- and knowledge-based industries.

Let us look outward, a little further. What happens when growth in the emerging markets finally levels off, say in 20 to 30 years? When these economies come to their own maturity, they will face the problem of today's advanced nations. They, too, will chafe at the prospect of a slow-growth manufacturing economy and will, in their turn, seek to move up the chain to services and knowledge creation.

At that point, perhaps, the north-south realignment – and its goal of geoeconomic integration between the developed and developing worlds – will have served its purpose, and we may then finally evolve toward a truly 'one world' approach.

Endnotes

1. Gerald F. Seib, "Looking Inward," *Wall Street Journal*, July 3, 1992 (A1).
2. Kenichi Ohmae, *Triad Power* (New York: The Free Press, 1985), p. xiii.
3. http://en.wikipedia.org/wiki/Chinese_economic_reform
4. Michael Shari (2003), "Malaysia after Mahathir," *Business Week International*, September 29.
5. http://www.businessweek.com/magazine/content/03_39/b3851015_mz046.htm
6. Charles I. Jones (2001), "Was an Industrial Revolution Inevitable? Economic Growth Over the Very Long Run," *Advances in Macroeconomics*, Vol. 1, Issue 2, p. 1028.
7. Ohmae, *Triad Power*.
8. William J. Baumol & Ralph E. Gomory (1998), "A Country's Maximal Gains from Trade and Conflicting National Interests," Working Papers 98–22, C.V. Starr Center for Applied Economics, New York University.
9. Robert Kagan (2003), *Of Paradise and Power*, New York: Vintage Books.
10. Winston Churchill, Speech at Zurich University, 19th September 1946.
11. Rugman, *The End of Globalization: Why Global Strategy Is a Myth & How to Profit from the Realities of Regional Markets* (New York: Amacom, 2000), p. 25.
12. The Economist, *World in Figures*, 2004.
13. Bjorn Hettne, Andras Inotai and Osvaldo Sunkel (eds) (1999), *Globalization and the New Regionalism*, London: Macmillan.
14. See Daniel R. Fusfeld, *The Age of the Economist* (Glenview, Ill.: Scott, Foresman, 1977), pp. 43–47, and Robert L. Heilbroner, *The Worldly Philosophers: The Lives, Times, and Ideas of the Great Economic Thinkers*, revised 7th ed. (New York: Touchstone/Simon & Schuster, 1999), pp. 75–104.

15. See Paul Kennedy, *The Rise and Fall of the Great Powers: Economic Change and Military Conflict from 1500 to 2000* (New York: Random House, 1987), pp. 143–156; 226–244.
16. Stuart Legg, "Trade and Capital: The Other Empire," in *The Horizon History of the British Empire*, ed. by Stephen W. Sears (New York: American Heritage/McGraw-Hill, 1973), p. 359.
17. For a more thorough, and engaging, analysis of Marx's critique of capitalism, see Heilbroner, *The Worldly Philosophers*, pp. 136–169.
18. Daniel Yergin and Joseph Stanislaw, *The Commanding Heights: The Battle for the World Economy* (New York: Touchstone/Simon & Schuster, 1998), p. xii.
19. Yergin and Stanislaw, pp. 26–27.
20. Yergin and Stanislaw, p. 204. See pp. 185–211 for the authors' full discussion of China's emergence into the world economy.
21. Thomas Friedman, *The Lexus and the Olive Tree: Understanding Globalization* (New York: Anchor Books, 2000), pp. 75–76.
22. "China's Hot, at Least for Now," *The New York Times*, Dec. 16, 2002 (C11).
23. Timothy Aeppel, "SARS Doesn't Take Long-Term Shine off China," *Wall Street Journal*, May 2, 2003 (A12).
24. Jonathan Heath, "Mexico Today: Bouncing Back from the Peso Crash," *Business Economics*, July 1999, pp. 14–21.
25. Friedman, *The Lexus and the Olive Tree*, p. 430.
26. Yergin and Stanislaw, p. 266. For the authors' discussion of Mexico's economic turnaround, see pp. 259–266.
27. Sebastian Moffet, "How Japan's Neighbors Give It a Lift," *Wall Street Journal*, Feb 13, 2003 (A10).
28. Ohmae, *Triad Power*, p. 163. For Ohmae's full discussion of the role of developing nations, see pp. 149–164.
29. Paul R. Krugman and Maurice Obstfeld, *International Economics: Theory and Policy* (New York: HarperCollins, 1994), p. 248.
30. Yergin and Stanislaw, p. xiii.
31. Yergin and Stanislaw, pp. 6–20.
32. Michael S. Teitelbaum and Philip L. Martin, "Is Turkey Ready for Europe?" *Foreign Affairs*, May/June 2003, pp. 97–111.
33. Yergin and Stanislaw, p. 318.
34. http://csfrance.amb-usa.fr/France2us2.pdf
35. Lester Thurow, *Head to Head: The Coming Economic Battle Among Japan, Europe, and America* (New York: William Morrow, 1992), p. 30.
36. Brian Hellauer, "IBM Bank Software Unit Gets Quality Stamp," *American Banker*, Sep 7, 1993, p. 16.
37. "U.S. Mission to EC Expands Services to Assist U.S. Exporters," *Business America*, Mar 8, 1993, p. 39.
38. Thurow, pp. 68–69.

39. Thurow, pp. 34–35.
40. Daniel Burstein, *Euroquake: Europe's Explosive Economic Challenge Will Change the World* (New York: Simon & Schuster, 1991), p. 327.
41. J. Lynn Lunsford, "U.S. Lawmakers Push Taiwan to Cancel Airbus Deal, Hire Boeing," *Wall Street Journal*, Sep 12, 2002, A13.
42. Daniel Michaels, "Airbus Goes into Overdrive," *Wall Street Journal*, Jan 14, 2003, B4.
43. John Tagliabue, "Airbus in $24 Billion Deal for Military Jets, *New York Times*, May 28, 2003, A1.
44. Alan Levin, "Near-Crash Uncovers Crack in Air Safety System," *USA Today*, May 27, 2003.
45. Alan Rugman, *The End of Globalization: Why Global Strategy Is a Myth & How to Profit from the Realities of Regional Markets* (New York: Amacom, 2000), p. 163.
46. Rugman, pp. 116–118.
47. "Poland: Europe's Tiger," *The Economist*, Aug 28, 1993, p. 48.
48. "Europe: Nice Holiday, Pity About the Job; Poland's Economy," *The Economist*, July 27, 2002, p. 46.
49. "Reaching for the European Union; The Czech Republic's Politics," *The Economist*, Mar 16, 2002, pp. 54–55.
50. Ernest S. McCrary, "Hungary Headed for the EU," *Global Finance*, Mar 2002, pp. 56–67.
51. "And Now Let's Have Another Look at the Road Map," *The Economist*, Dec 21, 2002, p. 67.
52. Thurow, pp. 91–111.
53. Michael Wines, "Putin Asks Europe to Open Borders," *New York Times*, Jun 1, 2003, p. 14.
54. Sabrina Tavernise, "Talks on Russian Entry into W.T.O. Hit Snag," *New York Times*, Oct 18, 2002, W1.
55. Vassily Likhachev, "Russia and the European Union," *International Affairs* (Moscow), Feb 2003, p. 55.
56. Guy Chazan, "Russian Revival," *Wall Street Journal*, Oct 14, 2002, R.4.
57. Chip Cummins and Jeanne Whalen, "BP Focuses on Six New Areas," *Wall Street Journal*, Feb 12, 2003, A3.
58. Thatcher, Margaret. *The Downing Street Years* (New York: HarperCollins, 1993), "unacceptable," p. 62; "'anchored' to the deutschmark," p. 690; "not prepared to compromise," p. 719; "supra-national institutions," p. 691; "philosophy justified centrism," p. 558; "centralist mindset," p. 536; "protectionist agenda," p. 727; "dominance from Brussels," p. 745; "its own defence," p. 814; "and fight," p. 728; "still proceeding," p. 726.
59. Peter Jenkins, *Mrs. Thatcher's Revolution*, p. 286.
60. Thatcher, p. 725.
61. "Chancellor to Fight VW Takeover Bid," *Automotive News*, Mar 4, 2002, p. 23.

62. Krugman and Obstfeld, pp. 178; 246.
63. Brandon Mitchener, "Silence, Please: It's Time to Sing the EU Anthem," *Wall Street Journal*, May 7, 2003, A1.
64. "Europe: All Aboard the Euro-train," *The Economist*, Apr 5, 2003, p. 50.
65. Cited in Daniel Yergin, *The Prize: The Epic Quest for Oil, Money, and Power* (New York: Simon & Schuster, 1991), p. 695.
66. Herbert Stein, *Presidential Economics* (New York: Simon & Schuster, 1984), p. 221.
67. Thurow, p. 183.
68. Stein, pp. 166–214.
69. Yergin and Stanislaw, pp. 31–38.
70. Stein, p. 191.
71. Yergin and Stanislaw, pp. 357–365.
72. Martin Anderson, *Revolution* (New York: Harcourt Brace, 1988), p. 117.
73. Lou Cannon, *President Reagan: The Role of a Lifetime* (New York: PublicAffairs, 1991), p. 489.
74. Cannon, p. 736.
75. Anderson, p. 260.
76. Cannon, p. 747.
77. Anderson, p. 180.
78. Cannon, p. 748.
79. "North, to Argentina" (editorial), *Wall Street Journal*, Nov 14, 1988.
80. Nels Ackerson, "U.S.-Canada Trade Pact May Founder on Autos," *Wall Street Journal*, Jun 23, 1987, p. 1.
81. Jeffrey Hawkins, "The Canada-U.S. Free Trade Agreement: An Interim Assessment," *Business America*, Apr 20, 1992, p. 2.
82. Peter C. Newman, "The End of Canada," *Maclean's*, Jan 8, 2001, pp. 18–20; and "Beware of Freer Trade," *Maclean's*, Dec 2, 2002, p. 46.
83. See Gregory N. Racz, "Perot Tells Senate Panel NAFTA Pact Will Cost Americans Three Million Jobs, *Wall Street Journal*, Apr 23, 1993, A7; and "Perot vs. Gore," *National Review*, Dec 13, 1993, p. 70.
84. "House Democratic Whip Escalates Attack on NAFTA," *Wall Street Journal*, Aug 30, 1993, A10.
85. Bob Davis and Asra Q. Nomani, "Jolt to NAFTA," *Wall Street Journal*, Jul 1, 1993, A1.
86. Dianne Solis, "NAFTA Negotiators Clear a Hurdle on Environmental Side Accord," *Wall Street Journal*, Jul 12, 1993, A9.
87. Ronald Reagan, "Tear Down the Trade Wall," *Wall Street Journal*, Sep 13, 1993, A16.
88. See Karen Elliot House, "Singapore Chief Wants NAFTA to Involve Asia," *Wall Street Journal*, Oct 4, 1993, B4; and Michael K. Frisby, "Clinton Makes 11th-hour Bid for NAFTA," *Wall Street Journal*, Nov 2, 1993, A2.
89. Bob Davis and Jackie Calmes, "The House Passes NAFTA," *Wall Street Journal*, Nov 18, 1993, A1.

90. Jeremy Brecher, "Global Village or Global Pillage?" *The Nation*, Dec 6, 1993, p. 685.
91. "Mexico's Second-Class Citizens Say Enough Is Enough," *The Economist*, Jan 8, 1994, p. 41.
92. "NAFTA: Working for U.S. Exports and Jobs," *Business America*, Dec 1994, p. 22.
93. "Happy Ever NAFTA?" *The Economist*, Dec 10, 1994, p. 23.
94. Paul Dacher, *Business America*, Aug 1996, p. 10.
95. "Against the NAFTA Naysayers," *Business Week*, Dec 9, 1996, p. 202.
96. "The Trucks That Hold Back NAFTA," *The Economist*, Dec 13, 1997, pp. 23–24.
97. Alan Zarembo, "Politics Trumps NAFTA," *Newsweek*, Feb 14, 2000, p. 54.
98. "The Americas: No Truck with Free Trade," *The Economist*, Aug 4, 2001, p. 35.
99. U.S. Department of State Dispatch, May 1995, p. 30.
100. Paul Magnusson, "Commentary: Beyond NAFTA," *Business Week*, Apr 21, 1997, p. 46.
101. Thomas Friedman, *The Lexus and the Olive Tree* (New York: Anchor Books, 2000), p. 336.
102. Paul Magnusson, "Farm Subsidies: A Blight on the Economy," *Business Week*, Sep 9, 2002, p. 50.
103. Geri Smith, "Mexico Pulls off Another Trade Coup," *Business Week*, Feb 7, 2000, p. 56.
104. John S. McClenahen, "NAFTA Works," *Industry Week*, Jan 10, 2000, pp. 5–6.
105. Cited in Yergin and Stanislaw, pp. 266–267.
106. Marilyn Geewax, "Protests Grow as Tech Jobs Move Offshore," *Atlanta Journal-Constitution*, Jun 27, 2003, E1.
107. Pauline Yoshihashi, "Predicted Shortage of Farm Labor Hasn't Materialized," *Wall Street Journal*, Sep 22, 1987, p. 1.
108. "Illegal Aliens," *The Economist*, Feb 20, 1993.
109. Dinesh D'Souza, *What's So Great About America* (New York: Penguin Books, 2002), pp. 77–78 ("moral triumph"); p. 175 ("material improvement"); p. 176 ("cultural relativism"); p. 84 ("your own destiny"); p. 169 ("face the truth").
110. Tony Emerson, "The Great Walls," *Newsweek*, Apr 23, 2001, p. 40.
111. Claudo Katz, "Free Trade Area of the Americas: NAFTA Marches South," *NACLA Report on the Americas*, Jan/Feb 2002, pp. 27–31.
112. Jeffrey E. Garten, "Why Bush Must Not Lose Sight of Latin America," *Business Week*, Dec 16, 2002, p. 26.
113. Mario Osava, "Trade-Americas: Brazil and U.S. Face Off in Decisive FTAA Talks," *Global Information Network*, May 29, 2003, p. 1.
114. Fareed Zakaria, "Banking on Mexico's Future," *Newsweek*, Jun 11, 2001, p. 4.

115. Michael Casey, "Argentina's High-Tech Chance," *Wall Street Journal*, Jul 24, 2003, A12.
116. Matt Moffett, "Land Rush," *Wall Street Journal*, Jul 10, 2003, A1.
117. Julie Creswell, "Investing in a Dangerous World," *Fortune*, Jun 16, 2003, p. 77.
118. "The Americas: Trade Wind; Brazilian Diplomacy," *The Economist*, Jun 28, 2003, p. 70.
119. Peter Richards, "Caribbean Leaders Agree to Step Up Drive for a Single Market," *Global Information Network*, Feb 20, 2003, p. 1.
120. Curt Hopkins, "Stitching Up a Deal," *Newsweek*, Jun 9, 2003, p. 37.
121. Geri Smith, "Chile—A Giant Step Toward Free Trade Across the Americas?" *Business Week*, Jun 16, 2003, p. 53.
122. Robert Sobel, *IBM vs. Japan: The Struggle for the Future* (New York: Stein and Day, 1986), p. 146.
123. Ezra F. Vogel, *Japan as Number One* (New York: Harper Colophon, 1978), p. 10.
124. Sobel, pp. 149–150 (four-step process); pp. 206–209 (television wars).
125. Sobel, p. 212.
126. Yergin and Stanislaw, p. 149.
127. Thurow, p. 248.
128. Vogel, p. 245.
129. Yergin and Stanislaw, p. 150.
130. Vogel, p. 250.
131. Yergin and Stanislaw, pp. 151–158.
132. Lee Kuan Yew, *From Third World to First: The Singapore Story, 1965–2000* (New York: HarperCollins, 2000), p. 3.
133. Lee Kuan Yew, pp. 52–55.
134. Lee Kuan Yew's discussion of the initial steps in Singapore's economic program is found in Chapter 4, "Surviving Without a Hinterland." See especially pp. 57–64.
135. Yergin and Stanislaw, pp. 168–169.
136. Lee Kuan Yew, p. 263.
137. Yergin and Stanislaw, p. 175.
138. Lee Kuan Yew, pp. 299–300.
139. See Chapter 20, "Asean—Unpromising Start, Promising Future" (pp. 329–342), for Lee Kuan Yew's discussion of the development of ASEAN.
140. Lim Chong Yah, *Southeast Asia: The Long Road Ahead* (New Jersey: World Scientific, 2001), p. 11; p. 160.
141. Lim Chong Yah, p. 49; p. 128.
142. Yergin and Stanislaw, pp. 177–178.
143. Lee Kuan Yew, p. 346.
144. Lee Kuan Yew, p. 345.
145. Yergin and Stanislaw, p. 179.

146. Lim Chong Yah, pp. 306–307.
147. Lee Kuan Yew, p. 344.
148. Lim Chong Yah, p. 311.
149. Yergin and Stanislaw, p. 183.
150. Lee Kuan Yew, p. 349.
151. "Never Mind the Quality," *The Economist*, Mar 1, 1997, p. 40.
152. "Expanding ASEAN," *The Economist*, May 3, 1997, p. 17.
153. "Nations: Tests for the ASEAN Nine," *Asiaweek*, Aug 1, 1997.
154. "Asia: A Slap on the Wrist," *The Economist*, Jun 21, 2003, p. 62.
155. "Asia Finds Its Voice on Myanmar," *New York Times*, Jun 17, 2003, A26.
156. Reprinted in *ASEAN Economic Bulletin*, Aug 2002, p. 211.
157. "Asia: Every Man for Himself," *The Economist*, Nov 2, 2002, p. 65.
158. Yergin and Stanislaw, p. 184.
159. Jonathan Story, *China: The Race to Market* (New York: Prentice-Hall/Financial Times, 2003), p. 14.
160. Story, pp. 65–71.
161. "The Booming Economy and China's Infrastructure," *NPR's Morning Edition*, Jun 14, 1995 (print version available online at ProQuest Information and Learning Company).
162. "Members Snag Infrastructure Contracts," *China Business Review*, Jan/Feb 1995, p. 13.
163. Henny Sender, "Li's Latest," *Far Eastern Economic Review*, Jul 11, 1996, p. 68.
164. Barry Wain, "New Leaders Help Revitalize Asian Group," *Wall Street Journal*, Sep 4, 2001, A17.
165. Story, pp. 72–73; p. 215.
166. Story, p. 220.
167. George Wehrfritz and Alexandra A. Seno, "Chugging Along," *Newsweek* (International ed.), Jun 23, 2003, p. 42.
168. Story, p. 66.
169. Wehrfritz and Seno, "Chugging Along," p. 42.
170. Michael Vatikiotis and David Murphy, "With Aggressive Trade Pacts, China Quietly Builds Clout in Region," *Wall Street Journal*, Mar 19, 2003, A12.
171. Story, pp. 76–77.
172. Charles R. Williamson and Drake Weisert, "Natural Gas: Fuel for the New Economy," *The China Business Review*, Sep/Oct 2001, p. 38.
173. Mark L. Clifford and Frederik Balfour, "Open Season," *Business Week*, Sep 9, 2002, p. 22.
174. Aoki Tamotsu, "Shanghai's Soft Power Shows the Way Forward," *Japan Echo*, Jun 2002, p. 58.
175. Story, p. 18.
176. Suvendrini Kakuchi, "Asia: China's Surging Economy Troubles the Japanese," *Global Information Network*, Mar 27, 2003, p. 1.

177. "China Briefing," *Far Eastern Economic Review*, Apr 17, 2003, p. 24.
178. James Pringle, "We've Got Nothing to Do," *Newsweek* (International ed.), May 5, 2003, p. 38.
179. Dalia Acosta, "Cuba: Miami Beckons," *Global Information Network*, May 8, 2003, p. 1.
180. Geri Smith, "Why Fidel Picked This Moment to Crack Down," *Business Week*, Apr 21, 2003, p. 59.
181. Patricia Grogg, "Cuba-Trade: Castro Abandons Bid to Join Cotonou," *Global Information Network*, May 20, 2003, p. 1.
182. Patricia Grogg, "Tourism-Cuba: New Slowdown for Motor of Economy," *Global Information Network*, Jan 11, 2003, p. 1.
183. Bert Wilkinson, "Castro Hosting Caribbean Leaders," *Global Information Network*, Dec 5, 2002, p. 1.
184. Dalia Acosta, "Cuba: Hoping Hard for a Strong Tourist Season," *Global Information Network*, Nov 7, 2002, p. 1.
185. Patricia Grogg, "Expanding Sugar Cane By-Products," *Global Information Network*, Jun 13, 2003, p. 1.
186. "Blacks in U.S. Flock to Cuba for Free Medical School," *Jet*, Feb 10, 2003, p. 61.
187. "$20 Million Cuban Trade Deal Offers Hope," *Jet*, Mar 24, 2003, p. 9.
188. Katrin Dauenhauer, "Bipartisan Support Grows for Ending Cuba Travel Ban," *Global Information Network*, Jul 24, 2003, p. 1.
189. Bradford Dillman, "Facing the Market in North Africa," *The Middle East Journal*, Spring 2001, pp. 198–215.
190. Aner Versi, "Tunisia: Relationship with the European Union," *Middle East*, Oct 2002, pp. 33–45; Josh Martin, "Morocco & Europe Talks," *Middle East*, Oct 2001, pp. 26–29.
191. Varsha Gupta d'Souza, "German Car Firms to Drive Funds into Eastern Cape," *Global Information Network*, Jul 25, 2003, p. 1.
192. Estelle Drew, "EU-South Africa Trade: Door Opens Just a Little Wider," *African Business*, Jul/Aug 2000, p. 20.
193. Dinesh D'Souza, *What's So Great About America* (New York: Penguin, 2002), p. 178.
194. Bernard Lewis, *What Went Wrong? Western Impact and Middle Eastern Response* (Oxford: Oxford Univ. Press, 2002), pp. 130–131.
195. Lewis, p. 73.
196. Emad Mekay, "U.S. Maps Ambitious Free Trade Deal with Middle East," *Global Information Network*, Jun 24, 2003.
197. Cam McGrath, "Boycott Fever Targets Israel, U.S. Brands," *Global Information Network*, May 9, 2002, p. 1.
198. "Bush Ties Aid to Israel to West Bank," *NPR—Weekend All Things Considered*, Sep 7, 1991 (print version available from ProQuest Information and Learning Company).

199. Paul Thanos, "Israel Faces New Economy and Challenges at 50," *Business America*, Sep 1998, p. 15.
200. "World Horticultural Trade and U.S. Export Opportunities" (PFP#712625252), pp. 6–7. On-line at www.usda.gov.
201. Sarosh Bana, "Now It Shines, Now It Doesn't," *Business India*, Aug 20, 2001.
202. Wade Boese, "Israeli Arms Exports to China of Growing Concern to U.S.," *Arms Control Today*, Mar 2003, p. 30.
203. Ferry Biedermann, "Hefty Defense Budget Has High Social Cost," *Global Information Network*, May 24, 2002.
204. Thanos, p. 15.
205. Tom Holland, "A Booming Economy Looks Overseas," *Far Eastern Economic Review*, Jun 5, 2003, p. 12.
206. Glenda Korporaal, "Oz Goes Offshore," *Far Eastern Economic Review*, Mar 7, 1991, p. 38.
207. Matthew Fletcher and Asif Shameen, "Australia: Staying Close to Asia," *Asiaweek*, Mar 11, 1996.
208. Kalinga Seneviratne, "Canberra Fears Possible Asian Tourist Boycott," *Inter Press Service*, Nov 4, 1997, p. 1.
209. "Australia's Fear and Loathing," *Asiaweek*, Oct 11, 1996.
210. Holland, p. 12.
211. Bruce Einhorn, "How Long Will Beijing Keep Playing It Cool on Taiwan?" *Business Week*, Sep 22, 2003, p. 63; also Bruce Einhorn, "China Is Taiwan's Sustenance—and Scourge," *Business Week Online*, Sep 18, 2003.
212. Murray Hiebert, Greg Jaffe, Jason Dean, Susan V. Lawrence, "Taiwan Shops for Missiles," *Far Eastern Economic Review*, May 15, 2003, p. 17.
213. Yergin and Stanislaw, pp. 158–164.
214. Leslie P. Norman, "Taiwanese Hold Big Stakes in Mainland Companies," *Barron's*, Sep 3, 2001, p. MW8.
215. Bruce Einhorn, "PC Makers: More Sales, Fewer Profits," *Business Week*, Sep 1, 2003, p. 46.
216. Michael Vatikiotis, Maureen Pao, "Just a Pawn in the Superpower Game," *Far Eastern Economic Review*, Apr. 26, 2001, p. 14.
217. Jason Dean, Michael Vatikiotis, "Politics First, the Economy Second," *Far Eastern Economic Review*, Jul 31, 2003, p. 12.
218. Dexter Roberts, "Greater China," *Business Week*, Dec 9, 2002, p. 50.
219. Mark L. Clifford and Frederik Balfour, "A Strong Tailwind," *Business Week*, Sep 8, 2003, p. 54.
220. Antoneta Bezlova, "Chief Exec Nixes Anti-Subversion Bill," *Global Information Network*, Sep 8, 2003, p. 1; also, "China's Efforts to Jumpstart Economy Working," *Global Information Network*, Sep 15, 2003, p. 1.
221. "A Seismic Shift Toward China," *Business Week*, Dec 9, 2002, p. 144.
222. Gurcharan Das, *India Unbound: The Social and Economic Revolution from Independence to the Global Information Age* (New York: Anchor Books, 2002), p. 98; "19 brands," p. 153; "proud new nation," p. 3.

223. Das, p. 83.
224. Das, pp. 220–221.
225. Das, p. 350.
226. Ranjit Devraj, "Software Trade with U.S. Mutes India's War Protests," *Global Information Network*, Mar 27, 2003, p. 1.
227. Jim Lobe, "U.S.-India-Israel Military Ties Growing Fast," *Global Information Network*, May 23, 2003, p. 1.
228. Manjeet Kripalani, "A Tempest Over Tech Outsourcing," *Business Week*, Jun 16, 2003, p. 55.
229. Das, pp. 337–338.
230. http://www.reaganfoundation.org/reagan/speeches/wall.asp
231. Three other "candidate" countries (Bulgaria, Romania, and Turkey) are waiting in the wings.
232. Jack Welch, *Jack: Straight From the Gut*, Warner Business Books, 2001.
233. Jagdish N. Sheth and Rajendra S. Sisodia (2004), "New Europe: Friend or Foe?"
234. http://teacherweb.ftl.pinecrest.edu/crawfor/apcg/unit3cap.htm
235. *Commanding Heights*, op. cit.
236. A Dictionary of Philosophical Terms and Names (http://www.philosophypages.com/dy/index.htm)
237. http://www.wilderdom.com/personality/L8-4StructureMindIdEgoSuperego.html; http://65.107.211.206/science/freud/Division_of_Mind.html; http://www.dummies.com/WileyCDA/DummiesArticle/id-1215.html
238. Michael Porter (1990), *The Competitive Advantage of Nation*, New York: The Free Press.
239. Rajendra Sisodia (1992), "Singapore Invests in the Nation-Corporation," *Harvard Business Review*, Vol. 70, No. 3 (May/June), pp. 40–50.
240. *The Economist*, "Arabia's Field of Dreams," May 27, 2004.
241. Marco Iansiti and Roy Levien, "Strategy as Ecology," *Harvard Business Review*, March 2004.
242. Benjamin Gomes-Casseres, "Group versus Group: How Alliance Networks Compete," *Harvard Business Review*, July 1994.
243. Gomes-Casseres, op. cit.
244. Jeffrey H. Dyer (1996), "How Chrysler Created an American Keiretsu," *Harvard Business Review*, July-August.
245. Ray Mac Sharry and Padraic White (2000), *The Making of the Celtic Tiger: The Inside Story of Ireland's Boom Economy*, Cork: Mercier Press.
246. Radio Free Europe / Radio Liberty Breffni O'Rourke, "EU: How Ireland Unleashed Its 'Celtic Tiger' Economy," http://www.rferl.org/features/2001/11/26112001091243.asp
247. The Birth of the Celtic Tiger, http://www.cordis.lu/itt/itt-en/04-2/dossier01.htm

248. From research firm eMarketer, cited in Justin Fox (2004), "The Great Paving," *Fortune*, Vol. 149, No. 2 (January 26), pp. 86–96.
249. http://www.acf.dhhs.gov/news/stats/6097rf.htm
250. http://www.alertnet.org/thenews/newsdesk/T132267.htm, accessed April 1, 2004.
251. *The Economist* (2002), "Special Report: Coming Home to Roost - Privatization in Europe," June 29, Volume 363, Issue 8279, p. 72.
252. Jay Solomon and Joanna Slater (2002), "Sales Call: India's Economy Gets a New Jolt From Mr. Shourie," *The Wall Street Journal*, January 9, p. A1.
253. Chi Hung Kwan, "Privatization of State – owned Enterprises Gathering Pace – Whither Chinese Socialism?" September 26, 2003, accessed at http://www.rieti.go.jp/en/china/03092601.html
254. Larry W. Penwell, "A Brief History of Total Quality Management in Japan," accessed at http://www2.mwc.edu/~lpenwell/Lectures/odc/history_tqc_japan.htm
255. Michael Pecht & William R. Boulton, "Quality Assurance and Reliability in the Japanese Electronics Industry," accessed at http://www.wtec.org/loyola/ep/c6s1.htm
256. http://www.tqe.com/hoshinHI.html
257. http://www.consumeraffairs.com/news04/hyundai_jdpowers.html
258. http://www.sinoptic.ch/scccgeneva/download/info/ccc/20030618_CCC_Dok.pdf
259. Keith Maskus (2000), *Intellectual Property Rights in the Global Economy*, Institute for International Economics.
260. Brent Schlender (2004), "Peter Drucker Sets Us Straight," *Fortune*, Vol. 149, No. 1 (January 12), pp. 114–118.
261. *The Economist* (2002), "Neighborly Lessons: European Unemployment," March 16, Vol. 362, Issue. 8264, p. 16.
262. Charles Oliver, "Greener, Cleaner All the Time," *Investor's Business Daily*, May 5, 1997.
263. Environmental Protection Agency (2004), "Latest Findings on National Air Quality: 2002 Status and Trends".
264. World Competitiveness Yearbook 2004, published by IMD; http://www01.imd.ch/wcy/
265. This section based partly on Rajendra S. Sisodia, "Singapore Invests in the Nation-Corporation," *Harvard Business Review*, May-June 1992, pp. 40–51.
266. Jagdish N. Sheth and Rajendra S. Sisodia (1993), "The Information Mall," *Telecommunications Policy*, July, pp. 376–389.
267. Sam Vaknin, "Infrastructure and Prosperity," http://www.theallineed.com/ad-business-4/business-012.htm
268. Roger Kahn (1991), "Building Information Highways," presentation at *Business Week* conference on *Information Highways: Linking America for*

Interactive Communications, September 11–12, New York.
269. Richard Mudge, "Infrastructure Investment Can Stimulate Growth," *Challenge*, March/April 1996, Vol. 39, Issue 2, pp. 4–8.
270. M. Ishaq Nadiri and Theofanis P. Mamuneas, "The Effects of Public Infrastructure and R&D Capital on the Cost Structure and Performance of U.S. Manufacturing Industries," *Review of Economics and Statistics*, Vol. 76, No. 1 (1994), pp. 22–37.
271. Arup Mitra, Aristomene Varoudakis, Marie-Ange Veganzones-Varoudakis, "Productivity and Technical Efficiency in Indian States' Manufacturing: The Role of Infrastructure," *Economic Development and Cultural Change*, January 2002, Vol. 50, Issue 2, pp. 395–426.
272. Andew F. Haughwout, "The Paradox of Infrastructure Investment," *The Brookings Review*, Summer 2000, Vol. 18, Issue 3, pp. 40–43.
273. Dominic Wilson and Roopa Purushothaman (2003), *Dreaming With BRICs: The Path to 2050*, Goldman Sachs Global Economics Paper No. 99, October 1, 2003, p. 13.
274. Satya Paul, "Effects of Public Infrastructure on Cost Structure and Productivity in the Private Sector," *The Economic Record*, December 2003, Vol. 79, No. 247, pp. 446–461; David Alan Aschauer, "Is Public Expenditure Productive?" *Journal of Monetary Economics*, March 23 1989, pp. 171–188; Alicia H. Munnell, "Why Has Productivity Declined?" *New England Economic Review*, Federal Reserve Bank of Boston, January/February 1990, pp. 3–22.
275. Mudge, op. cit.
276. http://www.geocities.com/ResearchTriangle/3896/comm5.html
277. Justin Fox (2004), "The Great Paving," *Fortune*, Vol. 149, No. 2 (January 26), pp. 86–96.
278. The Columbia Electronic Encyclopedia, 6th ed. Copyright © 2003, Columbia University Press; http://allsands.com/History/Events/railroadsinters_rtd_gn.htm
279. http://www.railneteurope.com/docs/railneteuropeconcept.pdf
280. Jason Singer (2003), "Lonesome Highways: In Japan, Big Tolls Drive Cars Away; Commuters Take Slow Road, Truckers Head for Exits; $50 to Cross a Bridge," *The Wall Street Journal*, September 15, p. A1.
281. Sheth, Jagdish N. and Rajendra S. Sisodia (1993), "The Information Mall," *Telecommunications Policy*, Vol. 17, No. 5 (July), pp. 376–389.
282. *M2 Presswire* (2003), "UK Government: Timms Calls for Universal Broadband Availability and Improved Co-Operation, November 12, p. 1.
283. Nuclear Issues Briefing Paper 11: World Energy Needs and Nuclear Power, July 2002, accessed at http://www.uic.com.au/nip11.htm
284. Nuclear Issues Briefing Paper 2: Asia's Nuclear Energy Growth, November 2003, accessed at http://www.uic.com.au/nip02.htm

285. http://quickstart.clari.net/qs_se/webnews/wed/cx/Bmd-usec.RRkJ_DSI.html
286. David Goodstein (2004), *Out of Gas: The End of the Age of Oil*, W.W. Norton & Company.
287. Peter Wonacott, Jeanne Whalen and Bhushan Bahree (2003), "Balance of Power: China's Growing Thirst for Oil Remakes the Global Market — Beijing's Buying Keeps Prices High — and Could Reshape Politics of Middle East — Growing Closer to the Saudis," *The Wall Street Journal*, December 3.
288. Daniel Yergin (1991), *Prize: The Epic Quest For Oil, Money & Power*, New York: The Free Press.
289. Joint Ministerial Statement ASEAN, China, Japan and Korea Energy Ministers Meeting (Manila AMEM+3) 9 June 2004, Makati City, Metro Manila, Philippines, accessed at http://www.aseansec.org/16144.htm
290. http://www.bankcard.net/hist.htm
291. http://www.didyouknow.cd/creditcards.htm
292. http://inventors.about.com/library/inventors/blmoney.htm
293. Brian Bremmer and Hiroko Tashiro, "Is Japan Back," *Business Week*, June 14, 2004, pp. 48–52.
294. Hitoshi Sasaki and Yuko Koga, "Trade Between Japan and China: Dramatic Expansion and Structural Changes," *Economic Commentary Number 2003–03*, Bank of Japan Research and Statistics Department, August 2003.
295. Choi Kyong-ae, "Korea Outdistances Japan in Shipbuilding Orders," *The Korea Times*, May 28, 2004.
296. http://www.auswaertiges-amt.de/www/en/laenderinfos/laender/laender_ausgabe_html?type_id=14&land_id=140
297. http://www.stratfor.com/
298. Roger Boyes, "Berlin Bows to Bush Over Moscow Axis," *The Times* (UK), April 09, 2001.
299. Martin Walker, "A Game of Hardball," posted Feb. 4, 2004, accessed at http://www.insightmag.com/news/2004/02/17/World/A.Game.Of.Hardball-597068.shtml
300. Walker, op. cit.
301. http://www.iatp.org/unctadxi/headlines.cfm?id=19253
302. A Brief History of TNC's, CorpWatch.org
303. www.wto.org/english/thewto_e/ minist_e/min96_e/invest.htm
304. http://www.businessweek.com/1998/35/b3593045.htm
305. Vito Tanzi (2001), "Globalization and the Work of Fiscal Termites," *Finance & Development*, March 2001, Volume 38, Number 1, accessed at http://www.imf.org/external/pubs/ft/fandd/2001/03/tanzi.htm
306. Chart from Alan Rugman (2001), *The End of Globalization*, New York: AMACOM.
307. "The Effects of NAFTA on US-Mexican Trade and GDP," *Congressional Budget Office*, May 2003.

308. "NAFTA at Ten," US Embassy in Mexico, accessed at www.usembassy-mexico.government/eNAFTA_figures.htm
309. The Economist (2004), *Pocket World in Figures.*
310. http://usinfo.state.gov/usa/infousa/facts/democrac/50.htm
311. Erich Marquardt, "China's Distant Threat to U.S. Dominance in Asia", *PINR: Power and Interest News Report*, September 8, 2003, accessed at http://www.pinr.com/index.php
312. *The Guardian Unlimited* (2001), "A History of Currency Unions," December 10, 2001, http://www.guardian.co.uk/euro/story/0,11306,616567,00.html
313. op. cit.
314. This section adapted from Rajendra S. Sisodia (1995), "Growth, Productivity and the Visible Hand – An Interview with Jagdish Sheth," *Journal of Asia Pacific Business*, Vol. 1, No. 1, pp. 121–134.
315. http://www.dnr.state.oh.us/recycling/awareness/facts/tires/ohiorubber.htm.
316. "How Akron became Tire Town," *Akron Beacon Journal*, May 18, 2004, accessed at http://www.ohio.com/mld/ohio/living/special_packages/newcomer_guide/8692144.htm?1c
317. Michael E. Porter (1998), "Clusters and the New Economics of Competition," *Harvard Business Review*, November-December.
318. Michael E. Porter (1990), *The Competitive Advantage of Nations*, New York: The Free Press, pp. 655–657.
319. CEC (1993), *XXIIIrd Report on Competition Policy*, Commission of the European Communities, Brussels.
320. Philip Raines (1996), "Labor Market Regulation and Foreign Direct Investment," Regional and Industrial Policy Research Paper Number 22, *European Policies Research Centre*, University of Strathclyde, November 1996, accessed at http://www.eprc.strath.ac.uk/eprc/PDF_files/R22LabMarkReg&ForDirInvest.pdf
321. H. Ramsay (1995), "Le Défi Européen: Multinational Restructuring, Labour and EU Policy," in A. Amin and J. Tomaney (eds.), *Behind the Myth of European Union*, Routledge, London.
322. Jagdish N. Sheth and Rajendra S. Sisodia (2002), *The Rule of Three: Surviving and Thriving in Competitive Markets*, New York: The Free Press.
323. Carl Mortished, "Siemens Considers Challenge to France's Rescue of Alstom," Times Online, May 20, 2004, accessed at http://business.timesonline.co.uk/article/0,,9067-1116943,00.html
324. *Associated Press*, "EU to Maintain Tough Merger Rules," November 7, 2002, accessed at http://www.globalpolicy.org/socecon/tncs/mergers/1107monti.htm
325. Jug Suraiya (2004), "Theatre of Conflict Bad for Biz," *The Times of India*, February 23, 2004.
326. *CNETAsia* (2003), "China Developing 'Super DVD' Format," October 28, 2003.
327. *Fortune*, Feb 23, 2004.

328. Brent Schlender (2004), "Peter Drucker Sets Us Straight," *Fortune*, Vol. 149, No. 1 (January 12), pp. 114–118.
329. http://en.wikipedia.org/wiki/Immigration
330. Brent Schlender (2004), "Peter Drucker Sets Us Straight," *Fortune*, Vol. 149, No. 1 (January 12), pp. 114–118.

Index

About the Authors

Jagdish N. Sheth is a renowned scholar and world authority in the field of marketing. His insights on global competition, strategic thinking, consumer behaviour, and relationship management are considered revolutionary.

Professor Sheth is the Charles H. Kellstadt Chair of Marketing in the Goizueta Business School at Emory University. Prior to this, he was the Robert E. Brooker Professor of Marketing at the University of Southern California, and a distinguished faculty at the University of Illinois, Columbia University and the Massachusetts Institute of Technology. He has also worked for numerous industries and companies in the US, Europe and Asia, both as an Advisor and as a Seminar leader. He is on the Board of Directors of several public companies.

A prolific writer, Jagdish Sheth has published a large number of books and research papers in different areas of marketing and business strategy, many of which are considered seminal references. His book *The Theory of Buyer Behavior* (1969) with John A. Howard is a classic in the field. His other publications include *Marketing Theory: Evolution and Evaluation* (1988), *Consumption Values and Market Choices* (1991), *The Rule of Three: How Competition Shapes Markets* (with Rajendra Sisodia), *Clients for*

Life (with Andrew Sobel) and *The Handbook of Relationship Marketing* (with Atul Parvatiyar).

Professor Sheth is the recipient of many awards including the 1989 Outstanding Outstanding Marketing Educator Award from the Academy of Marketing Science; the Outstanding Educator Award from the Sales and Marketing Executives International in both 1991 and 1999; and in 2004, both the Richard D. Irwin Distinguished Marketing Educator Award and the Charles Coolidge Parlin Award – the two highest awards given by the American Marketing Association. In 1996, Dr. Sheth was selected as a Distinguished Fellow of the Academy of Marketing Science. He is also a Fellow of the American Psychological Association.

Rajendra S. Sisodia is Professor of Marketing and the Founding Director of the Center for Marketing Technology at Bentley College, Waltham. An electrical engineer from BITS, Pilani, Dr. Sisodia has a Ph.D. in Marketing and Business Policy from Columbia University. His book, *The Rule of Three: How Competition Shapes Markets* (with Jagdish N. Sheth) has been translated into German, Italian, Polish, Japanese and Chinese. It was the subject of a seven-part television series by CNBC Asia, and was a finalist for the 2004 AMA Best Marketing Book Award. His forthcoming books (all with Jagdish N. Sheth) include *Does Marketing Need Reform?*, *Firms of Endearment*, and *The 4 As of Marketing*.

Dr. Sisodia has published about a hundred articles in publications such as the *Harvard Business Review*, *Journal of Marketing*, *Journal of Business Strategy*, *Journal of the Academy of Marketing Science*, *Journal of Marketing and Public Policy* and *The Wall Street Journal*. In 2003, he was cited as one of the '50 Leading Marketing Thinkers' by the UK-based Chartered Institute of Marketing (the largest marketing association in the world).

Local